Thank You, Jesus

Thank You, Jesus

Vinu V Das

Tabor Press

© 2025 Tabor Press. All rights reserved. No part of this publication may be reproduced, distributed, or transmitted in any form or by any means without the prior written permission of the publisher, except in the case of brief quotations embodied in critical reviews and certain other noncommercial uses permitted by copyright law.

ISBN 978-1-997541-19-6

Table of Contents

Chapter 1. Thank You, Jesus—The Name Above Every Name 13

  1.1 Recognizing His Identity 14

  1.2 Attributes Worthy of Praise 15

  1.3 Responding in Worship 17

  1.4 Biblical Titles and Their Rich Meanings 18

  1.5 The Power of His Name in Prayer and Warfare 19

  1.6 The Name Proclaimed Through History 20

  1.7 The Name in Worship and Liturgy 21

  1.8 Missional Implications of His Name 22

  1.9 The Eschatological Triumph of the Name 23

Chapter 2. Thank You, Jesus, for Coming to Us—The Miracle of Incarnation 25

  2.1 Heaven Touches Earth 26

  2.2 The Humble Birth in Bethlehem 27

  2.3 Early Life and Growth 28

  2.4 Fully God, Fully Man—The Hypostatic Union 29

  2.5 Living Among Humanity 30

  2.6 Revelation Through Embodied Teaching 31

  2.7 Implications for Creation and Redemption 32

  2.8 The Incarnational Call to the Church 33

  2.9 Celebrating the Incarnation 34

  2.10 Eschatological Fulfillment 34

Chapter 3. Thank You, Jesus, for Teaching Truth—Words of Life 36

   3.1 The Authority of His Teaching 37

   3.2 Unfolding the Kingdom Through Parables 38

   3.3 Reframing the Law and Prophets 40

   3.4 Life-Changing Dialogues 41

   3.5 Hard Sayings That Purify Motives 42

   3.6 Teaching Through Signs and Wonders 43

   3.7 Discipleship Lessons in Real Time 44

   3.8 Apocalyptic Discourse—Truth About the End 45

   3.9 Ethics for a Kingdom Community 46

   3.10 Legacy of the Living Word 47

Chapter 4 Thank You, Jesus, for the Cross—Our Redemption 49

   4.1 Prelude to Calvary: Gethsemane and Betrayal 50

   4.2 Trials and Condemnation 51

   4.3 Via Dolorosa—The Road of Suffering 53

   4.4 The Crucifixion Unveiled 54

   4.5 Seven Last Words—Windows into the Savior's Heart 55

   4.6 Cosmic Signs and the Veil Torn 56

   4.7 Theological Depths of the Cross 57

   4.8 The Cross and Covenant Fulfillment 58

   4.9 Application of Redemption to the Believer 59

   4.10 Sacramental Remembrance and Worship 60

   4.11 Embracing the Cross in Daily Discipleship 61

   4.12 Global Mission and the Message of the Cross 62

Chapter 5. Thank You, Jesus, for the Empty Tomb—Resurrection Hope 64

    5.1 Before Dawn: Waiting in the Shadow of Death 65

    5.2 Rolling Away the Stone—Heaven's Intervention.................66

    5.3 First Witnesses: Women Hear the Good News 68

    5.4 Verifying the Empty Tomb—Peter and John Run 69

    5.5 Personal Encounters with the Risen Lord 70

    5.6 Bodily Reality of Resurrection 71

    5.7 Theological Significance of the Resurrection......................72

    5.8 Firstfruits of the New Creation 73

    5.9 Union with Christ—Resurrection Life Now..........................74

    5.10 Ethics of Hope: Living in Light of the Empty Tomb 75

    5.11 Worship and Liturgy Shaped by Resurrection 76

    5.12 Mission Empowered by Resurrection Authority................77

    5.13 Eschatological Consummation—Our Future Resurrection 78

Chapter 6. Thank You, Jesus, for the Gift of the Spirit—Indwelling Presence...80

    6.1 Promise of the Paraclete 81

    6.2 Pentecost—The Spirit Poured Out 82

    6.3 Indwelling Presence and New Covenant 84

    6.4 Adoption and Assurance...86

    6.5 Sanctification and Fruit-Bearing 87

    6.6 Empowerment for Witness 88

    6.7 Gifts for Building the Body..90

    6.8 Guidance and Discernment 91

    6.9 Prayer and Worship in the Spirit 93

6.10 Unity and Diversity in the Spirit 94

6.11 Spiritual Warfare 95

6.12 Spirit-Filled Ethics in Daily Life 96

6.13 Revival, Renewal, and Global Mission 98

6.14 Eschatological Role of the Spirit 99

Chapter 7. Thank You, Jesus, for Daily Bread—Provision and Sustenance 102

7.1 Recognizing God as Provider 103

7.2 "Give Us This Day…"—Petition in the Lord's Prayer 104

7.3 Manna in the Wilderness—Lessons in Enough 106

7.4 Table Miracles of Jesus 107

7.5 Work, Vocation, and the Dignity of Labor 108

7.6 Contentment and Simplicity 109

7.7 Generosity—Blessed to Be a Blessing 110

7.8 Spiritual Bread—Word that Nourishes 110

7.9 Eucharist: Bread Broken, Grace Received 111

7.10 Freedom from Anxiety over Provision 112

7.11 Gratitude in Scarcity and Abundance 113

7.12 Eschatological Banquet—Ultimate Satisfaction 114

Chapter 8. Thank You, Jesus, for Healing—Body, Mind, and Spirit 116

8.1 Foundations of Divine Healing 117

8.2 The Healing Ministry of Jesus 118

8.3 Faith Encounters that Unlocked Miracles 120

8.4 Atonement & Healing at the Cross 121

8.5 Healing in the Acts Church 122

8.6 Gifts of Healing & Charismata Today 123

8.7 Emotional & Psychological Renewal 124

8.8 Deliverance from Spiritual Oppression 124

8.9 Community & Social Dimensions of Healing 125

8.10 Suffering, Mystery, and Unanswered Prayer 126

8.11 Practices that Cultivate a Healing Culture 127

8.12 Gratitude & Testimony 128

8.13 Eschatological Wholeness—The Ultimate Cure 128

Chapter 9. Thank You, Jesus, for Freedom—Chains Broken 130

9.1 Liberation From Sin's Power 131

9.2 Deliverance From Condemnation 132

9.3 Freedom From Legalism and Dead Religion 134

9.4 Freedom From Fear and Shame 135

9.5 Breaking Addictions and Strongholds 137

9.6 Spirit of Adoption—Free to Be Children 138

9.7 Walking in Newfound Liberty 139

9.8 Societal Dimensions of Freedom 141

9.9 Spiritual Warfare and Ongoing Victory 143

9.10 Worship as an Act of Freedom 144

9.11 Mission of Liberty—Proclaiming Freedom 146

9.12 Eschatological Freedom—Glorious Liberty of the Children of God 147

Chapter 10. Thank You, Jesus, for Peace in Storms—Comfort and Assurance 149

10.1 Portrait of Divine Peace 150

10.2 Prophetic Promises of Calming Presence 151

10.3 Jesus, the Storm-Silencer 153

10.4 Peace for Troubled Minds 154

10.5 Peace That Surpasses Understanding 156

10.6 Songs in the Night—Worship as Storm Shelter 158

10.7 Spiritual Warfare and the Shoes of Peace 159

10.8 Community Carriers of Christ's Calm 161

10.9 Peace amid Suffering and Persecution 162

10.10 Practical Practices for Storm-Time Peace 163

10.11 Eschatological Assurance—The Final Calm 165

Chapter 11. Thank You, Jesus, for the Fellowship of Believers—Community in Christ 167

11.1 Biblical Foundations of Christian Community 168

11.2 The Early Church Model 169

11.3 Means of Grace in Fellowship 171

11.4 Spiritual Gifts and Roles 172

11.5 Discipline, Restoration, and Forgiveness 174

11.6 Corporate Worship and Liturgical Rhythms 176

11.7 Mission, Witness, and Unity 177

11.8 Hospitality and Practical Care 179

11.9 Intergenerational and Multicultural Fellowship 181

11.10 Digital and Distance Community 183

11.11 Overcoming Conflict and Building Reconciliation 185

11.12 Eschatological Fellowship—The Banquet of the Lamb .. 187

Chapter 12. Thank You, Jesus, for Purpose—Calling and Service 190

12.1 Divine Calling and Commission 191

12.2 Spiritual Gifts and Vocation 192

12.3. Discipleship as Daily Calling 194

12.4 Models of Service in Scripture 196

12.5 Servant Leadership and Church Roles 197

12.6 Mission and the Great Commission 199

12.7 Stewardship of Time, Talent, and Treasure 200

12.8 Perseverance and Renewal in Service 202

12.9 Community Engagement and Social Witness 204

12.10 Collaboration, Teams, and Networks 205

12.11 Vision Casting and Discipleship Pathways 206

12.12 Eschatological Purpose and Eternal Rewards 208

Chapter 13. Thank You, Jesus, for Your Kingdom—Reign of Justice and Mercy 211

13.1 Kingdom in Prophecy and Promise 212

13.2 Jesus' Kingdom: Inauguration and Invitation 213

13.3 Kingdom Ethics: Justice, Mercy, and Humility 215

13.4 Kingdom Community: People of the King 216

13.5 Servant–King: Leadership in the Kingdom 218

13.6 Kingdom Mission: Extending Justice and Mercy 220

13.7 Kingdom Conflict and Victory 222

13.8 Kingdom Living: Present and Future 223

13.9 Songs and Symbols of the Kingdom 225

13.10 Living in Kingdom Citizenship 227

13.11 Kingdom Fellowship: Celebrating Together 228

13.12 Eschatological Consummation of the Kingdom 230

Chapter 14. Thank You, Jesus, for Eternal Glory—Hope Unfading

....233

14.1 Biblical Glimpses of Glory 234

14.2 Resurrection and the Firstfruits..236

14.3 New Resurrection Bodies 237

14.4 Eternal Inheritance 239

14.5 Living Hope 240

14.6 Hall of Faith 242

14.7 Glory through Suffering...244

14.8 Worship in Eternal Glory 246

14.9 Communion with the Redeemed 248

14.10 Renewal of Creation 249

14.11 Eternal Service and Sustenance....................................251

14.12 Crown of Unfading Hope 252

Chapter 1. Thank You, Jesus—The Name Above Every Name

Gratitude naturally rises in the human heart whenever greatness stoops low in loving concern, and nowhere is that mystery more radiant than in the person of Jesus Christ. From the first cry in Bethlehem's manger to the triumphant declaration "It is finished!" at Calvary, His name has gathered together every thread of God's self-revelation and woven them into a tapestry of saving grace. Long before the Church sang its earliest hymns, patriarchs and prophets whispered titles that hinted at One who would embody the holiness, compassion, and sovereign majesty of Yahweh in flesh and blood (Isa 9:6; Jer 23:5–6). In Jesus, those scattered promises reach their climactic "Yes" (2 Cor 1:20), inviting every tribe, tongue, and nation to bow in adoration. Because His name is not a mere label but a living declaration of identity, character, mission, and destiny, thanksgiving becomes more than polite religious speech; it becomes the atmosphere in which redeemed lives are meant to breathe. The following pages explore why that name eclipses every rival, how its power is experienced in daily discipleship, and what cosmic future awaits those who treasure it. As we trace Scripture's testimony across epochs, cultures, and liturgies, may a fresh song of gratitude swell within us, compelling both worshipful silence and world-shaking proclamation.

1.1 Recognizing His Identity

The Revelation of "I AM"

The burning bush episode (Ex 3:14) unveils God's self-designation as "I AM WHO I AM," a name brimming with inexhaustible being and covenant fidelity. Centuries later, Jesus echoes and embodies that declaration when He asserts, "Before Abraham was, I AM" (Jn 8:58), collapsing the gulf between eternity and time in a single breath. The claim scandalized His hearers, not because of semantic ambiguity, but because deity seemed to stand unmasked in human flesh. By appropriating the divine name, Christ reveals Himself as the self-existent One who depends on nothing yet chooses loving solidarity with humanity. Gratitude springs from realizing that the transcendent Creator entered our story, refusing to remain remote while sin marred His handiwork. His "I AM" means He is eternally present to redeem, never arriving too late to heal, forgive, or guide. Each time believers whisper "Thank You, Jesus," they align their confession with Moses' barefoot awe and the apostles' post-resurrection certainty that the bush still burns—now in the blazing heart of the risen Lord. That recognition reshapes identity, for those who belong to Jesus are anchored not in shifting cultural tides but in the unchanging One whose very name guarantees faithful presence.

Prophetic Titles Fulfilled in Christ

Isaiah heard heaven's courtroom announce a child who would be called Wonderful Counselor, Mighty God, Everlasting Father, Prince of Peace (Isa 9:6); Micah foresaw a ruler emerging from Bethlehem whose origins were "from days of eternity" (Mic 5:2). These titles were not poetic exaggerations but Spirit-breathed signposts pointing toward Jesus' uniqueness. In Matthew's infancy narrative, "Emmanuel—God with us" (Mt 1:23) frames the incarnation, assuring readers that Israel's God has drawn nearer than their wildest hopes. Each title paints a facet of His identity: Wonderful Counselor signals unfathomable wisdom; Mighty God proclaims divine power marshaled for human rescue; Everlasting Father conveys covenantal protection; Prince of Peace promises holistic shalom through His reign. Gratitude deepens when believers realize prophecy did not merely anticipate an event but introduced a Person whose name gathers up every redemptive epithet. Thanksgiving becomes the soul's echo of prophetic wonder, confessing that what poets longed for is now personally experienced.

Confession of Peter: "You Are the Christ"

When Jesus asked, "Who do you say that I am?" (Mt 16:15), Peter voiced the collective heartbeat of future generations: "You are the Christ, the Son of the living God." This confession split history, marking a pivot from curiosity to conviction. The term "Christ" (Messiah) affirms Jesus as the anointed King, priest, and prophet who fulfills Israel's deepest yearnings. "Son of the living God" anchors His identity in relationship, distinguishing Him from mere political liberators. Gratitude flows from knowing that faith is not rooted in private speculation but in a revelation the Father graciously grants (Mt 16:17). Every believer who utters "Thank You, Jesus" joins Peter on that windswept Caesarean ridge, confessing a truth that withstands martyrdom, empires, and millennia of doubt. This confession births community, for Jesus immediately speaks of building His Church upon such revealed faith (Mt 16:18). Thanksgiving therefore becomes both personal devotion and communal anthem, binding disciples across cultures to one unshakable cornerstone.

1.2 Attributes Worthy of Praise

Holiness That Inspires Awe

John's vision of seraphim crying "Holy, holy, holy" (Rev 4:8) unveils a realm where the name of Jesus elicits ceaseless wonder. Holiness, far from icy moral distance, radiates blazing beauty that attracts while it purifies. Jesus' earthly ministry exemplified this paradox: sinners felt safe near Him even as demons shrieked in terror. His holiness is relational, inviting transformation rather than mere compliance. Gratitude grows in proportion to the soul's apprehension of that glory; the cleaner the mirror is wiped, the more clearly Christ's perfection shines—and the more willingly believers surrender hidden corners of the heart. Biblical gratitude thus transcends casual thanks; it is the awe-filled response of creatures glimpsing majesty veiled in humility, a fire that never harms yet forever refines.

Compassion That Draws the Broken

Matthew observes that Jesus, seeing the crowds, "had compassion on them, because they were harassed and helpless" (Mt 9:36). The Greek term *splagchnizomai* suggests gut-wrenching empathy, as though divinity feels human pain from the inside out. Compassion propelled Him to touch lepers, converse with outcasts, and weep beside a friend's tomb (Jn 11:35). Gratitude erupts when wounded hearts realize they are not projects but beloved persons to the Shepherd who seeks lost sheep (Lk 15:4–7). His compassion redefines worth; no failure or stigma outruns the reach of nail-scarred hands. Saying "Thank You, Jesus" becomes a daily acknowledgment that divine pity has become personal rescue, that the One enthroned above cherubim stoops to lift the crushed in spirit.

Sovereign Authority Over All

Colossians crowns Christ as the One in whom "all things hold together" (Col 1:17), a cosmic glue binding galaxies and atoms. Storms obey His rebuke (Mk 4:39); legions of demons heed His single word (Mk 5:8–13); death itself relinquishes captives at His command (Jn 11:43–44). Such sovereignty is not detached determinism but love wielding omnipotence for redemption. Gratitude therefore merges reverence with rest: if Jesus governs quarks and kingdoms, then the believer's tomorrow is secure beneath His scepter. Thanksgiving becomes the steady heartbeat of trust, a confession that no headline, diagnosis, or crisis can eclipse the One whose name outranks principalities and powers (Eph 1:21).

1.3 Responding in Worship

Bowing the Heart in Adoration

Paul envisions a universal knee-bending before Jesus (Phil 2:10), yet authentic worship begins in the unseen posture of the heart. Adoration differs from gratitude in that it praises God simply for who He is, not merely what He gives. When believers quiet competing affections and center on Christ's worth, thanksgiving naturally follows as an overflow rather than an obligation. The Psalms model this movement: first beholding God's glory, then recounting His deeds. Bowing internally cultivates humility, dethroning ego and enthroning Christ in decision-making, relationships, and ambitions. "Thank You, Jesus" thus becomes more than liturgical filler; it is the exhalation of a soul delighting in its rightful King.

Proclaiming His Lordship Publicly

Peter's Pentecost sermon culminates in the declaration, "God has made this Jesus…both Lord and Christ" (Acts 2:36). Gratitude seeks amplification; joy in the heart longs to become testimony on the lips. Public proclamation includes but surpasses formal preaching—even casual conversations, digital posts, and artistic expressions can magnify His name. Courage to witness is often born from remembrance: recalling how Jesus rescued, healed, or guided provides fresh motive to share. Thanksgiving, therefore, is inherently missional; it refuses to hoard the treasure it celebrates. Each declaration—spoken or sung—echoes the shepherds who made known what they had seen in Bethlehem and the healed leper who returned glorifying God with a loud voice (Lk 17:15).

Glorifying His Name Through Service

"Whatever you do…do it all in the name of the Lord Jesus" (Col 3:17) reframes mundane tasks as liturgies of gratitude.

Serving coworkers, neighbors, or family becomes a canvas upon which Jesus' character is painted in kindness, excellence, and integrity. Early believers gained favor when opponents saw their good deeds and glorified God (1 Pet 2:12). Service roots thanksgiving in tangible love, protecting it from sentimentalism. It also dignifies vocations outside overt ministry, affirming that whether one codes software, changes diapers, or leads companies, each realm can reflect the King's beauty. Thus "Thank You, Jesus" finds echo in the silent sermon of daily work offered back to Him.

1.4 Biblical Titles and Their Rich Meanings

Alpha and Omega

Christ's self-designation as "Alpha and Omega" (Rev 22:13) compresses the Greek alphabet into a confession of total sovereignty over history's narrative arc. He authors the prologue and writes the epilogue, ensuring no plot twist escapes His editorial oversight. Gratitude rises from knowing life's chapters—birth, loss, success, aging—are bracketed by unwavering divine presence. The title also comforts persecuted communities in Revelation: the same Jesus who spoke galaxies into existence will have the final word over tyrants. Thanksgiving, therefore, is not naive optimism but defiant confidence rooted in the One who was, is, and is to come.

Lamb of God

John the Baptist's cry "Behold, the Lamb of God" (Jn 1:29) fuses Passover imagery with Isaiah's suffering servant. The innocent dies so the guilty may live, a truth sewn into Israel's liturgical memory and now unveiled in flesh. Gratitude toward the Lamb surpasses relief at personal pardon; it marvels that holiness would voluntarily embrace slaughter for love. Revelation's throne scene depicts an eternally scarred Lamb receiving universal worship (Rev 5:8–12), reminding saints that redemption cost heaven its dearest. Every "Thank You, Jesus" draws water from that well of sacrificial love, ensuring praise never drifts into cheap familiarity.

Lion of Judah

Contrasting the Lamb's meekness, Jesus is the "Lion of the tribe of Judah" who conquers (Rev 5:5). This paradox—lion and lamb—reveals that Christ's victories emerge through apparently vulnerable pathways. Gratitude arises from witnessing enemies routed by forgiveness, not force; by resurrection, not revenge. The Lion defends the oppressed and roars against injustice, assuring believers that evil's tenure is temporary. Thanksgiving, then, energizes courage: the same roar that topples darkness reverberates in disciples sent as ambassadors of reconciliation.

1.5 The Power of His Name in Prayer and Warfare

Asking in Jesus' Name

Jesus invites disciples to ask "in My name" so the Father may be glorified in the Son (Jn 14:13–14). This privilege is not a magical formula but alignment with Christ's character and purposes. Praying "Thank You, Jesus" before requests anchors petitions in gratitude, guarding against entitlement. Intercession becomes partnership: the believer, indwelt by the Spirit, discerns heaven's agenda and joins it. Countless testimonies—prodigals returning, doors opening, hearts softening—bear witness to prayers prayed confidently yet humbly in this name above names.

Authority Over Darkness

When the seventy-two returned rejoicing that "even the demons submit to us in Your name" (Lk 10:17), Jesus affirmed the authority He delegates to His Church. Gratitude and spiritual warfare intertwine, for thanksgiving magnifies the Victor and shrinks the adversary's intimidation. Naming Jesus over homes, cities, or troubled minds is not superstition; it is legal enforcement of Calvary's verdict. While believers avoid triumphalistic swagger, they refuse defeatism, knowing the darkness of this age cannot extinguish the light shining in His name (Jn 1:5).

Healing in His Name

Peter's words to the lame man—"In the name of Jesus Christ of Nazareth, walk" (Acts 3:6)—illustrate how Christ's ascended authority continues earthward through faith. Healing, whether instantaneous or progressive, testifies to the gospel's wholeness. Gratitude fuels expectancy: remembering past mercies emboldens fresh requests. Even when physical restoration tarries, the believer clings to the promise that ultimate healing is secured in the resurrection. Thus "Thank You, Jesus" can arise in hospital corridors and funeral homes alike, affirming that sickness does not hold the final script.

1.6 The Name Proclaimed Through History

Apostolic Preaching

Acts presents a relentless refrain: "There is no other name under heaven given to mankind by which we must be saved" (Acts 4:12). Apostles faced councils and prisons with unquenchable conviction because they had seen death's locks shattered. Gratitude propelled them; having freely received, they could not hoard the treasure. Their sermons stitched Scripture's promises to Jesus' story, inviting diverse audiences—Jews in Jerusalem, Gentiles in Athens—to repent and believe. Thanksgiving thus becomes historically rooted, joining modern voices to a two-thousand-year chorus that still rattles chains.

Martyrs and Confessors

From Stephen's forgiving plea (Acts 7:59–60) to Polycarp's steadfast confession and beyond, history records saints who valued Christ's name above life itself. Their blood became seed, and their gratitude—often sung in dungeons—unmasked the emptiness of tyrants' threats. Remembering them kindles present-day courage; persecution may differ in form, but the Lion-Lamb remains worthy. Thanksgiving honors their witness, refusing to let comfort dull the edge of devotion.

Contemporary Testimonies

Revelation celebrates those who "hold to the testimony of Jesus" (Rev 19:10), a reality unfolding today in refugee camps, boardrooms, universities, and remote villages. Stories of addicts delivered, marriages restored, and unreached peoples encountering Scripture in their heart language prove the name's undiminished potency. Gratitude widens when believers share testimonies, for a miracle told becomes hope extended. Each "Thank You, Jesus" voiced in modern dialects stitches fresh patches onto the quilt of redemptive history.

1.7 The Name in Worship and Liturgy

Hymns and Doxologies

Scholars recognize early Christian hymns embedded in passages like Philippians 2:6–11 and Colossians 1:15–20, where poetic cadence exalts Jesus' pre-existence, incarnation, and exaltation. Sung theology educated illiterate congregations and forged unity across cultural lines. Gratitude still bubbles up in song, for melody engages emotion, embedding truth deeper than prose alone. Whether Gregorian chant, gospel chorus, or modern worship anthem, the Church keeps discovering new ways to say "Thank You, Jesus," while never exhausting His worth.

Sacramental Invocation

When believers baptize "in the name of the Father and of the Son and of the Holy Spirit" (Mt 28:19) or partake of bread and cup "in remembrance of Me" (Lk 22:19), Christ's name is spoken over water and wine, ordinary elements that signify extraordinary grace. Gratitude saturates these acts: baptism celebrates burial with Christ into new life; communion rehearses covenant, proclaiming His death until He comes (1 Cor 11:26). Participating forms identity, reminding disciples that their stories are immersed in His.

Liturgical Seasons Focused on Christ

Advent trains hope toward the King's arrival; Epiphany broadens vision to Gentile inclusion; Lent invites repentance beneath the shadow of the cross; Easter thunders resurrection joy; Ascension and Pentecost extol enthronement and empowerment; Christ the King Sunday climaxes with cosmic sovereignty. Each season drapes a different color over the same radiant name, ensuring gratitude never grows monochrome. The Church calendar thus becomes a discipleship spiral, revisiting familiar mysteries with deeper awe each year.

1.8 Missional Implications of His Name

Global Evangelization

Jesus' Great Commission rests on the declaration "All authority in heaven and on earth has been given to Me" (Mt 28:18–20). Mission is therefore a grateful response, not a burdensome obligation: forgiven sinners long to see the King's beauty cherished by every people group. Translation projects labor to render His name intelligibly, preserving theological precision while honoring linguistic nuance. Thanksgiving fuels perseverance in hard places, for ambassadors remember the privilege of representing the Lord whose love first pursued them.

Translating the Name Across Cultures

Incarnational mission wrestles with how best to communicate "Jesus" where alphabets differ and historical baggage abounds. Should local believers use a phonetic approximation, a functional equivalent like "Savior," or a combination? Gratitude guides this discernment, refusing colonial imposition while guarding gospel integrity. Each successful translation becomes an act of worship: the name above every name finding new resonance in Maasai song, Mandarin poetry, or Quechua storytelling.

Justice & Mercy Ministries

Quoting Isaiah 61, Jesus announced good news to the poor and liberation for the oppressed (Lk 4:18-19). Gratitude for personal salvation overflows into societal engagement, challenging structures that degrade image-bearers. Feeding the hungry, advocating for the trafficked, and welcoming refugees become Christ-exalting acts when done "for the least of these" (Mt 25:40). Thanksgiving fuels perseverance amid slow progress, remembering that the Lion of Judah champions the marginalized.

1.9 The Eschatological Triumph of the Name

Every Knee Shall Bow

Paul depicts a cosmic courtroom where heavenly, earthly, and subterranean beings alike acknowledge Jesus' supremacy (Phil 2:9-11). Gratitude anticipates that day, tasting its certainty in worship gatherings where disparate demographics jointly exalt Christ. Far from escapist fantasy, this vision infuses present suffering with hope, assuring martyrs that vindication is scheduled. Each "Thank You, Jesus" now rehearses eternity's anthem, aligning affections with the storyline God will soon unveil publicly.

The Name Written on the Forehead

Revelation closes with servants seeing God's face and bearing His name on their foreheads (Rev 22:4). Ancient seals signified ownership and protection; here, the inscription marks intimate belonging. Gratitude swells at the promise of undiminished communion—no veil, temple, or sun required (Rev 21:22-23). Identity crises fade, for eternal destiny is anchored in an unerasable name. Thanksgiving today becomes the down payment on that future, reminding believers who they truly are amid cultural confusion.

Unending Worship of the Lamb

John hears cascades of voices—angels, elders, living creatures—praising the Lamb (Rev 5:11-13). The symphony swells until every corner of creation joins, suggesting gratitude is the native language of a healed cosmos. No fatigue, envy, or boredom disrupts the melody; worship is continual because revelation is ever fresh. Believers who practice thanksgiving now tune their hearts to that coming concert, training desire toward the day when sight replaces faith.

Conclusion

The name of Jesus spans the heights of heaven and the depths of human experience, gathering prophetic longing, sacrificial love, sovereign power, and eschatological hope into a single, radiant word. When lips whisper "Thank You," they do more than recite a polite phrase; they participate in a trans-historical, trans-cultural chorus that began in the promises of Eden and will crescendo in the worship halls of the New Jerusalem. Gratitude becomes strength in weakness, clarity in confusion, courage in battle, and melody in mundane tasks. It fashions ordinary believers into living letters, each stroke of obedience spelling out facets of the Savior's beauty for a watching world. While chapters and outlines must eventually end, the gratitude they summon does not, for the One who bears the name above every name is the Alpha and Omega of thanksgiving itself. May every breath until we see Him face to face be an echoed amen: "Thank You, Jesus."

Chapter 2. Thank You, Jesus, for Coming to Us—The Miracle of Incarnation

Long before shepherds knelt in fields near Bethlehem, the eternal Son of God delighted Himself in communion with the Father (Prov 8:30–31). Yet at the fullness of time, He chose to step into our broken chronology, wearing human flesh so that we might glimpse divine glory in a humble cradle (Gal 4:4–5). This miracle of incarnation profoundly reshapes every facet of our gratitude: God's nearness transforms doctrine into devotion, prophecy into presence, and cosmic sovereignty into personal compassion. As we trace the Word made flesh through prophetic promise, angelic proclamation, hidden childhood, and adult ministry, we discover that every manger mystery foreshadows the cross's cosmic victory (Jn 1:14; Phil 2:5–11). In beholding the incarnate Christ, we learn that true thanksgiving arises when we recognize God's majestic condescension—His willingness not merely to visit but to dwell among us (Jn 1:14). May this exploration awaken fresh wonder and draw us into deeper praise for the One who, though rich, became poor that we might become rich (2 Cor 8:9).

2.1 Heaven Touches Earth

Word Made Flesh: Pre-existent Logos Enters Time

In the opening of John's Gospel, the eternal Logos—through whom all things were made—"became flesh and dwelt among us" (Jn 1:14). This staggering declaration fuses the transcendence of Genesis 1 with the vulnerability of a human infant. Before Mary's womb received Him, He existed with God, fully sharing the divine nature (Jn 1:1; Phi 2:6). Yet He voluntarily embraced the constraints of time, space, and creaturely limitations, inviting humanity into intimate fellowship with the Creator. That descent into mortality did not dim His deity; rather, it illuminated the breadth of divine compassion. When we echo "Thank You, Jesus," we honor the paradox that the infinite God would become finite for our salvation. This act of kenosis—emptying Himself of independent divine privilege—anchors grace in history rather than abstraction (Phil 2:7).

Prophecies Foretelling God-with-Us

Centuries prior, Isaiah penned, "Behold, the virgin shall conceive… and they shall call His name Immanuel" (Isa 7:14). That name, meaning "God with us," provided Israel a beacon in exile and yearning in captivity. Micah pinpointed Bethlehem as the King's birthplace, foreshadowing a ruler whose origins were "from of old, from ancient days" (Mic 5:2). These prophecies, embedded in Israel's liturgy and expectation, converged in a single moment when earthly history and divine intention merged. To thank Jesus for His coming is to acknowledge God's unwavering fidelity: what He spoke in ages past, He fulfilled in a manger. Believers who ponder these texts during Advent engage in a tapestry of promise and fulfillment, experiencing gratitude as both remembrance and present reality.

Angelic Announcements: Gabriel's Message to Mary and Joseph

In Nazareth's ordinary stillness, the angel Gabriel declared to Mary, "You will conceive in your womb and bear a son, and you shall call His name Jesus" (Lk 1:31). Her response—"Behold, I am the servant of the Lord; let it be to me according to your word" (Lk 1:38)—models trust amid mystery. Simultaneously, an angel appeared to Joseph, assuring him that Mary's child was conceived by the Holy Spirit and urging him to name Him Jesus, "for He will save His people from their sins" (Mt 1:21). These heavenly communiqués did more than instruct; they invited humans into divine purpose and underscored the Son's dual identity as Messiah and Savior. Our thanksgiving deepens when we recognize that every announcement carried cosmic weight: angels announced the breach between God and man was being healed. Thus, believe that each "Thank You, Jesus" we speak resonates with angelic joy echoing across heaven (Lk 2:13–14).

2.2 The Humble Birth in Bethlehem

Bethlehem in Salvation History

Though small among Judah's towns, Bethlehem became a theological lightning rod when God promised, "Out of you will come for Me a ruler" (Mic 5:2). This "little town" would produce the Shepherd-King whose lineage traced back to David's throne, uniting royal promise with divine incarnation. Mary's journey from Nazareth to Bethlehem (Lk 2:4–5) fulfilled this oracle in humble circumstances, reminding us that God often chooses obscurity for His most significant reveals. When believers say "Thank You" for Jesus' birthplace, they exalt a pattern repeated throughout Scripture: God's grandeur often emerges from human insignificance. The manger's straw-strewn cradle thus becomes a throne room where cosmic glory and childlike wonder meet.

The Manger: Poverty and Presence

No inn would welcome Mary and Joseph, so Jesus entered the world amid animals and hay (Lk 2:7). This tableau of poverty wasn't oversight but divine strategy: the King of kings was accessible to the lowliest heart. The manger signifies God's refusal to distance Himself by luxury or formality; rather, He envelops humanity in His nearness. Only later would He teach that to welcome "one such child" is to welcome Him (Mt 18:5). Our gratitude intensifies when we grasp that simplicity amplifies presence: the same Creator who flung stars into space chose a feed trough as the first pulpit of incarnation.

First Witnesses: Shepherds and Cosmic Choir

Shepherds, marginalized and unclean by social standards, became first recipients of the Good News (Lk 2:8–12). Their fearful awe at the angelic proclamation transformed into jubilant proclamation to all who would listen (Lk 2:17–18). Simultaneously, a multitude of heavenly hosts burst into song, praising God with words of peace and goodwill (Lk 2:13–14). This juxtaposition—earthly lowliness and heavenly majesty—illustrates incarnation's dual axis: God stoops to sinners even as angels exalt Him. Our "Thank You, Jesus" today rides on their testimony, urging us to share wonder where least expected and to recognize that every human heart can become a worshiping shepherd.

2.3 Early Life and Growth

Flight to Egypt and Return to Nazareth

Before the first candle of Christmas cooled, Mary and Joseph fled to Egypt at Herod's murderous decree (Mt 2:13–15). This sojourn echoes Israel's own Exodus, recapitulating redemptive motifs and affirming the Son's solidarity with His people's trials. Joseph's dream-led obedience safeguarded Jesus until it was time to return, fulfilling Hosea's oracle, "Out of Egypt I called My Son" (Hos 11:1). Settlement in Nazareth—a locale of obscurity—prepared Him for a life of hidden obedience. Our gratitude extends to the protective provision that sustains the incarnate Christ through danger and displacement, reminding us that Divine Shepherd always guards His flock.

The Boy in the Temple: Growing in Wisdom and Stature

At twelve, Jesus astounded temple teachers with questions and answers, declaring He must be "in My Father's house" (Lk 2:49). His self-awareness—both human child and obedient Son—revealed the seamless unity of His dual nature. Mary and Joseph's mixture of anxiety and wonder at finding Him underscores incarnation's mystery: God learning obedience through what He suffered (Heb 5:8). As He increased in wisdom and favor (Lk 2:52), He modeled sanctified growth, demonstrating that maturity involves relational alignment with the Father. Our thanksgiving embraces Jesus' fully human journey, affirming that in our own upbringing and struggles, He is a sympathetic high priest able to empathize with every weakness (Heb 4:15).

Hidden Years: Sanctifying Ordinary Work

For decades Jesus lived in Nazareth, likely working as a carpenter (Mk 6:3), sanctifying the daily labor of artisanship. His invisibility to broader culture did not diminish His identity but deepened His empathy for working people. Those years of hidden service remind believers that significance is not always visible but is known by the Father who "sees what is done in secret" (Mt 6:4). Our gratitude extends to Christ's solidarity with the ordinary, anchoring human dignity in every honest vocation. As we strive in mundane tasks, we echo His footsteps, offering labor as worship.

2.4 Fully God, Fully Man—The Hypostatic Union

Kenosis: Voluntary Self-Emptying (Philippians 2)

Paul's hymn in Philippians 2 portrays the Son's self-emptying: though in the form of God, He "made Himself nothing" by taking "the form of a servant" (Phil 2:6–7). This kenotic descent is not subtractive but expressive: divine glory chose the garment of flesh to communicate love in palpable terms. The Word's becoming flesh did not dilute deity but displayed it through humility. Thanksgiving for incarnation stems from this paradox: strength is perfected in weakness, and heaven's royalty is revealed in servant-hood.

Sharing Human Emotions and Limitations

Jesus wept at Lazarus' tomb (Jn 11:35), hungered in the wilderness (Mt 4:2), and grew tired during travels (Jn 4:6). These glimpses of vulnerability invite awe: the infinite Son embraced creaturely needs so He could fully identify with our condition. Yet His emotions never stemmed from ignorance of pain or temptation; rather, they flowed from perfect empathy rooted in divine knowledge. Thanking Jesus involves gratitude for a Savior who does not stand aloof but enters our grief, our hunger, and our weariness—assuring us that in every human struggle, He has already been there.

Divine Authority Manifested in Humanity

Though limited in resources, Jesus exercised divine authority: calming storms (Mk 4:39), forgiving sins (Mk 2:5), and raising the dead (Jn 11:43–44). These miracles attest that His human nature was a genuine human experience empowered by unrestrained deity. Observers faced a startling reality: a man whose word compelled nature, spirits, and death itself. When we say "Thank You, Jesus," we praise a fully human figure whose authority ushers creation into restored harmony.

2.5 Living Among Humanity

Sharing Our Joys and Sorrows

Jesus' incarnation involved more than passive presence; He actively entered communal life—attending weddings (Jn 2:1–11), dining with tax collectors (Mt 9:10–11), and grieving with friends. His participation in human festivities and funerals signals that no experience is beneath His dignity. Gratitude swells when believers recall that Christ not only bore our shame but also celebrated every glimpse of beauty and goodness in fallen creation. Our joys become echo chambers of His delight, and our tears find solace in Him.

Perfect Obedience Modeled

As a boy and as an adult, Jesus consistently did the Father's will (Jn 4:34; Heb 10:7). His spotless obedience, even unto death, fulfills the law's highest demands on behalf of those under its curse (Gal 4:4–5). He transforms obedience from drudgery into delight, inviting gratitude through discovery that freedom emerges when one's will aligns with the divine. Each "Thank You, Jesus" thus honors a life lived as the ultimate obedient Son.

Identifying with the Marginalized and Outcast

Jesus' ministry prioritized those pushed to society's edges: He conversed with a Samaritan woman (Jn 4:7–26), healed lepers (Mk 1:40–45), and touched the unclean (Mk 5:27–34). His incarnation dismantled barriers of ethnicity, disease, and gender, displaying the kingdom's revolutionary inclusivity. Gratitude deepens when the marginalized find in Christ not only acceptance but restoration of dignity. The incarnate King baptizes boundaries with grace, and believers echo His welcome to all.

2.6 Revelation Through Embodied Teaching

Parables Rooted in Daily Life

Jesus spoke of farmers, fishermen, and merchants—stories drawn from daily toil that concealed profound truths about God's kingdom (Mt 13:3–23). By incarnating parables in relatable images, He bridged heaven's mysteries and human experience. Gratitude arises as we rediscover that divine truth is never remote but always incarnational—sprouting in the soil of ordinary life. Each parable invites thanksgiving for a teacher who meets us not on distant mountaintops but beside our worn paths.

Touching the Untouchable: Sacramental Encounters

The woman with the issue of blood dared to touch Jesus' garment (Mk 5:27–29), receiving healing not from a formula but through contact with living grace. Christ's physical ministry—laying hands on sick bodies, anointing with mud—foreshadowed sacraments that unite sign and reality. Gratitude for incarnation extends to baptism and communion, where water, bread, and wine convey tangible grace because the Word became flesh.

Table Fellowship: Hospitality as Theology

Jesus broke social norms by eating with sinners (Lk 5:29–32) and hosting feasts that illustrated the coming banquet of the kingdom (Lk 14:15–24). These table gatherings enacted the gospel: a community formed by mercy, not merit. Gratitude for Jesus' incarnational mission compels believers to practice hospitality, transforming meals into sacramental spaces where grace is both tasted and proclaimed.

2.7 Implications for Creation and Redemption

Material World Affirmed and Redeemed

Incarnation validates the goodness of creation: matter matters because God assumed it (Col 1:16). Jesus used dust to form eyes for a blind man (Jn 9:6–7), signaling that the physical realm participates in divine renewal. Gratitude deepens when Christians cherish environmental stewardship and artistry as forms of worship—honoring the very matter God chose for His advent.

Reversing the Curse: Healings and Miracles

By feeding multitudes (Mt 14:13–21), calming storms, and raising the dead, Jesus enacted Israel's redemption promises in bodily form. Each miracle proclaims that the curse upon creation will be undone. Thanking Jesus for incarnation includes rejoicing in God's commitment to heal a world groaning for renewal (Rom 8:22–23).

The Cross Foreshadowed in the Cradle

From the manger's vulnerability to the cross's atrocity, incarnation sets the stage for substitutionary atonement (Isa 53). The infant who would one day "be pierced for our transgressions" (Isa 53:5) bears the weight of future sacrifice in His womb. Gratitude intensifies as we trace how God's redemptive plan—conceived in eternity—unfolded in history's most tender moments.

2.8 The Incarnational Call to the Church

Being the Body of Christ Today

As Christ dwelt among us, so the Church is called to incarnate His presence in neighborhoods, workplaces, and schools (1 Cor 12:27). Believers, as living stones, are to reveal God's character in flesh-and-blood contexts. Gratitude for Jesus' coming fuels community practices that mirror His compassion and creativity.

Presence-Based Mission: Dwelling Among the Lost

Incarnational mission emphasizes presence over program: living among the marginalized, learning language, and bearing witness through shared life. This approach refuses quick fixes in favor of long-term solidarity. Thankfulness for the Word made flesh catalyzes a mission that risks comfort to incarnate Christ's love where it's needed most.

Incarnational Spiritual Disciplines: Hospitality, Simplicity, Justice

Following Jesus involves embracing rhythms that reflect His humility: opening homes to strangers, choosing simplicity over opulence, and pursuing justice for the oppressed (Isa 61:1–3). These disciplines embed gratitude in daily life, turning every act into a sacrament of incarnation.

2.9 Celebrating the Incarnation

Advent Expectation and Christmas Joy

The Church calendar's Advent season recaptures Israel's longing, weaving prophetic readings with candlelit anticipation. Christmas proclaims fulness of joy when the Word becomes flesh. Gratitude emerges as worship services burst into carols that enshrine incarnation's wonder for yet another generation.

Creeds and Hymns that Guard the Mystery

Historic creeds—Nicene, Apostles', Chalcedonian—protect the doctrine of Christ's full deity and true humanity. Hymns like "O Come, O Come, Emmanuel" and "Hark! The Herald Angels Sing" reenact that mystery poetically. Thankfulness for these confessional and musical treasures sustains robust faith amid doctrinal drift.

Eucharist: Ongoing Participation in the Word Made Flesh

When believers gather around bread and cup, they proclaim Christ's death and await His return (1 Cor 11:26). The sacrament, rooted in incarnation, unites the community with the incarnate Lord. Gratitude flows as worshipers touch tangible signs of the Word's dwelling among us.

2.10 Eschatological Fulfillment

Firstfruits of the New Creation

Christ's resurrection is the "firstfruits" guaranteeing believers' future body transformation (1 Cor 15:20–23). Incarnation's power extends beyond birth pangs into resurrection hope.

Thanking Jesus includes praise for the life to come—where flesh shall fully share divine glory.

The Second Advent of the Incarnate King

Just as He came in weakness, Jesus will return in power (Rev 19:11–16). The glory veiled in Bethlehem will blaze openly, vindicating every act of faith and every tear wiped away. Gratitude anchors present witness in the assured promise of His appearing.

Eternal Emmanuel: God Dwelling with Humanity Forever

Revelation's final vision portrays God's tabernacle among people, with no temple because the Lord and the Lamb are its temple (Rev 21:3–4). The eternal state fulfills incarnation's promise: God permanently residing with those He redeemed. Every "Thank You, Jesus" now echoes through unending halls of Heaven, where His presence is the everlasting wonder.

Conclusion

The incarnation stands at the heart of Christian gratitude: God-with-us in life's fragility and history's turmoil, bringing heaven's light into human darkness. From prophetic whispers to angelic shouts, from a cradle of straw to a throne of glory, the miracle of incarnation calls us to worship without end. When Jesus clothed Himself in our nature, He declared every human story worthy of divine attention. As we live in the tension of "already and not yet," our thanksgiving becomes a foretaste of eternity, where the Word made flesh will forever dwell among us—our Emmanuel, our Joy, our Hope. May every heartbeat affirm: Thank You, Jesus, for coming to us.

Chapter 3. Thank You, Jesus, for Teaching Truth—Words of Life

Teaching lies at the very center of Jesus' earthly mission. Long before the cross was sketched against the Judean sky, the Lord gathered crowds on Galilean hillsides, spoke mysteries beside inland seas, and carried private conversations far into the night, all to unveil realities hidden since the foundation of the world (Mt 13 : 35). His voice penetrated both the collective conscience of Israel and the individual hearts of fishermen, tax collectors, religious experts, and weary travelers. By wrapping eternal wisdom in everyday language—stories of soil, seeds, coins, banquets, barns, and vineyards—He dignified human experience while summoning it upward toward divine purpose. Whenever He concluded, "Whoever has ears, let them hear," He offered far more than information; He extended an invitation into the life of God, where truth heals, confronts, and ultimately liberates (Jn 8 : 31-32). Gratitude swells when disciples realize that the words reaching us through parchment and translation are the same Spirit-breathed utterances that once stilled storms of ignorance and sin. In the pages that follow we linger over some of those transformative lessons, thanking the Teacher whose syllables still carry resurrection power.

3.1 The Authority of His Teaching

Sermon on the Mount — Kingdom Manifesto

When Jesus ascended a Galilean slope and sat down, He adopted the authoritative posture of a rabbi; yet His opening words shattered conventional notions of blessedness (Mt 5 : 1-12). Declaring the poor in spirit heirs of a kingdom while calling the meek future landlords of the earth, He inverted social pyramids and exposed human cravings for status. His beatitudes sketch a portrait of flourishing that planets cannot provide: comfort to mourners, fullness to the famished, vision to the pure in heart, adoption to peacemakers. Far from moral platitudes, these announcements constitute royal edicts, for the King Himself guarantees the outcomes. Throughout chapters 5–7, every imperative—rejoice in persecution, let yes be yes, love enemies, pray unseen—rests on the bedrock promise of the Father's active care. Thus, thanksgiving erupts not merely for lofty ideals but for a new reality birthed by divine reign. Disciples reading these chapters today bow in awe before a Teacher whose words retain authority to expose private motives and empower radical obedience, all while assuring anxious hearts that heavenly provision runs deeper than lilies' colors and sparrows' songs (Mt 6 : 25-34).

Parabolic Method — Revealing to the Humble, Concealing from the Proud

Midway through His public ministry Jesus pivoted toward parables, embedding sharp truths in gentle tales (Mt 13 : 10-17). This strategy fulfilled Isaiah's prophecy that hearing ears might remain deaf when pride prevails, yet newborn humility would find hidden treasure in plain sight (Isa 6 : 9-10). Parables function like stained-glass windows: from outside they appear dull, but step inside the sanctuary of surrender and sunlight ignites color. Thus the same story both judges and saves: executives and peasants might share the same front-row seat, yet perception hinges on repentant posture. Gratitude wells up because the Teacher refuses coercion; He woos with narrative rather than nailing truth to forehead. Moreover, those who do lean in—the disciples who ask follow-up questions—receive fuller exposition, illustrating God's eagerness to grant revelation where curiosity is clothed in faith (Mk 4 : 34). Even now, believers detect fresh hues in familiar parables whenever they approach with childlike expectation, proving that Jesus' pedagogical genius remains inexhaustible.

"You Have Heard … But I Say" — Fulfilling and Deepening the Law

Six times in Matthew 5 Jesus contrasts inherited interpretations with His own authoritative voice. He does not discard Torah; rather, He stretches it from external conduct to interior architecture—anger equated with murder, lust with adultery, dishonest oaths with profanity of character. By pressing commandments into the hidden recesses of motive, He shows sin's seat within the heart while simultaneously illuminating a righteousness surpassing scribes and Pharisees (Mt 5 : 20). Yet His purpose is not despair but transformation. In fulfilling the Law (Mt 5 : 17), He embodies its intent: love that seeks neighbor's good even when neighbor proves enemy. Thanksgiving ascends because the same Author who once inscribed tablets on Sinai now inscribes compassion on fleshly hearts through His Spirit (Jer 31 : 33; 2 Cor 3 : 3). The teacher who deepens demands also supplies grace, inviting disciples to experience holiness as freedom rather than burden.

3.2 Unfolding the Kingdom Through Parables

Sower and Soils — Conditions of the Heart

In the opening parable of Matthew 13, seed remains constant while outcomes diverge according to soil texture (Mt 13 : 3-9, 18-23). Path, rocks, and thorns illustrate minds hardened by cynicism, wills shallow under pressure, and affections strangled by wealth. The good soil sees thirty, sixty, hundredfold harvest—evidence that the kingdom's expansion hinges on receptive hearts more than perfect circumstances. Followers thank Jesus for exposing internal landscapes we might never scrutinize, offering diagnosis and cure in the same breath. His explanation is agricultural tender-care: break fallow ground by repentance, remove stones of offense through trust, uproot choking desires via generosity. Each new willingness invites fresh sowing, proving that yesterday's wasteland can become tomorrow's granary under the Gardner's patient hand.

Mustard Seed & Leaven — Hidden, Subversive Growth

With two miniature analogies Jesus highlights disproportionate impact: a speck of mustard burgeons into a garden tree; a pinch of yeast pervades three measures of dough (Mt 13 : 31-33). Listeners expecting geopolitical spectacle learn that God delights in stealth operations. Gratitude arises for a kingdom unhindered by small beginnings—house-church prayers, whispered forgiveness, cups of cold water offered in alleys all carry leaven's quiet potency. History corroborates: despised fishermen seed a global Church, desert monks preserve Scripture, unknown translators ignite awakenings. Thanksgiving flows because significance is decoupled from size, tethered instead to divine vitality within the seemingly trivial.

Treasure & Pearl — Supreme Value That Demands Surrender

Two shoppers—one accidental, one deliberate—sell everything to secure a find beyond appraisal: buried treasure and dazzling pearl (Mt 13 : 44-46). Jesus paints the economics of discipleship: the gospel costs nothing and everything. True gratitude fuels such transactions; recognizing the incomparable worth of Christ compels joyful relinquishment of lesser securities. This joy-anchored sacrifice prevents asceticism from sourness; it is the delight of a merchant who knows he has traded baubles for brilliance. Here thanksgiving becomes the engine of holiness, not its garnish, reminding believers that lavish grace invites lavish response.

3.3 Reframing the Law and Prophets

Great Commandment — Love God and Neighbor

Pressed by religious lawyers to name the greatest command, Jesus laces Deuteronomy 6 with Leviticus 19, intertwining vertical devotion and horizontal compassion (Mt 22 : 34-40). He thus condenses six hundred plus statutes into a seamless garment of love, declaring all prophetic scrolls hang on this dual hinge. Gratitude awakens because complexity gives way to clarity: love becomes both compass and destination. Yet the Teacher's wisdom penetrates deeper—self-love is assumed, but reoriented; neighbor love mirrors self-concern, reflecting a healed identity anchored in divine affection. By praying, "Thank You, Jesus, for teaching truth," disciples celebrate liberation from checklist religion while embracing the all-embracing ethic that fulfills it.

Sabbath Made for Man — Rest Rooted in Mercy

Confronted over grain-picking and healing on the Sabbath, Jesus declares the day a gift, not a shackle, and identifies Himself as its Lord (Mk 2 : 23-28; Lk 13 : 10-17). By freeing a bent-over woman and justifying hungry disciples, He uncovers Sabbath's heart: restorative mercy grounded in God's own creative rhythm. Gratitude blossoms when weary modern souls hear that rest is not reward for efficiency but sacrament of trust. Jesus' teaching invites people to cease striving, delight in creatureliness, and join a weekly protest against Pharaoh-like systems that equate worth with output. Every Sabbath well kept whispers thanks to the Teacher who busts chains of legalism and hustle alike.

Weightier Matters — Justice, Mercy, Faithfulness

Pronouncing woes upon tithe-obsessed Pharisees, Jesus condemns their neglect of justice, mercy, and faithfulness—the heavier cargo of Torah (Mt 23 : 23-24). He affirms precise obedience in minor commands yet demands proportional passion for society's vulnerable. Gratitude for such blunt truth arises because it rescues religion from triviality; it re-centers worship where God's heart beats strongest: defending widows, welcoming strangers, dealing honestly. When churches recalibrate budgets, sermons, and calendars toward these weightier concerns, they enact thanksgiving, proving the Teacher's words continue steering conscience toward shalom.

3.4 Life-Changing Dialogues

Nicodemus — The Mystery of New Birth

Under nocturnal cover a respected teacher seeks greater light (Jn 3 : 1-21). Jesus bypasses credentials and prescribes rebirth—water and Spirit breezes unmanageable by pedigree. He discloses heavenly secrets: the Son must be lifted like Moses' serpent so that belief may usher eternal life. Thanksgiving ascends from hearts once baffled by second-birth paradox yet now delivered from condemnation through John 3 : 16's open invitation. Jesus' conversation affirms that no intellectual achievement substitutes for spiritual renovation; however sophisticated a skeptic, the Teacher engages patiently until darkness becomes dawn.

Samaritan Woman — Living Water for Thirsty Souls

At Jacob's well Jesus breaks social, ethnic, and moral taboos (Jn 4 : 4-42). He probes a five-husband history not to shame but to reveal unquenchable thirst misdirected toward fickle cisterns. His promise of living water evokes prophetic streams of Spirit-renewal (Jer 2 : 13; Isa 55 : 1-3). Gratitude overflows as outcasts hear themselves in her testimony—"He told me everything I ever did"—yet sense shame evaporating under sunrise of grace. Her village's revival underscores the ripple effect of personal conversations; disciples today thank Jesus that private wells can become public fountains when truth meets honesty.

Rich Young Ruler — The Cost of True Discipleship

An earnest seeker kneels, claiming law-abiding fidelity, yet exits sorrowful when told to liquidate wealth and follow Christ (Mk 10 : 17-27). Jesus' gaze of love pierces beyond commandments kept to idols clutched, illustrating that possessions may possess their owners. Gratitude for this unsettling encounter emerges because the Teacher refuses to dilute truth to inflate membership. He names the camel-through-needle impossibility only to unveil grace's hydraulics—"With God all things are possible." Those who yield find that relinquished riches pale beside treasure of companionship with Christ.

3.5 Hard Sayings That Purify Motives

"Eat My Flesh, Drink My Blood" — Radical Participation

In Capernaum's synagogue Jesus scandalizes listeners by equating eternal life with ingesting His very being (Jn 6 : 48-58). Many depart, offended by cannibalistic imagery. The metaphor anticipates cross and communion: believing means embracing sacrificial death as life's sustenance. Gratitude flourishes in hearts that have tasted the Eucharistic mystery—receiving grace not as abstract doctrine but as embodied nourishment. As Peter confesses, "You have the words of eternal life," the Church echoes thanksgiving for a sustenance deeper than manna, for flesh broken and blood poured becomes covenant hospitality.

"Hate Father and Mother" — Supreme Allegiance to Christ

Jesus employs Semitic hyperbole to demand discipleship loyalty surpassing filial ties (Lk 14 : 25-27). His stark language delineates kingdom priority: love for Him must be so unrivaled that all other loves, by comparison, look like hate. Gratitude awakens in realizing that such devotion liberates relationships from idolatry; when Christ reigns supreme, family affection flows purified of control. Hard words thus heal, pruning entanglements that choke spiritual fruitfulness. Thanksgiving embraces not only comfort but cutting truths that set hearts free.

Camel Through a Needle — Wealth and the Kingdom

Imagining a loaded camel squeezing through a city gate's eye, Jesus humorously exposes riches' capacity to inflate self-reliance (Mt 19 : 23-26). By highlighting impossibility, He redirects trust toward divine prowess. Gratitude springs forth when affluent and aspirational alike discover that salvation is a miracle, not a merger; kingdom entry cannot be purchased but only received. His hyperbole shatters illusions of control, inviting believers into childlike dependence where thanksgiving becomes the currency of grace.

3.6 Teaching Through Signs and Wonders

Feeding the Five Thousand — Bread of Life Revealed

With five loaves and two fish Jesus sets a banquet in wilderness, echoing Israel's manna and Elisha's multiplication (Mt 14 : 13-21; 2 Kg 4 : 42-44). He involves disciples in distribution, teaching stewardship of scarcity under divine sufficiency. Twelve baskets of leftovers symbolize provision for every tribe. Gratitude erupts as churches facing limited resources remember that thanksgiving precedes increase; Jesus looked up, blessed, broke, and abundance followed. The miracle becomes enacted parable of Himself as bread satisfying deepest hungers (Jn 6 : 35).

Walking on Water — " I AM" Over Chaos

After dismissing crowds, Jesus strides across storm-tossed waves toward terrified disciples (Mt 14 : 22-33). His self-identification, "It is I" (Greek ἐγώ εἰμι), evokes Yahweh's covenant name, asserting presence over elemental forces. Peter's brief water-walk exposes both daring faith and sinking doubt, yet Jesus lifts him, demonstrating that grace undergirds wobbling trust. Thanksgiving intensifies as believers recall nights of surging fear calmed by the same voice still echoing, "Take courage." The lesson: storms become corridors for fresh revelation when eyes fix on the Teacher rather than turmoil.

Healing on the Sabbath — Lord of Rest and Restoration

Repeatedly Jesus selects Sabbath settings to restore withered hands, blind eyes, and crippled backs (Mk 3 : 1-6; Jn 9 : 1-7). His healings proclaim liberation at the heart of Sabbath rest—shalom embodied, not rule-policing. Gratitude blooms where sick bodies and sin-burdened souls realize that God's rest is not passive cessation but active renewal. Each act of healing becomes sermon and signpost, pointing toward final Sabbath when creation itself will be healed.

3.7 Discipleship Lessons in Real Time

Washing Feet — Paradigm of Servant Leadership

On the eve of crucifixion Jesus removes outer garments, stoops with basin and towel, cleansing dust from disciples' feet—betrayer included (Jn 13 : 1-17). His enacted parable upends leadership hierarchies, defining greatness by service. Peter's protest and subsequent submission illustrate tension between prideful independence and grace-received humility. Gratitude for this lesson pulses whenever authority is wielded for another's good instead of self-promotion. Churches practicing foot washing—literal or metaphorical—testify that the Teacher's example still reforms power dynamics.

Storm on the Sea — Faith That Triumphs Over Fear

Earlier on Galilee, while waves threatened to swamp the boat, Jesus slept (Mk 4 : 35-41). Awakened, He rebuked wind and water, then questioned disciples' faith. The narrative frames fear as forgetfulness—ignoring the Teacher's promise to reach the other side. Gratitude arises when we realize that presence, not circumstance, secures destiny. Each crisis becomes classroom where anxiety can yield to worship—"Who then is this, that even wind and sea obey Him?"

Mission of the Seventy-Two — Apprenticeship in the Harvest

Sending trainees ahead in pairs with minimal supplies, Jesus empowers them to heal and announce the kingdom (Lk 10 : 1-20). Their joyful return over demons' submission elicits correction: rejoice not in power but in names written in heaven. Gratitude resonates in that recalibration—ministry identity rests in adoption, not performance. The Teacher delights to share His labor, schooling disciples through fieldwork rather than lecture alone. Thanksgiving today drives mission, remembering harvest belongs to the Lord of the harvest who still calls laborers.

3.8 Apocalyptic Discourse—Truth About the End

Birth Pains & Watchfulness — Signs of the Times

On Olivet's slopes Jesus blends immediate fall of Jerusalem with distant consummation, picturing wars, earthquakes, and persecution as labor contractions preceding new creation (Mt 24 : 3-14). His counsel stresses vigilance over date speculation: false messiahs will arise, but endurance marks true disciples. Gratitude for such forewarning equips believers to interpret turmoil without alarm, framing global upheaval as stage-setting for kingdom fullness. Hope anchored in the Teacher's sovereignty fortifies worship amid world volatility.

Ten Virgins — Readiness for the Bridegroom

A midnight cry finds five bridesmaids' lamps aflame and five flickering out (Mt 25 : 1-13). Jesus highlights personal responsibility: borrowed devotion cannot substitute prepared hearts. Gratitude for this parable pulses each time believers trim wicks through prayer, Scripture, and obedience, securing reserve oil of intimacy. Joyful anticipation, not dread, motivates readiness, for the Bridegroom's arrival means consummate celebration.

Sheep & Goats — Criteria of Final Judgment

In final courtroom imagery, nations divide by unnoticed acts of mercy toward "least of these" (Mt 25 : 31-46). The Judge identifies with hungry, stranger, prisoner, revealing that faith's authenticity manifests in concrete compassion. Gratitude trembles and thrills: trembles at justice's precision, thrills at opportunity to serve Christ incognito. Obedient love becomes thank-offering, echoing the Teacher's directive that greatness is measured by care for the vulnerable.

3.9 Ethics for a Kingdom Community

Seventy-Seven-Fold Forgiveness — The Economics of Grace

Peter's inquiry about forgiveness limits elicits arithmetic of mercy beyond calculation (Mt 18 : 21-22). Jesus then tells of a servant forgiven ten-thousand-talent debt who throttles another over pennies. In kingdom economy, forgiven debtors become lavish dispensers or face imprisonment of resentment. Thanksgiving fuels such generosity; remembering one's canceled ledger dismantles stinginess of spirit. Communities saturated with gratitude become healing zones where conflict becomes catalyst for deeper fellowship.

Restorative Discipline — Winning a Brother or Sister

Jesus outlines a redemptive process: private confrontation, escalation with witnesses, and finally community involvement—always aiming to regain the wanderer (Mt 18 : 15-17). Gratitude undergirds this ethic; valuing relational gift compels pursuit rather than passive withdrawal. The Teacher's framework balances holiness and mercy, protecting against gossip on one hand and permissiveness on the other. Thankful churches honor his guidance, treating discipline as spiritual hospitality—hard truth spoken for shared joy.

Beatitudes — Character Map of Blessed Citizens

Returning to the Sermon's opening promises, disciples recognize the beatitudes not only as descriptions but prescriptions empowered by Spirit. Poverty of spirit, mourning over sin, meek trust, hunger for righteousness, merciful posture, purity of heart, peacemaking, and persevering under persecution—this eight-fold jewel radiates kingdom culture. Gratitude for Jesus' teaching instills hunger to embody these traits, knowing blessing lies not in circumstance but in communion with the King who personifies every beatitude.

3.10 Legacy of the Living Word

Great Commission — Teaching All Nations to Obey

After resurrection Jesus anchors mission in His universal authority, commanding disciples to make disciples by baptizing and teaching obedience to His commands (Mt 28 : 18-20). Thanksgiving pulses through this charter: the Teacher entrusts His curriculum to former fishermen and doubters. Ongoing presence—"I am with you always"—assures efficacy. Every time the Church catechizes children, trains converts, or translates Scripture, it participates in this living mandate, echoing gratitude into future generations.

Gift of the Spirit of Truth — Ongoing Illumination

On farewell night Jesus promises another Paraclete who will teach all things and remind disciples of His words (Jn 14 : 26; 16 : 13). Pentecost inaugurates that internal tutor, ensuring Jesus' teaching never calcifies but remains fresh revelation. Gratitude for the Spirit safeguards against sterile academia; devotion becomes dialogue where ancient text encounters present context. Thus, sermons, study groups, and quiet meditations continue under the Teacher's supervision through His Spirit.

Apostolic Doctrine — Foundation Stones for the Church

Acts depicts early believers devoting themselves to apostles' teaching (Acts 2 : 42), crystallizing Jesus' oral instruction into letters, gospels, and pastoral counsel. This deposit, once hidden in scrolls, now saturates apps and airwaves, yet retains original potency because the Teacher's voice resonates behind every syllable. Gratitude moves Christians to guard, study, and live this doctrine, knowing that faithful transmission sustains global fellowship across centuries.

Conclusion

The words of Jesus never echo into emptiness; they create worlds, dismantle lies, kindle hope, and carve paths of righteousness where deserts once sprawled. Every parable, command, dialogue, and promise explored here reveals facets of a wisdom that flows from the heart of God yet stoops to instruct farmers, widows, scholars, and children alike. To thank Him for teaching truth is to acknowledge that without His illumination we would wander in intellectual brilliance yet spiritual night. Because He spoke, we know who we are, whose we are, where history heads, and how love manifests between now and then. May His living words dwell richly within us, shaping communities that mirror the kingdom manifesto, embrace divine inversion, and proclaim freedom to all who hunger for life. And may our perpetual refrain—spoken, sung, embodied—be this simple confession of wonder: "Thank You, Jesus, for the words that still give life."

Chapter 4. Thank You, Jesus, for the Cross—Our Redemption

The cross stands at the very heart of Christian faith, where divine love and cosmic justice converge in a single, shocking spectacle. It is both an execution device and an altar of mercy, where the innocent One bore the weight of human sin (2 Cor 5:21). In that moment, heaven's holiness and earth's brokenness collided, and the world was forever changed. Our gratitude for the cross stems not only from its demonstration of sacrificial love but also from its unveiling of God's redemptive purpose—turning shame into glory, curse into blessing, and death into life (Gal 3:13). As we trace the steps from Gethsemane's agony to the earthquake that shook the tomb, we will behold the depth of Christ's suffering and the breadth of His victory. Every drop of sweat and tear, every mock crown and jeering insult, carries the weight of our darkest deeds and the promise of our brightest hope. May this chapter lead our hearts into fresh praise for the One who endured the cross, despising its shame, that we might embrace the unending riches of His grace (Heb 12:2).

4.1 Prelude to Calvary: Gethsemane and Betrayal

Cup of Sorrow: Agony and Submission in the Garden

Before the cross's public horror, Jesus entered an even darker vale of suffering in Gethsemane, where He wrestled with the prospect of bearing humanity's sin (Mt 26:36–38). The weight of impending judgment pressed upon His soul so intensely that His sweat fell "like great drops of blood" (Lk 22:44), illustrating the physical cost of spiritual anguish. In that solitary hour, the Son of God confronted separation from the Father as He carried the world's guilt, revealing the absolute necessity of His sacrificial obedience. Yet amid overwhelming dread, He uttered the words that echo through ages: "Not my will, but yours, be done" (Lk 22:42). This submission frames our gratitude, for it was not resignation but loving surrender—choosing the cup of wrath so sinners might sip the cup of salvation. His agony teaches us that true obedience often involves suffering and that privileged position never negates sacrificial willingness. When we pause to say "Thank You, Jesus," we recall a garden prayer whose echo reverberates through Calvary's groans, securing our redemption.

Sleeping Disciples: Human Frailty Exposed

As Jesus pleaded for strength, He found His closest friends asleep, their weakness laid bare beneath olive trees (Mt 26:40–43). Peter, James, and John—who moments earlier professed unwavering loyalty—could not muster a single hour of watchfulness (Mk 14:37). Their slumber symbolizes every tendency to drift into spiritual drowsiness when faith demands vigilance, reminding us that even the most devoted followers need divine power to stand in trials. Jesus' gentle rebuke—"Could you not watch with me one hour?"—blends sorrow with mercy, exposing our frailty while still offering compassionate restoration (Mt 26:40). Gratitude springs from knowing that He stays awake for us, interceding even when our strength fails (Rom 8:34). The disciples' failure highlights both the cost of discipleship and the kindness of the Savior who does not abandon us in our weakness but bathes us again in grace.

Kiss of Betrayal: Judas and the Clash of Loyalties

Judas Iscariot's approach in the moonlight, lips brushing Jesus' cheek in a pretense of friendship, magnified evil's cunning cruelty (Mt 26:48–49). This "kiss of Judas" sealed the fate of the Innocent, displaying how proximity to Jesus does not guarantee loyalty. In that moment, betrayal pierced more deeply than the soldiers' swords to come, for it embodied the collective treachery of humanity—God's own receiving a kiss from those He loved most. Yet Jesus spoke to Judas with calm resolve, acknowledging Divine necessity even amidst treason. The betrayal teaches us that sin often masquerades as affection, requiring discernment born of prayer. Our gratitude extends to the One who faced betrayal without bitterness, absorbing treachery's sting so that our infidelity could be erased by His faithfulness (Ps 89:33). As we reflect on that kiss, we worship the steadfast Bridegroom whose love endures every false embrace.

4.2 Trials and Condemnation

Jewish Council: Charges of Blasphemy

Dragged before the Sanhedrin, Jesus faced religious rulers who accused Him of blasphemy for claiming to be the Son of God (Mk 14:61–64). Their courtroom combined pious veneer with political self-preservation, determined to silence the prophetic voice that exposed their hypocrisy. Under oath, Jesus affirmed His identity by invoking Daniel's vision of the Son of Man granted authority over all nations (Dan 7:13–14; Mt 26:64), an answer that enraged the council into rushing for stones. Their legalism, blind to truth, highlights how fear of losing power can corrupt religious devotion into murderous intent. Yet in that unjust verdict, the contours of divine justice emerge: the truly innocent standing condemned so the guilty might receive acquittal. Gratitude flows from recognizing the cross as God's courtroom where mercy triumphs over condemnation, and where the Law's demands are satisfied in the one perfect life.

Pilate's Judgment Seat: Political Expedience vs. Truth

Pontius Pilate, the Roman governor, navigated between his perception of truth and the political pressure of a volatile crowd (Jn 18:38–40). Though he found no fault warranting death, Pilate succumbed to expediency, handing Jesus over "to be crucified" to avoid unrest (Mk 15:14). His act reveals the tragic alliance between power and pragmatism, where truth becomes collateral damage. Pilate's symbolic washing of hands could not cleanse his conscience, a poignant reminder that moral compromise leaves indelible stains even on public reputations. The Son of God stood condemned by both religious zealots and political cynics, signaling that every human institution failed to uphold justice. Yet divine wisdom worked through this miscarriage to accomplish salvation. In Pilate's courtroom, we glimpse the cost of truth's rejection and bow in gratitude to the One who bore those false charges willingly.

Barabbas Exchanged: Innocence for the Guilty

In a cruel inversion of justice, the crowd chose to free Barabbas—a known insurrectionist—while delivering Jesus to crucifixion (Mk 15:6–15). Barabbas, stained by rebellion and bloodshed, walked to freedom as the spotless Lamb marched toward death. This exchange captures the essence of substitutionary atonement: the guilty set free, the innocent condemned. We see ourselves in Barabbas—captive to sin—yet through Christ's sacrifice, we are released from bondage (Rom 6:22). Every "Thank You, Jesus" acknowledges this exchange, where divine love orchestrated the greatest swap in history. The riotous crowd's roar becomes our anthem of praise, for in Barabbas' release, we see the shadow of our own justification secured on Calvary's hill.

4.3 Via Dolorosa—The Road of Suffering

Scourging and Mockery: Crown of Thorns, Robe of Shame

Before even reaching Golgotha, Jesus endured the brutality of Roman scourging—six strokes from the flagrum that tore flesh and ruptured vessels (Jn 19:1). Then soldiers wove a crown of thorns and draped Him in a purple robe, mocking His claim to kingship (Mk 15:16–20). Each thorn pressed into His brow, each lash across His back, symbolized the curse against human rebellion and the piercing of divine love for sinners (Gen 3:17–18). Their jeers—"Hail, King of the Jews!"—exposed the depth of human cruelty even as they unwittingly proclaimed His true identity. In those moments of shame, the Son became sin for us, shouldering every mockery so that our honor might be restored (2 Cor 5:21). Our gratitude swells when we remember that our Redeemer embraced the depths of humiliation to lift us into the heights of grace.

Bearing the Cross: Simon of Cyrene's Unexpected Service

Crippled by scourging, Jesus could not carry the heavy wooden beam alone, so Roman soldiers pressed Simon of Cyrene into service (Mk 15:21). In that forced encounter, Simon—perhaps a pilgrim from North Africa—became an unwitting partner in the Savior's mission. His reluctant obedience foreshadows the call to all disciples: to take up one's cross and follow Christ (Mt 16:24). Each step along the Via Dolorosa compressed the world's sin into a single procession toward judgment. Yet compassion shone through, as Simon's act mirrored the love that compels us to bear one another's burdens (Gal 6:2). Our gratitude acknowledges the hidden Simons—friends, family, strangers—through whose kindness Christ's yoke becomes lighter for us today.

Daughters of Jerusalem: Prophetic Warning Amid Lament

As Jesus trudged toward His execution, He paused to address the mourning women of Jerusalem, foretelling the city's coming desolation (Lk 23:27–31). His exhortation—"Weep not for me, but for yourselves and for your children"—laid bare the intertwined destinies of Messiah and nation. In their tears, we see the sorrow of humanity confronted by sin's consequences, and in His words, the call to sorrow that leads to repentance (2 Cor 7:10). Even on the road of suffering, Christ proclaimed truth and offered warning, embodying the prophet who loves compassion more than sacrifice (Hos 6:6). Our gratitude echoes in the tears we shed—both for our Savior's pain and for the broken world that still rejects His mercy.

4.4 The Crucifixion Unveiled

Place of the Skull: Historical and Theological Significance

Golgotha—Aramaic for "skull"—served as the bleak stage for the world's most consequential death (Jn 19:17). Tradition locates it outside Jerusalem's gate, a place of execution visible to worshipers in the temple. This location fulfilled prophetic foreshadowing, where the Passover lamb's blood was spat upon the doorpost, marking life amid death (Ex 12:7). On Golgotha's crest, justice and mercy met: the condemned One absorbed wrath so that His people might savor redemption. Our gratitude deepens as we contemplate that the cosmic Lamb bled in plain sight, declaring to all creation that there are no hidden sins beyond His capacity to forgive.

Nails and Blood: The Physical Cost of Redemption

Crucifixion was designed for maximum agony and public humiliation, as metal spikes pounded through wrists and ankles (Jn 20:25), stretches opening lungs to suffocation's edge. Yet those nails epitomized the startling reality that the Creator would be bound by humanity's cruelty. Streams of blood—from crown, scalp, and rib—inscribed a living gospel in the dust, testifying that life is in the blood (Lev 17:11) and that Christ's flowing veins renewed the covenant (Heb 9:22). Each scar on His body reflects a sin forgiven, a fear conquered, and a hope secured. Our murmured "Thank You, Jesus" cannot suffice to honor such costly love, but it ushers us into deeper worship of the One whose wounds became our healing (Isa 53:5).

Soldiers' Gambling: Fulfilled Prophecy in Seemingly Trivial Acts

As Jesus hung between heaven and earth, Roman soldiers cast lots for His seamless garment, fulfilling Psalm 22:18's ancient oracle. Their game—an apparently mundane footnote—reveals the divine orchestration underlying every detail of His passion. God sovereignly shaped history so that even soldiers' dice would testify to His Word's invincibility. The randomness of their play contrasts with the perfection of prophecy, showing that human cruelty cannot thwart redemptive purpose. Gratitude rises when we see the cross's minutiae as divine artistry, where no event is too small to proclaim God's unbreakable vow to save.

4.5 Seven Last Words—Windows into the Savior's Heart

Forgiveness Offered to Enemies

Amid excruciating pain, Jesus looked down upon the crowds and implored, "Father, forgive them, for they know not what they do" (Lk 23:34). This plea, uttered through torn lungs, epitomizes mercy's triumph over judgment. His forgiveness enveloped both violent executioners and indifferent spectators, demonstrating that divine love surpasses human resistance. In that moment, the cross became a confessional booth where even the worst offenders stand hopeful of pardon. Gratitude for this word of forgiveness shapes our own mercy, compelling us to forgive as we have been forgiven (Eph 4:32).

Promise of Paradise to the Penitent Thief

To the second thief who rebuked his companion, Jesus promised, "Today you will be with me in Paradise" (Lk 23:43). Stripped of earthly achievements and facing imminent death, this penitent sinner received the gift of eternal life through simple faith. His request—"Remember me when you come into your kingdom"—models the contrite heart that finds hope in mercy alone (Isa 66:2). Gratitude surges when we recall that no sin is too great to fall outside the cross's reach and that Christ's arms welcome the weakest who call upon His name (Rom 10:13).

Cry of Abandonment: Mystery of Divine Forsakenness

As the full weight of sin pressed upon Him, Jesus cried, "My God, my God, why have you forsaken me?" (Mt 27:46), quoting Psalm 22's lament. In that cry, He experienced the alienation due to sinners, enduring the Father's hiddenness so we might never be abandoned (Isa 49:15–16). The agony of separation underscores the seriousness with which God treats sin and the depth of His identification with human despair. Yet even in darkness, He trusted the Father's faithfulness, modeling prayer in defeat. Gratitude for this mystery arises as we realize that, because He endured forsakenness, we can cling to God's presence even in our darkest moments.

4.6 Cosmic Signs and the Veil Torn

Darkness at Noon: Creation Mourns Its Creator

From the sixth to the ninth hour, darkness engulfed the land as if creation itself repented (Mk 15:33). This supernatural eclipse declared that something cosmic had transpired—light meeting darkness in the person of Christ. The sun's refusal to shine mirrored the world's moral blindness and the gravity of the moment when sin's debt was paid. Gratitude deepens when we see creation join in Calvary's lament, affirming that Christ's work impacts every realm—from human hearts to heavenly bodies.

Temple Veil Split: Open Access to the Holy of Holies

At the moment of Jesus' death, the thick curtain separating the Holy of Holies tore in two from top to bottom (Mt 27:51), symbolizing the end of separation between God and humanity. No longer did a sinful people need an earthly high priest to mediate, for Christ inaugurated direct communion with the Father through His blood (Heb 10:19–20). This torn veil invites every believer into the sanctuary's inner chamber, where grace replaces fear. Our "Thank You, Jesus" resonates in worship that crosses former barriers—social, ethnic, gender—to stand boldly in God's presence.

Earthquake and Tombs Opened: Firstfruits of Resurrection

An earthquake shook the ground and opened tombs of many saints, whose bodies rose after Jesus' resurrection (Mt 27:52–53). These dramatic signs provided a foretaste of the general resurrection and the restoration of all creation. The trembling earth acknowledges Christ's victory over death, while the raised saints herald the promise that those in Christ will one day share in His triumph (1 Thess 4:16–17). Gratitude for these cosmic proclamations fuels hope amid mortality, reminding believers that our own tombs await the same life-giving quake.

4.7 Theological Depths of the Cross

Substitutionary Atonement: He Bore Our Sins

The doctrine of substitutionary atonement teaches that Christ stood in our place, bearing the penalty for sin we deserved (Isa 53:4–6). His willing sacrifice satisfies divine justice while extending mercy to the guilty. This profound exchange—our sin for His righteousness—forms the core of gospel gratitude, for it means that our standing before God rests not on fleeting performance but on the eternal work of Christ. Every "Thank You, Jesus" echoes this transaction, celebrating forgiveness purchased at infinite cost.

Ransom and Redemption: Price Paid for Freedom

Jesus Himself declared that He gave His life "as a ransom for many" (Mk 10:45), invoking imagery from Exodus, where the

Passover lamb's blood secured Israel's release (Ex 12:12–13). His death redeemed us from slavery to sin and fear, purchasing our liberty through shed blood (1 Pet 1:18–19). Gratitude swells when we consider that the eternal Son assumed the role of sacrificial lamb to liberate us from death's dominion. Our freedom is the cross's everlasting echo in every redeemed heart.

Christus Victor: Triumph over Powers and Principalities

Beyond individual forgiveness, the cross inaugurates Christ's victory over demonic forces and cosmic rulers (Col 2:15). His descent into the abyss and subsequent resurrection broke the chains of death and dismantled evil's strongholds. This "Christus Victor" motif portrays the cross as battlefield where King Jesus triumphed over every power that opposed God's reign. Gratitude ascends when we reflect on the cross's cosmic scope, where the triumph shouted in an empty tomb signals deliverance for the entire creation.

4.8 The Cross and Covenant Fulfillment

Passover Lamb Realized

Jesus died at the very hour the Passover lambs were being slaughtered, fulfilling the typology of Exodus (Jn 19:14). As the Lamb of God, He takes away the world's sin (Jn 1:29), embodying Israel's sacrificial system and surpassing its temporary efficacy. His blood, like the lamb's, marks us for salvation—only here its power is universal and eternal. Gratitude grows as we see the continuity of God's redemptive plan, where ancient rites find consummation in Christ's one perfect offering.

Blood of the New Covenant: Communion Foreshadowed

On the night He was betrayed, Jesus spoke of His blood as "the blood of the covenant, which is poured out for many for the forgiveness of sins" (Mt 26:28). This inaugurated a new covenant written on hearts rather than tablets of stone (Jer

31:33; Heb 8:10). The Lord's Supper continually commemorates that covenant, uniting believers with Christ's once-for-all sacrifice. Gratitude permeates each communion table, for every cup signifies a promise sealed by His blood that "never loses its power" (Rom 3:25).

Abrahamic Promise Ratified: Blessing for All Nations

The cross extends the blessing promised to Abraham to every nation (Gen 12:3), weaving Gentile believers into Israel's covenantal story (Gal 3:14). Through faith in Christ, the dividing wall of hostility is broken, and sons and daughters of Abraham emerge from every tribe and tongue. Gratitude swells as we recognize that the cross's scope is not limited by ethnicity or geography but reaches to the ends of the earth— a fulfillment of God's promise to bless all peoples.

4.9 Application of Redemption to the Believer

Justification: Declared Righteous by Faith

Through Christ's death, believers are declared righteous— justified not by works but by faith (Rom 3:24–26). This forensic declaration means that God treats us as if we had perfectly kept the law because Christ absorbed its penalty. Gratitude for justification reshapes our self-image: no longer condemned, we stand in grace, secure in God's verdict. Every "Thank You, Jesus" acknowledges that our legal standing rests on His finished work, not our shifting performance.

Adoption: From Orphans to Sons and Daughters

The cross does more than forgive; it adopts. By His blood, the Spirit testifies that we are God's children (Rom 8:15–16), heirs co-equal with Christ (Rom 8:17). This new identity imbues life with dignity, purpose, and belonging, replacing orphaned estrangement with familial intimacy. Gratitude wells up as we realize that the Son's death grants us entry into God's household, where love and security flow from Our Heavenly Father.

Reconciliation: Peace with God and One Another

Through the cross, enmity between God and humanity is abolished, creating peace (Eph 2:14–17). But this reconciliation extends further: believers are called to be ambassadors of peace (2 Cor 5:18–20), mending broken relationships through forgiveness. Gratitude for reconciliation propels us into active peacemaking, reflecting the cross's power to heal every rift—between spouses, cultures, or nations—and demonstrating that Christ's blood unites even the most divided.

4.10 Sacramental Remembrance and Worship

Lord's Supper: Proclaiming His Death Until He Comes

When Jesus instituted the Eucharist, He commanded, "Do this in remembrance of me" (Lk 22:19). Each celebration of bread and cup proclaims the cross's reality until His return (1 Cor 11:26). Gratitude for this sacrament arises as we taste the body broken and the blood shed, participating in a mystery that transcends time. Communion unites the local assembly with Calvary's drama, reminding us that every act of worship draws its power from the cross's once-for-all efficacy.

Baptism into Christ's Death and Resurrection

Baptism symbolizes burial with Christ and resurrection into new life (Rom 6:3–4). As believers are immersed, they identify with His death's cleansing power; as they emerge, they share in the hope of resurrection. Gratitude ripples through this rite of passage, for water and Spirit combine to inaugurate a lifelong embrace of the cross's transformative grace. Each baptized soul becomes a living testament to the cross's capacity to reshape mortality.

Cross-Centered Liturgy and Hymnody

Christian worship has historically centered on cross themes—from the ancient hymn in Philippians 2 to modern anthems like

"In Christ Alone." Liturgy that dwells on atoning sacrifice and triumphant victory nurtures a congregation's gratitude, anchoring hearts in gospel truths. Hymns that recount Calvary's story engage both emotion and intellect, forging communal identity around the cross. Every verse of praise exalts the Savior whose death paved the way for our worship.

4.11 Embracing the Cross in Daily Discipleship

Taking Up Our Cross: Cost of Following Jesus

Jesus declared that discipleship requires "taking up your cross daily" (Lk 9:23), an invitation not to ease but to sacrifice. This call means prioritizing Christ's mission over personal comfort, embracing suffering as participation in His redemptive work (Phil 1:29). Gratitude for this summons emerges when we realize that cross-bearing weeds out self-centeredness and cultivates Christ-likeness. Each hardship becomes a canvas upon which the cross's image is painted anew in our character.

Cruciform Ethics: Love, Service, and Self-Denial

The cross shapes Christian ethics: love that lays down life (Jn 15:13), service that stoops to others (Phil 2:5–7), and self-denial that resists lucrative shortcuts (1 Cor 9:24–27). Here, morality moves from rule-keeping to imitation of Christ's self-giving example. Gratitude deepens when we recognize that our moral compass is not external enforcement but internal formation by the Crucified One. In cruciform ethics, the world glimpses the gospel's power to rewrite moral narratives.

Suffering and Glory: Sharing in His Passion for Future Joy

Paul invites believers to "share in the sufferings of Christ" so that we may also share in His glory (Rom 8:17). This paradox grants suffering a purpose: training endurance and shaping hope. Gratitude for this perspective transforms trials from meaningless pain into purposeful refinement, as we anticipate "the glory that will be revealed in us" (Rom 8:18). Through suffering, we participate in Calvary's legacy, gaining insights that only cross-shaped lives can know.

4.12 Global Mission and the Message of the Cross

Foolishness to Greeks, Stumbling Block to Jews: Cultural Responses

Paul's sermons at Antioch and Athens revealed that the cross provokes divergent reactions—Greek philosophers deemed it madness, Jewish scholars saw it as scandal (1 Cor 1:23). Yet in this "foolishness," God's wisdom is hidden to shame human pride (1 Cor 1:27–29). Gratitude for the cross compels us to embrace its countercultural power, selling out to a message that defies popular sensibilities but transforms souls across cultural divides.

Power of God for Salvation: Evangelistic Proclamation

Preaching the cross remains "the power of God for salvation to everyone who believes" (Rom 1:16). The gospel's centrality ensures that apostolic mission does not pivot on social programs but on Christ crucified (1 Cor 2:2). Gratitude fuels evangelistic zeal, for each convert underscores the cross's enduring potency to break chains and kindle hope. As we bear witness, we join the apostolic legacy of proclaiming Christ's death and resurrection to every nation.

Unity at the Foot of the Cross: Breaking Barriers Worldwide

At Calvary, walls of hostility between Jew and Gentile were demolished (Eph 2:14), creating one new humanity in Christ. The cross thus becomes the great leveler and unifier, where tribal hatreds dissolve and walls of partition collapse. Gratitude for this unity inspires cross-cultural partnerships, shared worship gatherings, and collaborative service projects that reflect the kingdom's diversity within oneness. At the foot of the cross, every barrier is broken, revealing the heart of a Savior who gathers all peoples into His eternal banquet.

Conclusion

The cross is not primarily an event of the past but the wellspring of present grace and future hope. In its shadow, sin's penalty subsides, divine wrath finds satisfaction, and the pathway to intimacy with God swings wide open. Our "Thank You, Jesus" cannot be constrained to idle words but must resonate through lives transformed—through forgiveness extended, burdens borne, and communities reconciled. As we live under the cross's banner, we discover that suffering and joy co-exist in the landscape of redemption, where every tear is tenderly gathered and every joy is deepened by the memory of sacrifice. May our hearts continually return to that cruel wooden beam, finding in its weathered beams the promise that love's triumph endures forever.

Chapter 5. Thank You, Jesus, for the Empty Tomb—Resurrection Hope

No single event in human history has inspired as much awe, controversy, and hope as the resurrection of Jesus Christ. What began in the horror of a crucifixion reached its triumphant apex in an empty tomb—an event that transformed despair into joy and death's dominion into lifegiving power (Acts 2:24). For believers, the empty tomb is not merely an ancient report but the foundation of daily hope, confirming that God's promises extend beyond the grave (1 Cor 15:17–20). Even nature seemed to respond, as earth trembled and graves opened in testimony to the cosmic significance of that morning (Mt 27:51–53). Our gratitude for resurrection hope shapes every aspect of Christian identity: it fuels perseverance in trials, undergirds bold witness, and anchors us in the certainty that suffering is temporary and glory eternal. As we journey through the scenes before dawn to the cosmic consummation, may our hearts swell with renewed praise for the One who conquered the grave and secured life for all who believe.

5.1 Before Dawn: Waiting in the Shadow of Death

Sabbath Silence: The Day Hope Seemed Lost

After Jesus' death on Friday afternoon, the Sabbath commenced with an oppressive stillness over Jerusalem. No one expected the Savior's story to end at a tomb, yet religious authorities secured the burial site with a seal and soldiers, determined to prevent any postmortem deception (Mt 27:62–66). In those hours of Sabbath rest, grief weighed heavily on the disciples' hearts, for they believed all had been lost. The silence of Jerusalem's streets echoed their despair, as the city prepared for a holy day devoid of the Messiah's presence. Yet that Sabbath "rest" was not God's final word, for in divine wisdom He paused creation's rhythms to prepare heaven's intervention. Our thanksgiving begins here—recognizing that even God's apparent inactivity heralds the dawn of resurrection power (Ex 16:23–25). In the shadow of death, hope's seed lay dormant, waiting for the Father's appointed hour.

Women Who Watched: Faithful Love Amid Grief

While male disciples fled in fear, a band of devoted women—Mary Magdalene, Mary the mother of James, and Salome—remained near the place of execution, caring for Jesus' body (Mk 15:40–41). Their fierce loyalty drove them to return before dawn, carrying spices to honor the Teacher's corpse. These women risked danger, ridicule, and heartbreak to serve One who had taught them love in action (Lk 8:1–3). Their grief was raw, marked by tears and trembling hope that perhaps anointing would bring closure. Yet they went not out of duty alone but from a devotion that refused to be silenced by crucifixion. In their vigil we see that true love persists in the darkest hours, sustained by the memory of kindness received. As we thank Jesus for resurrection hope, we must also honor those whose faith stands firm when hope itself seems buried.

Guarded Tomb: Roman Seal and Pharisaic Fear

Religious leaders, fearing Jesus' followers might steal His body and claim resurrection, petitioned Pilate for a guard and seal (Mt 27:64). The Roman seal—a symbol of imperial authority—and armed soldiers introduced terror amidst the mourners. What began as a security measure revealed the deep anxiety engendered by Jesus' prophetic words: "I will rise again" (Mt 20:19). The empty tomb would not be an accident but a divine spectacle that exposed both human fear and God's sovereignty. Our gratitude intensifies when we remember that every precaution to contain Jesus' influence backfired: the same soldiers who guarded the grave became unwitting heralds of the greatest liberation. In their guarded watch we glimpse the futility of human schemes against resurrection's unstoppable power.

5.2 Rolling Away the Stone—Heaven's Intervention

Earthquake and Angelic Descent

At the precise moment God appointed, an angel descended from heaven, his appearance like lightning and his clothing brilliant as snow (Mt 28:2). The ground shook violently, and the massive stone sealing the tomb's entrance was rolled away, not by human hand but by divine command. This earthquake signaled creation's participation in redemption, as the cosmos itself seems to endorse the triumph of life over death. The angel's presence—the first messenger of the resurrection—shattered both the seal and the silence of the Sabbath night. In that seismic event, the helplessness of tomb-captives was reversed: what once marked finality became a signpost of new beginnings. Our "Thank You, Jesus" resonates with the trembling earth, praising the Father who intervenes when all seems lost. That angelic descent reminds us that heaven's glory cannot be long restrained by earthly barriers.

Stone Dislodged: Sign, Not Escape Hatch

While skeptics have sometimes claimed Jesus used the rolled-away stone as an exit, Scripture emphasizes it as a sign rather than a mere escape route (Jn 20:1–2). The stone's removal served to display the empty grave to witnesses, inviting them into faith rather than concealment. It declared publicly that death's boundary had been breached and that no barrier could contain the life-giving power of God. The witnesses—women and later Peter and John—marveled at its displacement, for in that moment faith found tangible proof beyond rumor or wishful thinking. The stone thus stands as both tomb-shutter and resurrection billboard, proclaiming Christ's victory to any willing to look. Gratitude flows as we remember that God's truths are often boldly announced in visible wonders, calling us from skepticism into worship.

Terrified Guards: Power Confronts Empire

The Roman soldiers assigned to guard the tomb fell into convulsions of fear at the angel's descent, appearing to many as dead men (Mt 28:4). Their collapse underscores that the resurrection is not a private spiritual phenomenon but a public, undeniable encounter with divine power. When they recovered, they reported the events to the chief priests, who bribed them to spread a cover-up story blaming the disciples for theft (Mt 28:11–15). Yet even their conspiracy inadvertently attested to the empty tomb's reality. The terrified guard's collapse and the subsequent bribery illustrate empire's impotence and corruption before God's truth. In their fear we glimpse the cosmic stakes at play: the resurrection does not merely unsettle religious pretenders but rattles the foundations of human authority. Our thanksgiving intensifies as we recall that no force on earth can stand against the risen Lord.

5.3 First Witnesses: Women Hear the Good News

Mary Magdalene and Companions at Sunrise

Before the sun had fully risen, Mary Magdalene and the other Mary made their way to the tomb, hearts pounding with sorrow and anxious hope (Mt 28:1). As light braced the eastern sky, their grief-stricken pace converted into astonished wonder when they saw the stone rolled away. They were among the first to encounter the angelic messenger and to hear the words that would forever transform history: "He is not here, for He has risen, as He said" (Mt 28:6). These women's presence at dawn emphasizes resurrection's explosion into life when darkness yields to light. Their faith in action—rising early, braving the unknown—becomes our model for encountering Christ. Gratitude for their courage deepens our own resolve to seek Jesus even when circumstances seem stark. In their joyful fear, we see hope's birth at the intersection of grief and glory.

"He Is Not Here": Angelic Proclamation of Victory

The angel's declaration "He is not here" (Lk 24:6) focused attention not on the absence of death but on the presence of life. This message subverted all expectations: the tomb that once testified to crucifixion became proof of resurrection. Angels, who declared Christ's birth, now herald His victory over death, bookending His redemptive mission with supernatural proclamation. The phrase "as He said" underscores Jesus' own predictions, affirming His reliability and divinity (Mk 9:31). Thanksgiving swells at the recognition that God keeps His word, transforming tombs of doubt into altars of trust. The angelic proclamation continues to ring in every believer's ear, inviting us to leave behind the wrappings of old hopes and step into living reality.

Fear, Joy, and Commission to Tell the Disciples

Trembling and bewildered, the women were given a mandate: "Go quickly and tell His disciples... that He is risen from the dead" (Mt 28:7). Their initial fear gave way to exuberant obedience as they embraced the commission. This pattern—emotion stirred by divine encounter, followed by faithful action—characterizes all who meet the risen Lord. Despite cultural biases against women's testimony, God entrusted them as the first heralds of resurrection hope, demonstrating that kingdom values invert human hierarchies (Jn 20:17–18). Our gratitude for this commissioning recalls that every believer is called not only to receive gospel truth but to proclaim it, regardless of status or circumstance. In their joyful flight from the tomb, we see the urgency of resurrection witness echoing through the centuries.

5.4 Verifying the Empty Tomb—Peter and John Run

Race to the Grave: Eager Skepticism

Upon hearing the women's report, Peter and the "other disciple" (traditionally John) sprinted toward the tomb (Jn 20:3–4). Their run blended skepticism and hope, for they had struggled to believe earlier predictions of resurrection (Mk 9:32). Yet the possibility stirred them into action, demonstrating that even doubtful hearts can be catalysts for discovery when curiosity meets spiritual invitation. In their haste, they left behind decorum, showing that faith often requires abandoning caution. Our gratitude aligns with their eagerness—recognizing that honest questions, when pursued with sincerity, can lead to life-changing revelation.

Graveclothes Left Behind: Order amid Miracle

John entered the tomb first, "saw and believed" at the sight of the neatly folded graveclothes (Jn 20:8–9). Peter, upon entering, noted the linen wrappings lying apart and the face cloth rolled up in its place (Jn 20:6–7). These details testify not to a body stolen in chaos but to a deliberate, orderly departure—Christ Himself stewarding the scene. The graveclothes symbolize death's discarded vestments, now obsolete before resurrection's power. Gratitude flows as we meditate on this precision, for it reassures us that resurrection is not myth but a reality accompanied by recognizable evidence. The preserved order invites faith rooted in tangible truth, rather than wishful illusions.

Belief Born in an Empty Space

Though John witnessed and believed, he still struggled to fully understand until Jesus appeared later (Jn 20:11–16). Yet the empty space, once a sign of loss, became the birthplace of belief, as absence underscored presence. This paradox teaches us that sometimes God's most powerful revelations emerge in the voids He creates—spaces where expectations collapse and divine glory dawns. Our thanksgiving resonates as we recall personal "empty tomb" experiences—moments when loss turned into life, doubt into conviction, and silence into song. In the emptiness of the grave, we find reason to believe and reasons to bless His name.

5.5 Personal Encounters with the Risen Lord

Mary's Name Called in the Garden

While lingering weeping outside the tomb, Mary Magdalene heard someone speak her name: "Mary" (Jn 20:16). At that moment, grief exploded into joy as she recognized the risen Christ. This intimate address—by name—reveals resurrection's personal dimension: the Savior knows each of His children and calls them into relationship. Mary's transformation from sorrowful mourner to ecstatic witness charts the path from death's darkness to life's light. Gratitude swells when we realize that the same voice that spoke Mary's name echoes through centuries, calling each believer from despair into hope. In that garden encounter, love reclaimed its beloved, and new creation began.

Road to Emmaus: Hearts Burning with Revelation

Two disciples traveling to Emmaus encountered a stranger who explained Scripture's messianic meaning, culminating in their recognition of Him in the breaking of bread (Lk 24:13–35). Their hearts "burned" within them as He opened the Old

Testament to unveil the promise of resurrection (Lk 24:32). This discipleship model—Scripture interpreted in community, sacrament, and fellowship—continues to ignite faith today. Their return to Jerusalem, breathless with excitement, demonstrates that encountering the risen Christ compels us to testify. Gratitude for Emmaus teaches that resurrection hope flourishes where Word and table converge, fueling both understanding and action.

Upper Room: Peace to Fearful Disciples

Hiding behind locked doors in fear, the disciples were suddenly greeted by Jesus' voice: "Peace be with you" (Jn 20:19). His appearance transcended physical barriers, infusing their trembling hearts with calm assurance. He showed them His wounds—proof that He was the very One they had crucified—and breathed the Spirit upon them, commissioning them to forgive sins (Jn 20:20–23). This encounter reshaped their identity from frightened followers into empowered apostles. Gratitude arises as we realize that the risen Lord brings peace amid panic, transforms isolation into community, and imparts mission alongside mercy. The Upper Room scene remains a microcosm of resurrection's power to disarm fear and embolden witness.

5.6 Bodily Reality of Resurrection

Touch My Hands and Side: Empirical Evidence

Thomas, absent at the first appearance, doubted until he could touch Jesus' nail-pierced hands and side (Jn 20:24–29). When Jesus graciously invited him—"Do not disbelieve, but believe"—Thomas exclaimed, "My Lord and my God!" (Jn 20:28). This interaction underscores the physicality of resurrection: it was not a mere spirit or vision but a bodily return. Jesus' wounds were not erased but glorified, proving continuity between His pre- and post-resurrection identity. Gratitude for this reality reassures us that our future resurrection involves redeemed bodies, not disembodied souls. In Thomas's confession we find our own testimony: that faith grounded in visible wounds is blessed above blind belief.

Eating Fish in Galilee: Fellowship Restored

On the shore of the Sea of Tiberias, the risen Jesus prepared breakfast for seven disciples, broiling fish and bread (Jn 21:1–14). This simple meal reestablished fraternity disrupted by denial and fear, illustrating that resurrection restores relationships. The shared act of eating underscored Jesus' tangibility and the goodness of ordinary provision suffused by divine presence. Gratitude for this scene emerges as we appreciate that resurrection life is as much about community and daily bread as it is about cosmic triumph. In fellowship with the Risen Lord, routine becomes sacrament, and broken bonds find healing.

Thomas's Doubt Turned Confession

Thomas's initial skepticism and subsequent proclamation—"My Lord and my God!"—trace a journey from rational question to worshipful confession (Jn 20:28). Jesus did not condemn his doubt but invited investigation, demonstrating that honest inquiry can lead to deeper faith. This episode models pastoral care for seekers, showing that resurrection accounts welcome both questions and reverent response. Gratitude for Thomas's story grows as we recognize that our own doubts can become doorways to encounter, and that Christ meets us in our uncertainties with patience and grace.

5.7 Theological Significance of the Resurrection

Vindication of the Son: God's "Amen" to the Cross

The resurrection is God's definitive affirmation of Jesus' identity and sacrificial work (Rom 1:4). In raising Him from the dead, the Father declared that the atoning sacrifice was acceptable, vindicating the crucified One as the righteous sufferer. This divine "Amen" silences every accusation against Christ and confirms His authority to forgive sins (Acts 2:24–32). Our thanksgiving begins here: resurrection vindicates every promise, testifies to God's fidelity, and assures us that death could not invalidate Christ's mission. In the resurrection, divine justice and mercy meet in perfect harmony.

Defeat of Death: Sting Removed, Grave Conquered

Paul exults that through Christ, death's "sting" is removed and the grave's "victory" swallowed up in life (1 Cor 15:54–57). Resurrection inaugurates the end of death's reign, offering believers both present empowerment and future hope. Death no longer holds horror for those united with Christ; instead, it becomes the gateway to eternal joy. Gratitude for this triumph shapes Christian preaching and practice, turning funerals into memorials of hope rather than mere remembrances of loss. In resurrection power, the final enemy is vanquished.

Justification Sealed: Righteousness Imputed

The resurrection not only validates Christ's work but secures our justification before God (Rom 4:25). Just as His death dealt with sin's penalty, His rising demonstrates its complete removal. Believers, united to Him by faith, share in this justification, standing before God as righteous recipients of grace (Rom 5:1–2). Gratitude deepens as we realize that justification is not tentative but sealed by resurrection's invincible power. In Christ's rising, every believer's acquittal is forever irrevocable.

5.8 Firstfruits of the New Creation

Christ the Prototype of Glorified Humanity

Paul calls Christ the "firstfruits" of those who have fallen asleep (1 Cor 15:20), indicating that His resurrection is the pattern for our own bodily renewal. His glorified body—recognizable yet transformed—assures us that resurrection entails continuity and transformation. As the prototype, He inaugurates the new humanity God intends to recreate, free from corruption, sickness, and death (Phil 3:20–21). Gratitude for this truth bolsters hope in trials, reminding us that our present bodies are destined for imperishable glory.

Creation Groans for Its Own Resurrection

Romans 8 portrays creation itself as groaning for the revealing of God's children (Rom 8:19–22). The resurrection of Christ is the first chapter in cosmic renewal, signaling that the entire universe will one day share redemption. Mountains will sing, waters clap hands, and fields blossom in unbroken harmony (Is 55:12). Gratitude for resurrection hope thus extends beyond personal salvation to environmental restoration, inspiring stewardship that reflects future consummation.

Cosmic Renewal Foreshadowed

The empty tomb foreshadows the day when new heavens and a new earth will emerge, where sorrow, crying, and death are no more (Rev 21:1–4). Resurrection hope fuels mission to proclaim this future to every tribe and tongue, inviting all creation to anticipate its liberation. Gratitude for this cosmic horizon shapes worship that lifts eyes from present woes to eternal glory. In the empty tomb, we glimpse the blueprint for all that God will renew.

5.9 Union with Christ—Resurrection Life Now

Raised with Him: Spiritual Regeneration

Believers are united with Christ in His death and resurrection through baptism (Rom 6:3–5). This spiritual regeneration signifies that we are no longer slaves to sin but alive to God, empowered by the same life that raised Jesus from the dead. Gratitude for this union transforms daily living, as we reckon ourselves dead to sin and alive in Christ (Rom 6:11). Resurrection life begins now, enabling holiness and joyful obedience.

Walking in Newness of Life: Sanctification Power

Resurrection hope is not only future but present: the Spirit who raised Jesus dwells in us, enabling progressive transformation (Rom 8:11). Each moment becomes an opportunity to "set our minds on things above" (Col 3:1–2), reflecting Jesus' resurrected values in thoughts and actions. Gratitude for sanctification power sustains us through battles with sin, reminding us that victory is not achieved by human effort alone but by life-giving Spirit.

Spirit of Him Who Raised Jesus Dwells in You

Paul assures believers that the same Spirit who raised Christ from the dead lives in us (Rom 8:11). This indwelling presence guarantees both future resurrection and present empowerment. Even when our bodies groan under weakness, the Spirit bears witness with our spirit that we are God's children (Rom 8:16). Gratitude for the Spirit's residency celebrates the profound mystery that resurrection life has descended into our mortal frame, ensuring that death's sting is already being neutralized from within.

5.10 Ethics of Hope: Living in Light of the Empty Tomb

Courage in Persecution: Nothing to Fear but Unbelief

Knowing that Christ has risen emboldens believers to face persecution with courage (Acts 4:13–20). Fear of death loses its grip when we understand that physical demise is not the final chapter. Many early martyrs testified that "to die is gain" (Phil 1:21), for they longed to be with Christ in resurrection glory. Gratitude for this perspective sustains faithfulness under trial, transforming prisons into pulpits and martyrdom into witness.

Holiness Motivated by Future Glory

Resurrection hope propels ethical living: if we are destined for incorruptible bodies, then present impurity stands in stark contrast to our future calling (1 Cor 15:42–44). Paul exhorts believers to "make every effort" to be found blameless and at peace when Christ returns (2 Pet 3:14). Gratitude for future glory fuels present holiness, as we view ethical choices not as burdens but as expressions of anticipated transformation.

Stewardship of the Body: Honor the Coming Resurrection

Paul warns that our bodies are "temples of the Holy Spirit" and will be raised imperishable (1 Cor 6:19–20; 15:42). This truth calls us to honor God with our physical selves—through care, purity, and sacrificial service. Gratitude for bodily resurrection shapes lifestyle choices—diet, rest, sexuality, and generosity—reflecting that our mortal frame participates in God's redemptive story. In stewarding our bodies, we worship the One who will one day transform them completely.

5.11 Worship and Liturgy Shaped by Resurrection

Lord's Day Observance: Sunday as Victory Day

Early Christians gathered on the first day of the week—"the Lord's Day"—to commemorate Jesus' resurrection (Acts 20:7; Rev 1:10). Sunday worship testifies that the week's work ends not in Saturday's rest but in Sunday's celebration of new life. Gratitude for this liturgical rhythm infuses corporate gatherings with joy, as hymns, prayers, and sacraments pivot around resurrection themes. Each gathering becomes a mini-Easter, rehearsing the defeat of death and the promise of life.

Easter Vigil and Paschal Hymns

The Easter Vigil service—spanning darkness to light—culminates in baptisms, renewal of vows, and the Paschal preface, proclaiming "Christ our light" (Ex 14:27; Lk 24:32). Paschal hymns like the "Exultet" and "Christians, to the Paschal Victim" weave theology and poetry, immersing congregations in resurrection's wonder. Gratitude for these ancient rites affirms that Christian worship is inherently Easter-shaped, ensuring that resurrection remains central to faith expression.

Sacramental Echoes: Baptism and Eucharist

Baptism and the Lord's Supper continually point back to the empty tomb. In baptism we identify with Christ's burial and rising; in communion we partake of the body broken and the blood shed, looking forward to His return (1 Cor 11:26). Gratitude for these sacraments anchors our faith in tangible encounter, reminding us that resurrection is not an abstract doctrine but a present reality to be received and shared.

5.12 Mission Empowered by Resurrection Authority

Great Commission Rooted in Risen Lordship

Jesus' final command—"All authority in heaven and on earth has been given to me... go and make disciples" (Mt 28:18–20)—rests on His resurrection vindication. Mission springs from His sovereign lordship, ensuring that every proclamation of gospel truth carries divine backing. Gratitude for resurrection authority fuels bold evangelism, confident that the same power that raised Jesus will advance the kingdom through faithful witnesses.

Preaching "Jesus and the Resurrection" in Acts

Peter's Pentecost sermon centered on resurrection, declaring Jesus both Lord and Christ (Acts 2:22–36). Philip's outreach in Samaria and Paul's testimony in Athens likewise emphasized the empty tomb as proof of divine promise (Acts 13:26–39; 17:31). Gratitude for the apostles' resurrection preaching inspires modern proclamation strategies: to speak not only of moral teachings but of a living Savior who meets needs and fulfills destinies.

Martyr Witness: Death Is Gain

The early church's martyrs—such as Stephen, Polycarp, and Perpetua—faced death singing resurrection hymns, convinced that "to die is gain" (Phil 1:21). Their blood became seed, spreading faith across hostile territories. Gratitude for their witness challenges contemporary believers to view sacrifice not as loss but as participation in resurrection's triumph. At the foot of the cross and before the empty tomb, martyrdom becomes the ultimate sermon.

5.13 Eschatological Consummation—Our Future Resurrection

Trumpet Blast and Dead in Christ Rise

1 Thessalonians 4 depicts the Lord's return with a shout and trumpet call, raising the dead before catching up living believers to meet Him (1 Thess 4:16–17). This dramatic reunion illustrates resurrection's communal dimension: death's breach is closed, and the body's destiny shifts from decay to immortality. Gratitude for this promise sustains saints as they await the final trumpet, assured that separation will be undone and reunion eternal.

Transformation of Mortal Bodies

Paul envisions our perishable, weak bodies being transformed "in a moment, in the twinkling of an eye" into imperishable, glorious forms (1 Cor 15:51–53). This metamorphosis demonstrates that resurrection restores both soul and body, fulfilling the creation mandate to populate heaven with redeemed humanity. Gratitude deepens as we anticipate the freedom from pain, illness, and limitation—conditions for which our spirits long and our bodies were made.

New Heavens and New Earth: Dwelling with God Forever

Revelation's final vision portrays the Holy City descending and God dwelling among His people, wiping away every tear (Rev 21:1–4). No sun is needed, for the Lamb illuminates all—a fitting culmination of resurrection hope. Gratitude for this consummation shapes present living, as we steward creation, love neighbors, and proclaim the gospel in light of eternity's realities. The empty tomb thus points not only to personal renewal but to cosmic restoration—a forever dwelling where death is banished and joy endures without end.

Conclusion

The empty tomb stands as the cornerstone of Christian hope, demonstrating that God's redemptive work did not end with crucifixion but burst forth in resurrection glory. Every scene—from the dawn vigil of grieving women to the cosmic tremors at Calvary—reveals layers of meaning that feed our faith and fire our worship. Resurrection transforms theology into lived experience: it heals grief, fuels mission, and guarantees that suffering is not the final word. As believers, we live between the empty tomb and the promised new creation, sustained by the assurance that He who rose once will raise us also (1 Cor 6:14). Therefore, with hearts full of gratitude and voices lifted in praise, we say anew: Thank You, Jesus, for the empty tomb and the hope it secures for time and for eternity.

Chapter 6. Thank You, Jesus, for the Gift of the Spirit—Indwelling Presence

The resurrection of Jesus did not mark the end of His earthly activity but the beginning of a new epoch in which His very life would be poured into His followers through the Holy Spirit. Immediately before His ascension, the risen Christ lifted His nail-scarred hands over a still-confused band of disciples and promised that "power from on high" would soon clothe them (Luke 24:49). That promise was not an afterthought but the climactic goal of the incarnate mission: God dwelling with humanity by dwelling within humanity (John 14:16-18). Whereas Old-Covenant saints experienced the Spirit as an external anointing that occasionally rested upon judges, prophets, and kings, New-Covenant believers receive the Spirit as a permanent resident, transforming every believer into a living temple (1 Corinthians 3:16). The indwelling Presence is therefore both intensely personal—He knows our innermost groans—and profoundly corporate—He constructs us, stone by stone, into a worldwide sanctuary of praise (Ephesians 2:21-22). Gratitude for this gift must run deeper than mere acknowledgment; it ought to suffuse our prayers, animate our obedience, and embolden our witness. Across the following sections we will explore the many-faceted ministry of the Spirit promised by Jesus, poured out at Pentecost, and active in the Church to the very end of the age. May every line awaken fresh thanksgiving for the Helper who abides, empowers, teaches, convicts, and seals us for the day of final redemption.

6.1 Promise of the Paraclete

Farewell Discourses: "I Will Not Leave You Orphans"

On the night of His betrayal, Jesus sounded a note of consolation that would reverberate through centuries: He would not abandon His disciples as orphans (John 14:18). Their faces were already registering panic at hints of His departure, yet He redirected their grief toward a greater hope—the coming of Another Helper. The Greek term *paraklētos* carries the warmth of an advocate, comforter, and counsellor who stands alongside in every circumstance. Jesus framed the Spirit's arrival as an upgrade rather than a mere consolation prize, insisting that His bodily absence would make way for universal divine presence (John 16:7). The assurance reached backward to Isaiah's orphan imagery and forward to the epistles' robust doctrine of adoption, knitting testaments into a single tapestry of covenant care. By promising permanent companionship, Jesus sealed the fracture sin introduced in Eden, re-establishing unbroken fellowship between God and humanity. Gratitude swells when we realize that every moment of loneliness, every season of uncertainty, is intersected by the Spirit who whispers, "You belong."

Spirit of Truth: Guiding Into All Reality

Three times in the Farewell Discourses Jesus called the Paraclete the "Spirit of truth," underscoring continuity with His own identity as Truth incarnate (John 14:17; 15:26; 16:13). Whereas the Law inscribed regulations on stone tablets, the Spirit engraves divine reality onto tender hearts, enabling discernment that transcends mere information. He does not fabricate new doctrines independent of Christ; rather, He takes what belongs to the Son and unveils its richness to receptive minds. This guiding ministry is progressive yet anchored, unfolding layers of gospel depth without deviating from apostolic foundations. In an age drowning in data yet parched for wisdom, the Spirit's illumination equips believers to sift counterfeit narratives and stand firm in revealed truth. The promise of guidance removes paralyzing fear that we might drift into error, for the Spirit faithfully course-corrects those who seek light over self-validation. Thanksgiving erupts when sermons pierce our conscience, when Scripture leaps alive in morning devotions, and when ordinary decisions are steered by extraordinary insight.

Another Helper: Continuity of Jesus' Ministry

By calling the Spirit "another" Helper (John 14:16), Jesus signaled both similarity and distinction, implying that the Spirit would prolong and universalize the Messiah's earthly works. The Spirit would teach, as Jesus had taught, drawing from the same well of divine wisdom to remind disciples of everything the Master said (John 14:26). He would convict the world of sin, righteousness, and judgment (John 16:8), echoing Jesus' prophetic critiques while widening the audience beyond Galilean hillsides. He would glorify the Son by spotlighting the cross and resurrection, thereby perpetuating Christ-centered worship long after eyewitnesses died (John 16:14). This continuity guards Christians from nostalgia; we need not long for a first-century shoreline because the same power operates in twenty-first-century living rooms. The Spirit shapes physicians in hospitals, parents at breakfast tables, and missionaries on remote islands, ensuring that Jesus' ministry flourishes in every locale. Gratitude deepens as we awaken each day confident that the Helper who walked with Jesus now walks within us, enabling kingdom exploits impossible in mere human strength.

6.2 Pentecost—The Spirit Poured Out

Sound of Wind and Tongues of Fire

Fifty days after Passover, Jerusalem's avenues filled with pilgrims celebrating Shavuot when a violent wind rattled the upper room (Acts 2:1-2). The rushing sound recalled Ezekiel's valley where God breathed life into dry bones, announcing that spiritual resurrection was underway (Ezekiel 37:9-10). What appeared as flames separated and rested upon each gathered believer, evoking Sinai's fiery theophany but now distributed over many instead of one (Exodus 19:18). The imagery signaled that every follower, not only prophets or rulers, would carry the blazing presence of Yahweh. Filled with the Spirit, they erupted in previously unlearned languages, reversing Babel's fragmentation by enabling worship intelligible to diverse nations (Acts 2:3-4). This sensory spectacle established that Christianity's birth was not philosophical speculation but a supernatural invasion of divine life into human history. Thanksgiving arises whenever we remember that the same wind still blows across spiritual deserts, and the same fire still ignites timid hearts for bold witness.

Reversal of Babel: Unified Proclamation

Genesis records how human pride built a tower reaching for heaven, prompting God to scatter languages and slow the tide of self-exaltation (Genesis 11:4-9). At Pentecost, God did not erase linguistic diversity but orchestrated unity within it, enabling worshipers to hear "the mighty works of God" in their native tongues (Acts 2:11). This miracle inaugurated a missionary trajectory oriented toward translation, contextualization, and the conviction that no culture is peripheral to salvation history. The gospel's leaping across language barriers in a single morning prefigured Bible translators laboring centuries later to render Scripture in every dialect. By reversing Babel's curse, the Spirit affirmed that diversity need not threaten unity when Christ is exalted above all tribal allegiances. Gratitude fuels cross-cultural humility, urging believers to honor accents, idioms, and customs as vessels through which the Spirit may declare God's glory. Each time we witness songs of praise rising in Swahili, Korean, or Quechua, we celebrate a Pentecost that continues to reverberate through global worship.

Peter's Prophetic Interpretation (Joel 2)

Confronted with accusations of drunkenness, Peter lifted his voice and linked the event to Joel's prophecy of an end-time outpouring upon "all flesh" (Acts 2:14-17; Joel 2:28-32). Young and old, male and female, slave and free would prophesy, dream, and envision, erasing socio-economic boundaries previously governing religious privilege. Peter's exegesis located Pentecost within eschatological timelines: the last days had begun, and the Spirit's arrival was the down payment of consummation. He connected cosmic signs—blood, fire, and vapor of smoke—with Christ's crucifixion and resurrection, framing salvation as both personal deliverance and cosmic upheaval. His sermon climaxed in a call to repent and receive "the gift of the Holy Spirit," promising inclusion to those far off, geographically and generationally (Acts 2:38-39). Gratitude for this interpretive key reminds us that every genuine move of the Spirit should be tethered to Scripture, guarding fervor with fidelity. As we study Joel's scroll today, our hearts burn anew, recognizing that we, too, stand in the flow of prophetic fulfillment inaugurated that Pentecost morning.

6.3 Indwelling Presence and New Covenant

Heart of Stone to Heart of Flesh (Ezekiel 36)

Centuries before Christ, Ezekiel envisioned a day when God would replace Israel's stony hearts with responsive flesh, breathing His Spirit within them (Ezekiel 36:26-27). This radical internal change contrasted with mere external adherence to Torah, promising intrinsic motivation for obedience. Pentecost fulfilled that vision, demonstrating that holiness is no longer sustained by threat of exile but by love infused into human will. Indwelling Presence transforms moral effort from grim striving into Spirit-energized delight, enabling believers to fulfill the law's righteous requirements (Romans 8:4). The surgery of regeneration removes callouses formed by habitual sin, restoring sensitivity to conviction and joy in righteousness. Gratitude flows when we observe attitudes once rigid with self-interest melting into compassion, patience, and mercy—evidence of stone becoming flesh. Each testimony of heart-level overhaul echoes Ezekiel's promise and magnifies the Surgeon who operates with nail-scarred hands.

Law Written Within: Internal Transformation

Jeremiah foresaw a covenant in which God's law would be inscribed on minds and hearts rather than tablets of stone (Jeremiah 31:33). The Spirit serves as divine ink, etching kingdom values deeper than cultural mores or institutional codes. Conscience, once unreliable due to sin's distortion, is recalibrated to resonate with righteousness's frequency. This inner inscription democratizes holiness: illiterate peasants and educated scholars alike can discern God's will through Spirit-shaped intuition. It also safeguards against legalism, for obedience arises from affection, not fear, aligning ethics with love's intent. Gratitude intensifies when temptation loses allure because inward desire now harmonizes with heaven's melody. Spiritual disciplines—prayer, fasting, meditation—become not ladders to God but settings in which the Spirit further chisels Christ's likeness into believers' cores.

Spirit as Down Payment of Inheritance

Paul describes the Spirit as an "arrabōn"—a guarantee or first installment—of believers' full inheritance (Ephesians 1:13-14). Like an engagement ring promising future union, the Spirit's present work foreshadows bodily resurrection and unmediated fellowship. This down payment secures our status even amid unfinished sanctification, assuring us that what God starts He will complete (Philippians 1:6). It also redefines suffering: present groans are contractions heralding the birth of glory, not signs of abandonment (Romans 8:23). Gratitude for the guarantee steadies shaky faith during loss or persecution, reminding us that the best wine is saved for last. The Spirit's gifts, joy, and peace are appetizers, whetting appetites for the marriage supper of the Lamb. Each whisper of Abba, each surge of courage, each moment of inexplicable peace declares that the promised inheritance is already breaking into the present.

6.4 Adoption and Assurance

Spirit of Sonship: Crying "Abba, Father"

Through the Spirit of adoption, believers transfer from slavery to intimacy, addressing God with the Aramaic term of familial affection, "Abba" (Romans 8:15). This cry is spontaneous, not scripted, evidencing relational authenticity rather than religious performance. First uttered by Jesus in Gethsemane (Mark 14:36), "Abba" becomes the shared language of all who are in Christ, binding Master and disciples in one familial expression. The Spirit liberates prayer from transactional bargaining, inviting childlike confidence in a Father who knows our needs. Abba-prayer dismantles orphan mindsets—fear of rejection, anxiety over provision, striving for approval—and replaces them with restful trust. Gratitude for sonship surfaces when worshipers sense God's delight independent of productivity, basking simply in being beloved. Every "Abba" rising from believers' lips across continents testifies that the Spirit is forging one global household marked by tender reliance on the Father's heart.

Witness With Our Spirit: Security in Salvation

Assurance is not a psychological pep talk but a joint witness between the Holy Spirit and our regenerated spirit that we are God's children (Romans 8:16). This dual testimony silences Satanic accusations and internal self-doubt, anchoring identity in divine declaration rather than shifting emotion. The Spirit seals believers, stamping heavenly ownership on their hearts and destinies (2 Corinthians 1:22). Holy assurance produces humble boldness, empowering saints to approach God's throne with confidence (Hebrews 4:16). It also spurs perseverance; those convinced of God's hold on them press forward despite persecution or failure. Gratitude bursts forth when Scripture leaps alive, circumstances align providentially, or inner peace overrides logical anxiety—moments when the Spirit's witness reverberates. Such assurance is not complacency but fuel for mission, for those secure in Christ freely expend themselves for others without fear of losing divine favor.

Firstfruits of Redemption: Hope Amid Groaning

Paul admits that creation groans under decay, and believers groan inwardly as they await bodily redemption (Romans 8:22-23). Yet the same passage calls the Spirit "firstfruits," agricultural imagery depicting an initial harvest sample guaranteeing more to come. The tension of "already/not yet" keeps gratitude realistic: pain is acknowledged, but despair is banished. We mourn losses, protest injustice, and battle sickness, but the Spirit's presence within signals that these troubles are temporary. Thanksgiving glimmers in hospital rooms when hymns rise through tears, proclaiming that resurrection life pulses beneath fragile flesh. The Spirit also groans with us, translating wordless sighs into intercession aligned with God's will (Romans 8:26-27). Every answered prayer, every unexpected comfort, every glimpse of justice realized is a down payment of the full redemption on the horizon.

6.5 Sanctification and Fruit-Bearing

Walking by the Spirit vs. Desires of the Flesh

In Galatians, Paul contrasts walking by the Spirit with gratifying fleshly desires, offering a dynamic framework for daily holiness (Galatians 5:16-17). The verb *peripateō* (walk) conveys continuous, habitual strides; spirituality is not an occasional sprint but a lifelong pilgrimage. Flesh here denotes the self-centered nature inherited from Adam, perpetually lobbying for autonomy. The Spirit wages counter-desires, not by suppressing personality but by re-orienting affections towards God. Victory emerges not through sheer grit but through yielded partnership—choosing Spirit-prompted pathways over knee-jerk impulses. Gratitude strengthens resolve; thankful hearts more readily detect Spirit whispers amid competing voices. Each crucified craving and each Spirit-led act becomes a testimony to the transforming friendship promised by Christ.

Ninefold Fruit: Character of Christ Formed Within

The singular "fruit of the Spirit" in Galatians 5:22-23 blossoms into nine facets—love, joy, peace, patience, kindness, goodness, faithfulness, gentleness, self-control. Unlike gifts, which vary among believers, fruit is universal evidence of Spirit life, reflecting Jesus' own character. Agricultural imagery stresses organic growth; fruit ripens through abiding, not frantic effort (John 15:4-5). Community context is essential—patience is exercised with difficult people, kindness extended in hostile environments. The Spirit cultivates these virtues simultaneously, steadily balancing temperament quirks into Christlike harmony. Gratitude accelerates cultivation; focusing on God's generosity softens soil hardened by criticism or entitlement. When congregations display this fruit collectively, the aroma of Christ attracts seekers more powerfully than polished programs.

Ongoing Renewal: From Glory to Glory

Paul describes believers beholding the Lord's glory "with unveiled faces," being transformed into the same image from one degree of glory to another (2 Corinthians 3:18). This metamorphosis (*metamorphoō*) denotes internal change that eventually radiates outward, driven by the Spirit's artistry, not self-manufacture. Sanctification is thus progressive and participatory; we cooperate by fixing gaze on Jesus through Scripture, worship, and obedience. Each incremental shift—growing patience, deepening humility, expanding compassion—signals a glory upgrade orchestrated by divine hands. Gratitude guards against discouragement over slow progress, celebrating that any resemblance to Christ is miraculous new-creation evidence. The promise of "ever-increasing glory" subverts cultural obsessions with fading beauty, anchoring identity in imperishable splendor. Ultimately, the Spirit's renewal will climax in bodily resurrection, but He delights to sketch tomorrow's glory on today's canvas.

6.6 Empowerment for Witness

"You Shall Receive Power": Missional Mandate

Jesus tethered the Great Commission to the gift of power, declaring that the Spirit would enable witness "to the ends of the earth" (Acts 1:8). The Greek *dynamis* suggests explosive energy, yet its goal is not self-aggrandizement but gospel proclamation. First-century disciples, formerly silenced by fear, became unstoppable heralds once clothed with this power. The promise remains active: church planting in restricted nations, prison ministry breakthroughs, and digital evangelism all rely on Spirit-infused boldness. Gratitude fuels courage; remembering past empowerments emboldens present risk-taking. Without the Spirit, mission deteriorates into marketing; with Him, frail vessels convey treasure that transforms eternity. Every conversion story is a monument to promised power recreating dead hearts into living testimonies.

Boldness in Persecution: Acts as Case Study

When authorities threatened Peter and John, they prayed not for safety but for boldness; the place shook and they spoke the word with courage (Acts 4:29-31). Stephen, full of the Spirit, faced death with radiant peace, seeing the Son of Man standing at God's right hand (Acts 7:55-60). Paul's stoning in Lystra and imprisonment in Philippi did not muffle his testimony; songs erupted from jail cells, shaking doors and hearts alike (Acts 16:25-34). The pattern is unmistakable: Spirit-filled witnesses value obedience above survival, trusting resurrection hope to eclipse temporal loss. Gratitude for historical examples steels modern believers facing censorship, ridicule, or violence. Such boldness is not brashness but love refusing to stay silent while darkness enslaves souls. The Spirit continues to amplify humble voices, confounding persecutors and awakening seekers in every generation.

Spirit-Led Evangelism: Philip & the Ethiopian

An angel redirected Philip from Samaria's revival to a desert road, where the Spirit then prompted him to approach an Ethiopian official reading Isaiah (Acts 8:26-29). The encounter demonstrates evangelism orchestrated by divine GPS, matching open hearts with prepared messengers. Philip's obedience bridged ethnic and geographic gaps, planting gospel seeds that would ripple through Africa. The Spirit leveraged Scripture study questions into baptismal confession, illustrating how He illumines both messenger and listener. Gratitude for such orchestration encourages believers to treat every nudge seriously—whether to speak, listen, or travel an inconvenient path. Evangelistic strategies thus expand beyond formulas to Spirit-prompted improvisation, responsive to individual narratives. Each Spirit-arranged appointment affirms that heaven relentlessly pursues the lost, and gratitude bursts forth when we witness divine choreography unfold.

6.7 Gifts for Building the Body

Varieties of Gifts, Same Spirit (1 Corinthians 12)

Paul enumerates diverse manifestations—wisdom, knowledge, faith, healings, miracles, prophecy, discernment, tongues, interpretation—yet emphasizes one Giver (1 Corinthians 12:4-11). The Trinity orchestrates gifting: the Spirit distributes, the Son administers, the Father empowers, fostering humility and interdependence. Gifts are "for the common good," dismantling consumerist attitudes that measure value by platform visibility. Gratitude arises when we celebrate others' gifts without jealousy, recognizing that the Spirit custom-fits abilities for communal flourishing. Diversity combats uniformity; a body needs eyes, hands, ears, and feet functioning harmoniously. Abuse or neglect of gifts injures corporate health, but Spirit-energized stewardship catalyzes mission, worship, and discipleship. Thanksgiving thrives in gatherings where shy intercessors, articulate teachers, compassionate servants, and prophetic voices honor the same Head.

Motivation, Manifestation, and Ministry Gifts

Romans 12 lists motivational gifts—service, teaching, exhortation, giving, leadership, mercy—that shape believers' internal drives. Ephesians 4 outlines ministry offices—apostles, prophets, evangelists, pastors, teachers—given to equip saints. First Corinthians highlights manifestation gifts—visible operations that reveal God's power in real time. This tripartite framework ensures holistic expression: inward passion, outward role, and supernatural sign converge under the Spirit's governance. Gratitude flourishes when churches help members discern gift mixes, affirm unique contributions, and provide contexts for expression. In such ecosystems, spiritual gifts cease to be competitive badges and become collaborative tools. The Spirit's generosity overflows in synergy, painting a mosaic of grace across congregational life.

Love as the Governing Way (1 Corinthians 13)

Sandwiched between chapters on gifts, Paul's hymn to love declares that spiritual endowments devoid of love are noisy gongs and empty boasts. Love redirects gifts from spotlight-seeking to sacrificial service, mirroring the Son who washed feet. Patience, kindness, and humility ground prophetic words, healing prayers, and tongues in Christlike ethos. Gifts will cease when perfection comes, but love endures, making it the ultimate metric of Spirit vitality. Gratitude for love's supremacy protects churches from sensationalism, anchoring charisms in covenant fidelity. When congregations pursue love first, gifts edify rather than divide, testify rather than terrify. Thus, thanking Jesus for the Spirit includes thanking Him for knitting charisma and agapē into inseparable strands of kingdom ministry.

6.8 Guidance and Discernment

Spirit's Check in Decision-Making (Acts 16)

On Paul's second missionary journey, the Spirit forbade entrance to Asia and Bithynia, redirecting him through a Macedonian vision (Acts 16:6-10). Guidance sometimes manifests as closed doors, requiring sensitivity to interpret red lights as divine rerouting rather than defeat. Obedience positioned Paul to plant churches that would later send aid to Jerusalem and contribute epistles to Scripture. The Spirit's GPS balances strategic planning with prophetic interruption, weaving human initiative into divine sovereignty. Gratitude grows when hindsight reveals wisdom behind detours—relationships forged, dangers avoided, breakthroughs gained. Learning to pause, listen, and pivot fosters agile discipleship attuned to subtle promptings. Every Spirit-led decision, big or small, advances kingdom purposes far beyond immediate calculation.

Testing the Spirits: Safeguarding Truth

John exhorts believers to test spirits, because deception often masquerades as enlightenment (1 John 4:1). Criteria include Christological fidelity—confessing Jesus' incarnation—and alignment with apostolic teaching. The Spirit of truth never contradicts Scripture; counterfeit influences twist or truncate gospel essentials. Discernment functions communally; isolated individuals risk confirmation bias, whereas councils of Spirit-filled believers refine conclusions. Gratitude for protective discernment averts gullibility and cynicism alike, nurturing mature faith. Spiritual disciplines—fasting, prayer, Scripture meditation—sharpen discernment faculties like exercise tones muscles. In safeguarding truth, the Spirit preserves the bride's purity, enabling her to shine unblemished before the Bridegroom.

Conscience Illuminated: Ethics in the Spirit

Paul speaks of consciences washed by the Spirit, no longer seared but sensitive (1 Timothy 1:5; Hebrews 9:14). Conscience acts as an internal referee informed by Scripture and calibrated by the Spirit's nudges. Ethical grey areas—media choices, business practices, social engagement—require Spirit-saturated discernment beyond black-and-white commands. The Spirit elevates motivations over technicalities, probing why as much as what. Gratitude for enlightened conscience prevents legalistic rigidity and laissez-faire relativism, steering believers toward integrity. Community accountability complements personal conviction, ensuring that private peace aligns with corporate holiness. Ultimately, Spirit-illuminated conscience beautifies witness, for the world notices lives governed by unseen yet undeniable convictions.

6.9 Prayer and Worship in the Spirit

Spirit Helps Our Weakness in Prayer (Romans 8)

Human vocabulary falters when facing grief, injustice, or mystery, but the Spirit intercedes with groans too deep for words (Romans 8:26). These inexpressible petitions harmonize with the Father's will, guaranteeing effective advocacy beyond our comprehension. Knowing this, believers pray boldly even when emotions are numb or thoughts scattered, trusting the Spirit to translate sighs into symphonies. Gratitude for this assistance alleviates prayer guilt, inviting honesty over eloquence. The Spirit's intercession also sustains endurance: when prayer feels futile, He carries the weight. Many testify that breakthrough followed seasons where only tears flowed—a sign the Spirit was laboring within. Thus, prayer becomes collaboration rather than duty, energizing communion with God at soul-deep levels.

Praying in the Spirit: Diversity of Expression

Jude urges believers to "pray in the Holy Spirit," a phrase encompassing intelligible requests, spontaneous praise, and Spirit-given tongues (Jude 20; 1 Corinthians 14:15). Diversity of expression honors varied temperaments and cultural styles, from contemplative silence to exuberant intercession. Glossolalia edifies personal devotion when private, and prophetic tongues edify the body when interpreted, showcasing Spirit creativity. Structured liturgies, too, become Spirit-energized when hearts engage rather than recite. Gratitude celebrates freedom within order, refusing to restrict the Spirit to one volume or vocabulary. Musical worship likewise spans genres—hymns, gospel, contemporary, indigenous chants—each a conduit for Spirit-breathed adoration. In every sincere expression, the Spirit magnifies Jesus, drawing diverse voices into unified chorus before the throne.

True Worshipers in Spirit and Truth (John 4)

Jesus told the Samaritan woman that true worship is not tied to geographic mountains but springs from Spirit and truth convergence (John 4:23-24). Truth anchors worship in doctrinal fidelity; Spirit infuses it with living reality, preventing dead orthodoxy. This paradigm shatters cultural elitism—peasants and priests alike can access the Father through regenerated hearts. Spirit-empowered worship transcends ritual, transforming everyday tasks—laundry, spreadsheets, nursing—into sanctuaries of praise. Gratitude for indwelling Presence turns commutes into prayer walks and board meetings into mission fields. Corporate gatherings become rehearsals for eternity, where Spirit-lifted hearts preview the unending anthem of Revelation 7:9-10. When worship aligns Spirit and truth, earth kisses heaven, and Jesus receives the glory for which He bled.

6.10 Unity and Diversity in the Spirit

One Body, One Spirit, One Baptism (Ephesians 4)

Paul roots church unity in shared spiritual realities: one hope, Lord, faith, baptism, and God who is over all (Ephesians 4:4-6). Unity is therefore ontological before organizational, produced by the Spirit, not manufactured by committees. Believers guard, not create, this unity by refusing gossip, extending forgiveness, and prioritizing reconciliation. Doctrinal essentials anchor unity while allowing diversity in non-essentials—a tension navigable only through Spirit humility. Gratitude for unity critiques factionalism and tribalism, recalling that Christ is not divided. Ecumenical dialogues flourish when participants approach tables conscious of shared Spirit indwelling. Each multicultural worship service manifests the manifold wisdom of God to heavenly powers (Ephesians 3:10).

Breaking Down Ethnic & Social Barriers

In Corinth, socioeconomic divides threatened the Lord's Supper, prompting Paul to invoke Spirit equality (1 Corinthians 11:17-22). Galatians proclaims neither Jew nor Greek, slave nor free, male nor female can claim superiority, for all are one in Christ (Galatians 3:28). The Spirit engineers a counter-cultural society where seating charts ignore caste and inheritance. Practical steps—shared meals, resource redistribution, power-sharing—embody theological convictions. Gratitude motivates inclusion initiatives, not as political correctness but as gospel necessity. Churches that resist Spirit-led integration forfeit a facet of resurrection witness. When diversity harmonizes, the world glimpses a foretaste of the coming kingdom feast.

Mutual Submission and Collaborative Mission

Paul instructs believers to submit to one another out of reverence for Christ, a command contextualized within Spirit-filled living (Ephesians 5:18-21). Mutual submission overturns hierarchies of dominance, inviting servant leadership modeled by Jesus. Decisions become discerning conversations rather than top-down decrees, leveraging collective wisdom. Spiritual gifts flourish in such environments, for each member's contribution is valued. Gratitude fuels willingness to yield preferences for communal edification, trusting the Spirit to vindicate humility. Collaborative mission—church networks, interdenominational projects, missional business ventures—thrives under this ethos. When believers submit to one another joyfully, skeptics observe a love impossible apart from supernatural Source.

6.11 Spiritual Warfare

Armor Empowered by the Spirit (Ephesians 6)

Spiritual armor—truth belt, righteousness breastplate, gospel shoes, faith shield, salvation helmet, Word sword—requires Spirit activation (Ephesians 6:10-18). Prayer "in the Spirit" brackets the armor list, highlighting dependence, not self-armoring bravado. The Spirit illuminates Scripture to parry deception, fans faith to extinguish fiery darts, and reminds hearts of salvation certainty. Warfare mindset is defensive and offensive; believers stand firm and advance ground through truth proclamation. Gratitude for Spirit-supplied armor dissipates fear of unseen forces, anchoring confidence in

Christ's victory. Consistent armor maintenance—confession, study, fellowship—prevents chinks that invite enemy exploitation. Battle-tested saints radiate peace amid turbulence, bearing witness to the Spirit's protective power.

Authority Over Darkness: Acts Illustrations

In Philippi, Paul cast a divination spirit from a slave girl, liberating her and unsettling profiteers (Acts 16:16-18). Ephesus witnessed mass renunciation of occult practices as the Spirit magnified Jesus' name (Acts 19:17-20). These narratives demonstrate that evangelism often collides with territorial spirits controlling economies and ideologies. Authority flows from union with Christ, not ritual formulas—sons of Sceva learned this painfully (Acts 19:13-16). Gratitude for delegated authority humbles, reminding believers they wield power as stewards, not sorcerers. Spiritual warfare thus combines proclamation, compassion, and confrontation under Spirit guidance. Victories serve mission, freeing captives to join the worship chorus, expanding kingdom borders.

Victory Through Resistance and Dependence

James instructs, "Submit to God, resist the devil, and he will flee" (James 4:7), coupling resistance with dependence. Submission aligns hearts with divine priorities, stripping the enemy of footholds. Resistance employs truth, worship, and community accountability—Spirit-energized habits breaking sin cycles. Dependence fosters prayerful watchfulness, acknowledging weakness that invites greater grace. Gratitude celebrates each delivered temptation as evidence of Spirit faithfulness. Over time, believers mature from reflexive defeat to reflexive reliance, forging resilience. Ultimate victory awaits Christ's return, but daily skirmishes forge character and testify to a kingdom already advancing.

6.12 Spirit-Filled Ethics in Daily Life

Household Codes Reimagined (Ephesians 5–6)

Paul addresses wives, husbands, children, fathers, slaves, and masters, framing roles within Spirit-filled mutual submission (Ephesians 5:21). Wives respect husbands; husbands sacrificially love wives; children obey; fathers nurture; slaves serve sincerely; masters forego threats. These instructions subvert patriarchal abuses by routing authority through Christlike self-giving. The Spirit empowers each party to transcend cultural norms, embodying kingdom counterculture. Gratitude turns duty into worship; spouses forgive, parents apologize, employees excel, employers honor. Household harmony becomes evangelistic, displaying gospel plausibility within watching neighborhoods. Modern equivalents—co-workers, roommates—likewise thrive when Spirit ethics govern interactions.

Marketplace Integrity and Creativity

Filled with the Spirit, Bezalel crafted tabernacle art, demonstrating that vocational skill can be Spirit-inspired (Exodus 31:1-5). Today, entrepreneurs, scientists, and artists receive innovative ideas originating from the same creative Spirit. Honesty in contracts, generosity in profit sharing, and justice in supply chains reflect kingdom values. The Spirit convicts against exploitation, redirecting ventures toward stewardship and community uplift. Gratitude fuels excellence, for work becomes participation in divine creativity rather than mere income pursuit. Witness emerges when colleagues note joy, diligence, and ethical consistency that transcend corporate culture. Through Spirit-empowered marketplace engagement, the earth is filled with knowledge of the Lord as waters cover the sea (Habakkuk 2:14).

Generosity, Justice, and Social Witness

The Jerusalem church practiced radical generosity, selling property to meet needs (Acts 4:34-35). Such economics flowed from Spirit unity, not coercive redistribution; hearts liberated from greed released resources joyfully. Advocacy for widows, orphans, immigrants, and prisoners springs from the Spirit's compassion (Isaiah 61:1). Gratitude propels justice initiatives, framing them as thanksgiving offerings rather than guilt payments. The Spirit equips prophets to challenge oppressive systems while empowering servants to meet practical needs. Social witness without Spirit power becomes burnout; Spirit enthusiasm without justice becomes hollow. Integrated disciples represent Christ holistically, proclaiming and demonstrating good news to body and soul.

6.13 Revival, Renewal, and Global Mission

Historical Outpourings: From Acts to Today

The Spirit's waves have crashed repeatedly—Augustine's Hippo, Moravian prayer vigils, Welsh revival, Azusa Street—each rekindling dormant embers. Common threads: fervent prayer, contrite repentance, and renewed passion for Scripture and mission. While manifestations differ, fruit remains—church planting, social reform, missionary sending. Gratitude for past revivals stokes expectancy, countering cynicism that God no longer moves mightily. Historical hindsight also warns against quenching Spirit fire through institutional control or moral compromise. Documenting testimonies preserves legacy, inspiring future generations to seek fresh wind. Revival narratives remind us that the Spirit delights to revive parched hearts, communities, and nations.

Spirit and the Ends of the Earth

Acts structures geographically—Jerusalem, Judea, Samaria, ends of the earth—tracing Spirit momentum outward (Acts 1:8). Today, vibrant growth surges in the Global South, illustrating Spirit impartiality toward geography. Indigenous movements contextualize liturgy, music, and theology without Western filter, manifesting Pentecost pluralism. Gratitude fuels partnership over paternalism, honoring Spirit leadership in every culture. Diaspora populations bring renewal to host nations, reversing missionary flows as immigrants plant churches in erstwhile sending countries. Technology extends Spirit witness via digital Bible apps, online discipleship, and virtual prayer gatherings. The promise remains: the earth will be filled with the Spirit's glory through multiplying Spirit-empowered witnesses.

Praying for Fresh Wind: Anticipating Future Waves

Every revival was preceded by united, persistent intercession that refused resignation to spiritual stagnation. The Spirit partners with human hunger; empty vessels invite filling. Corporate repentance dismantles barriers—unforgiveness, complacency, worldliness—that grieve the Spirit (Ephesians 4:30). Gratitude for past mercies anchors petitions for greater outpourings, blending memory with expectation. Prayer movements today—24-7 boiler rooms, house of prayer networks, student awakenings—signal rumblings of next waves. The Spirit responds not to formula but to desperation rooted in gospel passion. Believers who watch and pray position themselves to ride forthcoming gusts of kingdom advance.

6.14 Eschatological Role of the Spirit

Seal Until the Day of Redemption

Paul instructs believers not to grieve the Spirit "by whom you were sealed for the day of redemption" (Ephesians 4:30). This seal functions as royal insignia, protecting against tampering until final unveiling. Eschatology, therefore, is not escapist fantasy but Spirit-guarded inheritance. Gratitude for the seal generates resilience; storms may batter, but the scroll of destiny is secure. The Spirit's seal also implies accountability—lives marked by holiness honor the royal stamp. Each communion cup, baptismal immersion, and answered prayer reminds us of the seal's permanence. When Christ returns, the Spirit's work of sealing will culminate in glorification, unveiling sons and daughters radiant with divine likeness.

Spirit and the Bride Say "Come"

Scripture concludes with a duet: "The Spirit and the Bride say, 'Come!'" inviting thirsty souls to drink freely (Revelation 22:17). This eschatological chorus reveals the Spirit's longing for consummation, harmonized with the Church's anticipation. Evangelism becomes eschatology in motion—offering living water ahead of the river flowing from the Lamb's throne. Gratitude propels this invitation, for recipients of grace cannot help but extend grace. The Spirit stokes bridal affection, guarding against fading first love (Revelation 2:4). Every revival of worship, purity, and mission is a rehearsal dinner before the marriage supper. Thus, the Spirit sustains a posture of longing and welcoming until the Bridegroom appears.

Foretaste of New Creation Glory

Isaiah envisioned a renovated cosmos—wolf dwelling with lamb, deserts blooming, nations streaming to Zion (Isaiah 11; 35). The Spirit now sprinkles prophetic dew on parched hearts, previewing that reality through signs, wonders, and reconciled communities. Environmental stewardship by Spirit-led believers prefigures creation's liberation from decay (Romans 8:21). Artistic expressions—music, paintings, poetry—often pulse with Spirit-inspired beauty hinting at Eden restored. Gratitude sharpens perception, allowing believers to recognize foretastes rather than dismiss them as coincidence. Sacraments, too, are appetizers: baptism mirrors future resurrection; Eucharist anticipates the wedding feast. Living in the Spirit, therefore, is living in the overlap of ages, tasting tomorrow's harvest today and inviting the world to the banquet.

Conclusion

From the upper-room wind of Pentecost to the whispered "Abba" in a believer's heart, the Holy Spirit manifests Jesus' promise to dwell with and within His people. He is the down payment of our inheritance, the animator of evangelistic power, the artisan sculpting Christlike character, and the compass steering the Church toward consummation. Every miracle witnessed, every sin conquered, every hymn sung in Spirit and truth amplifies thanksgiving to the Giver of the greatest gift short of glory itself. As we cherish His indwelling Presence—consulting His guidance, relying on His strength, and yielding to His sanctifying flame—we preview the day when sealed saints will stand in unveiled splendor before

God's throne. Until then, may our lives echo ceaseless gratitude: "Thank You, Jesus, for sending the Spirit, for through Him Your life beats within our own."

Chapter 7. Thank You, Jesus, for Daily Bread—Provision and Sustenance

When Jesus invites us to pray, "Give us this day our daily bread" (Mt 6:11), He is not merely teaching polite table grace; He is re-calibrating our entire outlook on life. In a single phrase He links the humblest need—another bite of food—to the glorious generosity of our Father in heaven. Scripture presents provision as one of God's signature attributes, stretching from Eden's lush abundance (Gen 2:8-10) to the final marriage supper of the Lamb (Rev 19:9). Between those bookends, covenant history reveals countless moments when the Lord feeds, clothes, shelters, and sustains His people, not only preserving biological existence but fostering trust, community, and worship. To say, "Thank You, Jesus, for daily bread" is therefore to praise the One who still multiplies loaves, still opens storehouses in drought, and still nourishes souls with living bread that never perishes. In the pages that follow we will trace this theme through Scripture and experience, discovering how divine provision shapes a kingdom economy of contentment, generosity, and unshakable hope. May each paragraph plant fresh confidence that the God who numbers hairs (Mt 10:30) is more than able to fill pantries, pay bills, strengthen bodies, and satisfy hearts.

7.1 Recognizing God as Provider

Source of Every Good Gift: The Father's Open Hand

From the outset the Bible introduces a God who delights to give. Eden overflows with edible trees "pleasant to the sight and good for food" (Gen 2:9), underscoring that human survival and enjoyment spring from divine largesse. Later, James distills that pattern into a principle: "Every good and perfect gift is from above, coming down from the Father of lights" (Jas 1:17). Creation itself is therefore a standing testimony to providence—a vast pantry stocked with grains, fruits, water, and sunlight long before humanity plants a single seed. Recognizing God as Provider counters the modern illusion of self-sufficiency, reminding us that paychecks, grocery stores, and irrigation systems are secondary causes undergirded by a primary Giver. Gratitude opens our eyes to everyday graces we tend to overlook: the fragrant steam curling from coffee, the sweetness locked in a strawberry, the humble loaf sliced at breakfast. When we bless a meal we are not adding spirituality to something secular; we are acknowledging reality—that the Father's open hand precedes every bite. Such recognition nurtures humility, curbs entitlement, and prepares the heart to trust even when cupboards look bare.

Providence in Creation: Seasons, Sun, and Soil

Psalm 104 paints a panoramic portrait of God's ecological provision: clouds as watering cans, grass sprouting for cattle, wine gladdening hearts, and bread strengthening mortals (Ps 104:10-15). The cyclical dance of seedtime and harvest (Gen 8:22) testifies that the Creator has hard-wired rhythms of sustenance into the planet. Sunlight triggers photosynthesis; soils teem with microbes breaking down nutrients; pollinators shuttle life from bloom to bloom. Far from being mechanistic phenomena, these processes are expressions of ongoing providence—God "sending rain on the righteous and the unrighteous" (Mt 5:45). For believers, studying agronomy or meteorology becomes a doxological exercise, unveiling the wisdom that choreographs climate patterns and soil fertility. Gratitude wells up not only at the dinner table but in gardens, markets, and weather reports, as each forecast and harvest testifies afresh that the earth is the Lord's pantry entrusted to humanity's stewardship.

Jesus Reveals the Generous Heart of God

While creation shows God's generosity, Jesus embodies it. Feeding hungry crowds (Mk 6:30-44), reframing worry with illustrations of birds and lilies (Mt 6:25-34), and turning water into celebratory wine (Jn 2:1-11), He reveals a Father who overflows rather than rations. Each miracle highlights both compassion and abundance: baskets of leftovers, gallons of vintage wine, nets straining with fish (Lk 5:6-7). Even in teaching, Jesus' metaphors presume divine generosity—a shepherd finding lush pasture (Jn 10:9) or a banquet host filling his house (Lk 14:23). When we thank Jesus for daily bread, we confess that scarcity is not heaven's default setting; abundance is. Our gratitude therefore becomes an act of faith, declaring that the same heart that pitied itinerant fishermen and overlooked wedding planners still throbs with desire to care for modern disciples navigating rent, tuition, and grocery inflation.

7.2 "Give Us This Day..."—Petition in the Lord's Prayer

Daily Dependence vs. Weekly Stockpiling

Jesus intentionally chooses "this day" rather than "this month," steering hearts toward rhythmic reliance. Like the Israelites who collected manna one dawn at a time (Ex 16:4-5), disciples learn that faith matures in daily increments, not once-for-all windfalls. Modern economics praises stockpiling—retirement accounts, pantries, data storage—but the kingdom invites ongoing conversation with the Giver. Praying for today's bread honors prudent planning while resisting the illusion that tomorrow is guaranteed (Jas 4:13-15). Gratitude blossoms in this daily cadence, for each provision is recognized as fresh grace rather than background entitlement. When believers awaken to find mercies renewed (Lam 3:22-23), they discover joy untethered from bank statements and anchored in relational trust.

Bread as Symbol of All Essentials

In first-century Palestine bread was staple food, the baseline of sustenance. By teaching disciples to request bread, Jesus sanctions asking for every legitimate necessity—food, shelter, clothing, companionship, wisdom for decisions. The petition rejects both ascetic denial and consumeristic excess, situating need between those ditches. It also dignifies physicality; spirituality that neglects stomachs is foreign to biblical faith. Gratitude, then, includes thanksgiving for heaters in winter, clean water, and safe neighborhoods, holding them alongside prayer meetings and Bible study. Bread's ordinariness whispers that nothing mundane is beneath the Father's attention; every diaper, invoice, and grocery bag can be an altar of thanks.

Prayer that Forms a Trusting Heart

Petition is as much about formation as acquisition. Asking daily cultivates awareness of dependency, dismantling the fortress of self-reliance brick by brick. Over time, believers detect subtle shifts: anxiety mutates into anticipation, cynicism into childlike expectancy. Gratitude accelerates this renovation, because thankful recollection fuels present confidence—what God did last week He can do again. Thus "Give us this day" becomes a spiritual posture: open palms replacing clenched fists. Even unanswered prayers nurture trust, for silence trains ears to discern provision in unexpected timetables or forms.

7.3 Manna in the Wilderness—Lessons in Enough

Morning Dew of Mercy: Gathering without Hoarding

The wilderness manna miracle (Ex 16) stands as Scripture's archetype of daily provision. Each dawn Israelites found "flakes like frost," enough for everyone yet impossible to stockpile (Ex 16:14-18). Attempts to hoard bred maggots, illustrating that sufficiency is discovered in obedience, not anxiety. Modern parallels abound—in hoarded wealth rotting in unused bank accounts, in over-scheduled calendars leaving no space for rest. Gratitude guards us from such maggoty excess, teaching delight in sufficiency rather than compulsion for surplus. When we gather what God apportions—money, energy, opportunities—we find contentment free of decay.

Sabbath Portion: Resting in Divine Sufficiency

On the sixth day manna doubled, enabling Sabbath rest without lack (Ex 16:22-30). Provision, therefore, is linked to rhythm: six days of gathering, one of trusting God to keep the bread from spoiling. In a culture idolizing productivity, the Sabbath principle confronts the fear that rest will reduce supply. Gratitude empowers obedience here, persuading hearts that God's math still works—that revenues can meet budgets despite a closed laptop on Sunday, that bodies regenerate more through rest than through relentless output. Practicing Sabbath becomes a living doxology, announcing to self and society that the Lord of manna still sustains.

Remembering with a Jar in the Ark

God ordered a jar of manna preserved before the Testimony (Ex 16:32-34), memorializing provision for future generations. Tangible reminders—journals of answered prayers, framed photographs of early apartments furnished by miracles— serve the same function today. They silence amnesia during lean months, when doubts hiss that bread will fail. Gratitude curates these memory jars, elevating testimony from private nostalgia to community encouragement. Every retelling of

God's faithfulness becomes fresh bread for listeners slogging through their own deserts.

7.4 Table Miracles of Jesus

Wedding at Cana: Scarcity Turns to Celebration

In Cana's understated crisis—wine depleted before the festivities ended—Jesus converted plain water into gallons of fine vintage (Jn 2:1-11). The miracle affirms that God's provision extends beyond bare calories to convivial joy. Scarcity threatened communal embarrassment; abundance fostered celebration. Gratitude perceives such extravagance not as frivolity but as kingdom foretaste, where joy overflows. When believers toast milestones, share desserts, or host neighborhood barbecues, they reenact Cana, proclaiming a Messiah who rescues parties from running dry.

Feeding the Five Thousand: Multiplication in the Hands of Christ

All four gospels record the seaside picnic where five barley loaves and two fish satisfied a stadium-sized crowd (Mk 6:38-44). The sequence—Jesus blesses, breaks, hands to disciples, who distribute—models how divine provision often travels through human hands. Gratitude thus motivates availability; what we surrender, however meager, can multiply once entrusted to Jesus. Twelve baskets of leftovers underscore kingdom economics: generosity begets abundance, never lack. Recalling this miracle infuses modern stewardship—sharing lunch with colleagues, funding missionaries—with resurrection-charged expectancy.

Breakfast on the Shore: Provision After Failure

Post-resurrection, Jesus meets weary fishermen at dawn, fills their nets, and cooks breakfast (Jn 21:1-14). The scene follows Peter's denial, hinting that provision flows even after moral collapse. Charcoal coals (mirroring the courtyard of denial) become a grill for grace, turning shame into fellowship.

Gratitude thrives here, freeing believers to receive resources without disqualifying themselves through guilt. Daily bread, then, is not payment for performance but gift from a Lord who restores with coffee-and-fish hospitality.

7.5 Work, Vocation, and the Dignity of Labor

Adam's Garden Mandate Revisited

Before sin, God placed Adam in Eden "to work it and keep it" (Gen 2:15). Labor predates the curse; toil's frustration is the curse's intrusion (Gen 3:17-19). Redemption in Christ re-dignifies work as partnership with the Provider—cultivating, inventing, organizing resources so creation's potential flourishes. Whether coding software or cleaning hotel rooms, vocation becomes an altar where bread is coaxed from earth. Gratitude converts daily tasks from drudgery to worship, recognizing each pay stub as God's indirect provision.

Paul's Tentmaking Model

Paul declined Corinthian patronage, supporting ministry through tentmaking (Acts 18:1-3) and teaching that "anyone unwilling to work should not eat" (2 Th 3:10). His example balances supernatural supply with vocational responsibility. Gratitude embraces both—a heart open to miracles and hands committed to craftsmanship. When salaries arrive, thankful souls praise Jehovah-Jireh as fervently as after unexpected checks, discerning the same Provider behind both.

Balancing Industry and Idolatry of Work

Work can mutate into idol—identity tethered to productivity. Sabbath, prayer pauses, and relational commitments counter this slide, reminding that provision ultimately rests in God. Gratitude loosens white-knuckled grip on career ladders, enabling rest without dread and generosity without fear. When job loss or retirement shifts income streams, thankful hearts trust provision beyond a specific role, echoing David's assurance: "I have not seen the righteous forsaken" (Ps 37:25).

7.6 Contentment and Simplicity

Lilies of the Field: Beauty Without Toil

Jesus directs anxious disciples to observe wildflowers clothed more splendidly than Solomon (Mt 6:28-30). The comparison rebukes worry not by denying needs but by elevating trust in a God who beautifies weeds. Gratitude enhances this lesson: noting small wonders—a robin's nest, a thrift-store treasure—renews confidence that Creator cares for details. Contentment grows as eyes catalog beauty detached from price tags.

Apostle Paul's Secret in Plenty and Want

Writing from prison, Paul claims he has learned to be content in every circumstance (Phil 4:11-13). The secret? Union with Christ, empowering sufficiency beyond external supply. Gratitude is integral to that school—thanking God for meager rations and palace fare alike. Such practiced gratitude immunizes hearts against envy in abundance and despair in scarcity, producing the rare freedom to enjoy wealth without chains and survive lack without panic.

Practicing Simplicity in a Culture of Excess

Simplicity is gratitude's sibling: both acknowledge that happiness is not cumulative but relational. Spiritual disciplines—decluttering, fasting from media, buying secondhand—train appetites to delight in enough. Far from ascetic gloom, simplicity makes room to savor gifts—unhurried meals, deeper friendships—often eclipsed by clutter. Gratitude fuels these practices, cheering the soul with evidence that less can indeed feel like more when Jesus satisfies deepest hungers.

7.7 Generosity—Blessed to Be a Blessing

Loaves Shared, Not Stored

A boy's lunch fed thousands because it was offered (Jn 6:9). Proverbs echoes: "One gives freely, yet grows all the richer" (Prov 11:24). Kingdom economics equate generosity with multiplication, hoarding with loss. Gratitude disarms scarcity mentality, converting receivers into conduits. When pay raises or harvests arrive, thankful hearts inquire, "Who else's table can this bread adorn?"

Early-Church Radical Giving (Acts 4)

Jerusalem believers sold property to erase poverty among them (Acts 4:34-35). Their generosity sprouted from "great grace" resting on all—experience of divine provision birthed openhandedness. Modern parallels surface in benevolence funds, medical bill crowdfunding, and hospitality to refugees. Gratitude motivates such giving, remembering the undeserved nature of our own resources.

Principles of Cheerful, Proportionate Stewardship

Paul instructs Corinth: give "not reluctantly or under compulsion" but cheerfully (2 Cor 9:7). He commends proportional giving—"as God has prospered" (1 Cor 16:2)—ensuring fairness. Gratitude transforms percentages into praise, shifting focus from obligation to opportunity. Whether tithing, tipping generously, or sponsoring wells, cheerful stewardship testifies that God's provision never diminishes when shared; it multiplies in eternal dividends.

7.8 Spiritual Bread—Word that Nourishes

"Man Shall Not Live by Bread Alone"

Jesus' wilderness reply to Satan (Mt 4:4; Deut 8:3) elevates Scripture as sustenance for soul. Physical bread sustains bodies briefly; God's Word nourishes eternally. Gratitude for physical provision thus finds complement in thanksgiving for verses that steady emotions, counsel decisions, and reveal Christ. Neglecting daily Bible intake is spiritual starvation masquerading as busyness.

Daily Meditation as Soul Sustenance

The righteous person "meditates day and night" (Ps 1:2), rooting like a tree by streams. Such meditation is more than reading; it is chewing, savoring, and assimilating truth until it forms character. Gratitude motivates consistency—returning day after day to a table where the Host never exhausts courses. Journaling insights, memorizing passages, or discussing with friends enhances flavor, deepening the feast.

Teaching Our Children to Feast on Scripture

Israel was charged to teach God's words diligently to children (Deut 6:6-7). Modern parents, mentors, and teachers extend that mandate—bedtime stories, youth devotionals, Scripture art on refrigerators. Gratitude propels this transmission, viewing Scripture not as homework but heritage. When young voices recite Psalm 23 at family prayers, generations echo thanks for bread that never molds.

7.9 Eucharist: Bread Broken, Grace Received

From Passover to Lord's Supper

Jesus re-interprets Passover bread as His body, instituting communion (Lk 22:19). Provision language peaks here: the Giver gives Himself. Gratitude at the table transcends sentiment, recognizing that every loaf sliced by believers worldwide proclaims substitutionary sacrifice sustaining spiritual life. Each bite testifies: our deepest hunger is satisfied in Christ alone.

Communion as Weekly Re-centering on Christ

Early Christians "broke bread" on the first day of the week (Acts 20:7), recentering identity around gospel grace before scattering to work. The Table equalizes classes—slave beside magistrate—each receiving identical portions. Gratitude levels hearts, uprooting superiority or shame, focusing gaze on the Host who paid all seats with blood, not coins.

Anticipating the Marriage Supper of the Lamb

The Eucharist is appetizer for eschatological banquet (Rev 19:9). Each celebration whispers of that coming feast where hunger and thirst cease forever (Rev 7:16). Gratitude blends remembrance with anticipation, tasting future fullness in present morsels. Thus communion fuels mission: until every people group receives invitation, the Church distributes spiritual bread worldwide.

7.10 Freedom from Anxiety over Provision

Birds of the Air: Theology of Carefree Trust

Jesus points to ravens who neither sow nor reap but are fed by God (Lk 12:24). He does not endorse laziness; He targets anxiety birthed by unbelief. If feathered creatures merit such care, how much more image-bearers? Gratitude rehearses this logic, calming nerves with avian theology—every chirping sparrow a sermon against worry.

Casting Cares through Prayer and Supplication

Paul counsels Philippians: exchange anxiety for grateful petition, and peace will guard hearts (Phil 4:6-7). Gratitude is crucial—thanksgiving reframes circumstances, recalling past faithfulness. As cares are cast, God's shalom garrisons minds, stabilizing decisions. Those who practice this rhythm often testify that provision meets them mid-prayer, arriving in envelopes, job leads, or unexplainable calm.

Replacing Worry with Worship

Worry rehearses potential loss; worship recounts proven love. Singing doxologies in kitchens or cars shifts focus from deficits to divine sufficiency. Gratitude fuels this shift: hymns like "Great Is Thy Faithfulness" or "Jireh" summon memories of rent paid, illnesses healed. Over time, worship becomes reflex when bills arrive, defeating anxiety before it metastasizes.

7.11 Gratitude in Scarcity and Abundance

Ten Lepers: The One Who Returned

Only one healed leper returned to thank Jesus (Lk 17:11-19), and he was a Samaritan. Thanksgiving distinguished him, turning physical healing into holistic salvation—"Your faith has made you well." Gratitude thus deepens gifts into relationship. In plenty or need, returning to God with praise ensures provision promotes intimacy, not mere consumption.

Ebenezer Stones: Markers of Past Faithfulness

Samuel erected a stone, naming it Ebenezer— "Till now the Lord has helped us" (1 Sam 7:12). Journals, framed verses, or annual gratitude feasts replicate this practice, stockpiling memories of provision. During famine seasons, these markers speak louder than empty pantries, anchoring faith in historical kindness.

Testimonies that Strengthen Community Faith

Revelation says believers overcome "by the word of their testimony" (Rev 12:11). Sharing provision stories in small groups fuels collective trust—job miraculously secured, groceries gifted anonymously, tuition covered. Gratitude spreads contagiously; hearing others' bread miracles enlarges expectation, prompting fresh prayers and bold generosity.

7.12 Eschatological Banquet—Ultimate Satisfaction

Isaiah's Mountain Feast of Rich Wine and Fat Things

Isaiah envisions the Lord hosting a feast of rich food, aged wine, swallowing death forever (Isa 25:6-8). Provision culminates in resurrection celebration, where tears are wiped away. Gratitude stokes longing for this finale, comforting mourners missing loved ones at earthly tables.

Parables of the Wedding Banquet: Invitations and Responses

Jesus' parables (Mt 22:1-14; Lk 14:15-24) depict a king inviting guests who make excuses, so servants gather the marginalized. Daily bread gratitude compels acceptance of this invitation—refusing distractions of field and business—while urging us to extend invitations to others, especially society's overlooked.

"Come, Buy Without Money": Final Fulfillment in the New Creation

Isaiah 55 portrays a marketplace where essentials cost nothing because the Servant paid the price. Revelation echoes with invitations to drink freely (Rev 22:17). When believers thank Jesus for daily provision now, they rehearse eternal gratitude for inexhaustible satisfaction ahead. Scarcity will vanish; abundance will be norm. Until then, every loaf is a down payment of that future feast.

Conclusion

From Genesis bread that sprouts effortlessly in Eden's sod to Revelation's banquet groaning with unending abundance, Scripture sings of a God who loves to feed His people. Jesus, the living loaf broken for the world, invites us to trust, receive, and share. Daily bread—whether harvested through diligent labor, multiplied by miracle, or received through the kindness of others—arrives with a tag that reads, "From the Father, with love." Gratitude is the appropriate response, not merely as table prayers but as lifestyles marked by contentment, simplicity, generosity, and joyous expectancy. As we cultivate thankful hearts, anxiety loses its grip, communities knit together in sharing, and the watching world tastes and sees that the Lord is good. One day our provisional meals will give way to the wedding supper where hunger and want are forever obsolete. Until then, may every slice of bread, every paycheck, every answered prayer elicit the confession that fuels all other worship: Thank You, Jesus, for daily bread.

Chapter 8. Thank You, Jesus, for Healing—Body, Mind, and Spirit

Woven through the biblical story is God's unwavering intention to restore broken creation to the wholeness He envisioned in Eden. From the first promise of a serpent-crushing Redeemer (Gen 3:15) to the climactic vision of leaves that heal the nations (Rev 22:1-2), Scripture reveals divine compassion reaching into every sphere where disorder, pain, and sin have wreaked havoc. Jesus Christ embodies that compassion in flesh, touching lepers, calming tormented minds, and shattering the grip of demonic darkness. Yet His earthly ministry is only the opening movement of a healing symphony that continues in the Church through the Holy Spirit. To thank Jesus for healing, then, is to celebrate more than isolated miracles; it is to praise the Lord who re-weaves body, soul, relationships, and societies into the tapestry of shalom. The following pages explore that tapestry thread by thread—biblical foundations, gospel narratives, apostolic practice, gifts of the Spirit, and the eschatological promise that every tear will be wiped away. May each testimony and text nurture confident gratitude that the Great Physician is still on call, still writing prescriptions of grace for every kind of ache.

8.1 Foundations of Divine Healing

Creation & Shalom: Wholeness in Eden

Healing begins, paradoxically, in a place where no one was sick. Genesis presents Eden as a realm of integrated flourishing—humans enjoying unhindered fellowship with God, harmonious relationships with each other, and perfect synergy with the earth's ecology (Gen 1:31; 2:25). This original shalom establishes wholeness as God's default intention, framing sickness not as a divine design but as an alien intruder. The very rhythms of Eden—balanced work and rest, abundant nutrition, untainted emotional intimacy—model holistic wellness that medicine often tries to replicate. When we thank Jesus for healing, we are thanking Him for restoring a lost design, reconnecting fractured realities to their Edenic blueprint. Every miracle, therefore, is simultaneously forward-looking toward new creation and backward-looking toward Eden's wholeness. Gratitude for today's relief becomes worship for a Creator who never abandoned His original plan. Such a worldview energizes healthcare, counseling, and social justice, recognizing that restoring bodies, minds, and communities aligns with God's primordial "very good."

Fracture at the Fall: Sickness, Sin, and Separation

The entrance of sin in Genesis 3 detonates a chain reaction that ripples through every human cell and social structure. Physical decay, psychological distress, and relational hostility—all traceable to the rupture with God—signal that sickness is symptomatic of deeper alienation (Rom 5:12). The curse on the ground introduces toil that strains the body; pain in childbirth hints at obstetric peril; fig-leaf shame foreshadows emotional disintegration (Gen 3:16-19). Scripture never simplistically equates individual sin with specific disease (Jn 9:2-3), yet it portrays the totality of sickness as fruit of systemic fallenness. Grasping this linkage guards us from fatalism: if sickness entered through rebellion, it can exit through redemption. Gratitude for healing, then, honors Jesus as the Second Adam who absorbs the curse to reroute history toward life (1 Cor 15:22). Each testimony of recovery whispers that Calvary's antidote is outworking in real time, reversing the entropy sin unleashed.

Covenant Compassion: Yahweh-Rapha Revealed in Exodus

When Israel emerges from the Red Sea, God introduces Himself with a new title: "I am the Lord, your healer" (YHWH-Rapha, Ex 15:26). This covenant clause couples obedience with wellness, linking faith to flourishing in the harshness of Sinai's wilderness. The bitter waters of Marah sweetened by divine intervention illustrate God's readiness to transform harmful environments into sources of life. Subsequent Torah legislation on quarantine, sanitation, and diet complements miraculous intervention with practical wisdom, revealing a holistic therapeutic framework centuries ahead of medical science. Israel's hymnbook later praises Yahweh who "forgives all your iniquity and heals all your diseases" (Ps 103:3), merging moral and physical restoration into a single act of mercy. Thanking Jesus for healing stands in continuity with that covenant revelation, acknowledging Him as the incarnate expression of Yahweh-Rapha. His touch on fevers and forgiveness of sinners are twin streams from the same fountain of compassion first unveiled beside Marah's spring.

8.2 The Healing Ministry of Jesus

Touching the Untouchable: Lepers, Bleeding Woman, Outcasts

In first-century Judea, illness often carried social quarantine, yet Jesus repeatedly extended His hand where culture recoiled. A leper bowed, saying, "If You will, You can make me clean," and Jesus' immediate touch simultaneously cured disease and restored human dignity (Mk 1:40-42). Likewise, the woman hemorrhaging for twelve years stole a forbidden touch of His garment and heard herself publicly affirmed as "daughter." (Mk 5:25-34). Each interaction rewrites communal boundaries, proving that divine holiness is not contaminated by sickness but contagious with wholeness. Grateful reflection on these stories assures marginalized sufferers—addicts, chronically ill, stigmatized minorities—that Christ's compassion overrides taboo. Modern believers emulate this touch through hospital chaplaincy, hospice care, and friendship with society's quarantined. Thanksgiving fuels such risky love, remembering that we, too, were touched while unclean and invited into the embrace of the Healer who breaks exclusion.

Word of Authority: Paralytics Rise, Fevers Flee

Jesus need not always touch; sometimes He speaks. A royal official's son is healed at a forty-kilometer distance (Jn 4:50-53). Peter's mother-in-law's fever disappears when He "rebukes" it like an unruly wind (Lk 4:39). Most dramatically, four friends lower a paralytic through a roof, and Jesus pairs the physical command "Rise, take up your mat" with the spiritual pronouncement "Your sins are forgiven" (Mk 2:5-12). His authoritative word reveals illness as subject, not sovereign; viruses and vertebrae alike obey their Creator's voice. Gratitude for such authority emboldens prayer today: we petition a living Lord whose vocabulary still contains imperatives stronger than pathology. Whether healing manifests instantly, gradually through medicine, or ultimately in resurrection, faith rests on the One who merely "sends out His word and heals" (Ps 107:20).

Holistic Restoration: Body, Emotions, Relationships

Gospel healings rarely stop at tissue repair; they ripple into psychological and social domains. The Gerasene demoniac ends clothed and "in his right mind," ready for mission (Mk 5:15-20). Jairus's daughter receives not only life but instructions for a nourishing meal, hinting at ongoing care (Mk 5:43). Ten lepers are cleansed, yet only the thankful Samaritan hears the fuller blessing of salvation (Lk 17:19). Jesus' healings thus model integration—physical, emotional, relational, spiritual—anticipating modern integrative medicine. Thanksgiving for such holistic ministry spurs churches to pair prayer lines with counseling referrals, food pantries, and reconciliation initiatives, continuing the multifaceted restoration that characterized the Master's touch.

8.3 Faith Encounters that Unlocked Miracles

Centurion's "Just Say the Word" Confidence

A Roman officer appeals on behalf of his paralyzed servant, confessing unworthiness for Jesus to enter his Gentile home yet affirming that a command will suffice (Mt 8:8-10). Jesus marvels, spotlighting Gentile faith surpassing Israeli expectation. The narrative underscores faith's essence: perceiving authority in Christ and entrusting the problem to His sovereignty. Gratitude grows when believers emulate the centurion—interceding for others, acknowledging Jesus' supremacy over distance, diagnoses, and social boundaries. Modern testimonies of long-distance healings—prayers over video calls, letters, or digital messages—echo this ancient precedent, proving that faith's reach matches Christ's reign.

Friends on the Roof: Persistent Intercession

Four companions dismantle a rooftop to lower their paralyzed friend before Jesus (Mk 2:4-5). Scripture notes "Jesus saw their faith," attributing healing partly to communal persistence. This story validates corporate intercession and creative obstacles-busting love. Gratitude here is communal; healings become shared celebrations that knit friendships tighter. Churches practicing prayer chains, hospital visits, and meal trains participate in rooftop faith, thanking Jesus together when miracles manifest.

Bartimaeus' Cry: Recognizing Messianic Mercy

Blind Bartimaeus shouts "Son of David, have mercy on me!" despite crowd rebukes (Mk 10:46-52). His messianic title signals theological insight; his persistence illustrates determined faith. Jesus asks, "What do you want?" inviting explicit request. Gratitude for Bartimaeus' story encourages vocal, specific petitions today, even when culture hushes desperation. His immediate sight recovery testifies that acknowledging Jesus' identity catalyzes healing power. Each worship chorus proclaiming Christ's lordship becomes a Bartimaean cry, drawing mercy into present darkness.

8.4 Atonement & Healing at the Cross

"By His Stripes We Are Healed" (Isa 53)

Isaiah's Servant Song couples substitutionary suffering with healing: "He bore our griefs... with His wounds we are healed" (Isa 53:4-5). Matthew cites this text after a flurry of miracles, linking Jesus' clinical work to His impending crucifixion (Mt 8:16-17). Peter later anchors believers' sanctification and bodily wholeness in the same wounds (1 Pet 2:24). Gratitude recognizes Calvary as the legal basis for every healing, whether partial now or perfected in resurrection. The cross demolishes the lie that sickness is immune from redemption's reach; the same blood that pardons guilt can reverse decay.

Forgiveness and Physical Recovery in One Breath

In Capernaum, Jesus fuses pardon and healing, confronting skeptics with the rhetorical question, "Which is easier...?" (Mk 2:9). This tandem act declares that sin and sickness, though distinct, share a remedy in Christ. Under the new covenant, communion cup and bread signify both—blood for sin, body for brokenness (1 Cor 11:23-30). Gratitude at the Table therefore encompasses both moral cleansing and somatic renewal. Many testify to physical improvements during Eucharist services, hinting at the meal's holistic power rooted in Calvary.

Eucharist as Ongoing Participation in Christ's Wholeness

Paul warns Corinthians that careless communion results in weakness and sickness, implying the inverse: reverent participation mediates strength and health (1 Cor 11:29-30). Early church fathers viewed the Table as "medicine of immortality." Modern charismatic traditions often include healing prayer during communion, seeing bread as contact point with Christ's risen life. Gratitude transforms ritual into expectancy; each bite becomes a sacramental plea: "Lord, let Your wholeness permeate my cells, thoughts, and relationships."

8.5 Healing in the Acts Church

Gate Beautiful: Lame Man Walking & Leaping

Peter and John encounter a forty-year cripple at the temple gate; invoking Jesus' name, they lift him to instantaneous mobility (Acts 3:1-10). The miracle attracts a crowd, offering evangelistic platform that yields five thousand converts (Acts 4:4). Healing thus functions as sign and sermon, validating the risen Christ. Gratitude for historical record stirs contemporary prayer teams who minister at street outreaches, hospitals, and refugee camps, anticipating similar "walking and leaping and praising God."

Shadow and Apron: Extraordinary Means, Ordinary People

Peter's shadow heals (Acts 5:15) and cloths from Paul's body drive out disease and demons (Acts 19:11-12). Scripture labels these events "extraordinary," reminding that God sometimes employs unconventional conduits. Gratitude guards against formula fixation, honoring the Spirit's creativity. Testimonies of healings via phone recordings, handkerchiefs, or even worship flags find precedent here; the focus remains on Jesus, not methodology.

Integration with Evangelism: Signs That Confirm the Word

Acts consistently pairs preaching with power: Samaritans heed Philip after demons flee (Acts 8:6-8); Lystra's cripple sparks attention before Paul's sermon (Acts 14:8-18). Mark's ending anticipates this pattern: signs confirm proclaimed gospel (Mk 16:20). Gratitude for healing spurs missional boldness—mercy ministry, street evangelism, and cross-cultural missions all enriched by expectancy that God will authenticate His Word through tangible compassion.

8.6 Gifts of Healing & Charismata Today

Diversity of Manifestations, Same Spirit

Paul lists "gifts of healings" (plural) implying varied specializations—migraine relief, orthopedic miracles, emotional deliverance (1 Cor 12:9). The Spirit distributes as He wills, preventing monopolies and fostering interdependence. Gratitude honors each manifestation without envy; a back-pain testimony inspires faith even for cancer breakthroughs. Churches that celebrate small recoveries cultivate climate for larger wonders.

Discernment, Order, and Love as Governing Frames

Healing ministry risks excess—manipulation, hype, or shaming those not healed. Paul embeds charisms within chapters on body life and love (1 Cor 12–14). Discernment tests motives; order ensures edification; love protects dignity. Gratitude itself moderates extremes: thankful healers remember they are conduits, not sources, avoiding celebrity pitfalls. Congregations governing ministry with Scriptural parameters safeguard witness and maximize fruit.

Practical Guidelines for Prayer Lines & Anointing

James prescribes elders anointing the sick with oil, prayer of faith, confession of sin (Jas 5:14-16). Modern application includes trauma-informed ministry: obtain consent, respect privacy, follow safeguarding policies. Teams blend listening to Spirit with medical advice—blessing medicine as gift while seeking miracle. Gratitude undergirds follow-up: testimonies recorded, medications tapered responsibly, discipleship offered to healed persons. Such protocols honor Jesus and serve communities with integrity.

8.7 Emotional & Psychological Renewal

Jesus Heals the Broken-hearted (Lk 4)

Quoting Isaiah 61, Jesus claims mandate to bind broken hearts (Lk 4:18). Encounters with grief—widow of Nain, Jairus's household—show Him confronting emotional devastation as seriously as disease. His tears at Lazarus's tomb validate lament (Jn 11:35). Gratitude draws sufferers to a Savior who feels with them, dismantling stigma around therapy and counseling. Churches partnering with Christian psychologists extend Jesus' mission today, merging prayer with evidence-based care.

From Anxiety to Peace: "Cast All Your Cares"

Peter exhorts believers to cast anxieties on God "because He cares" (1 Pet 5:7). Paul echoes: prayer plus thanksgiving guards hearts with peace surpassing understanding (Phil 4:6-7). Neuroscience confirms gratitude rewires anxiety circuits. Practicing daily thankfulness—journals, breath prayers—becomes spiritual cognitive therapy. Healing thus includes rewiring thought life through Spirit-empowered gratitude.

Transforming Thought Patterns: Renewing the Mind

Romans 12:2 links transformation to renewed minds. Inner healing ministries guide believers to replace lies ("I'm worthless") with truth ("I am God's workmanship," Eph 2:10). Gratitude accelerates this exchange, spotlighting evidences of God's goodness that debunk despair. Cognitive Behavioral Therapy aligns with biblical metanoia, and when saturated in prayer, fuels deep psychological resilience.

8.8 Deliverance from Spiritual Oppression

Jesus vs. Legion: Authority over Darkness

A man inhabited by a legion of demons experiences self-harm and isolation until Jesus commands them into pigs (Mk 5:1-

13). Deliverance restores him to sanity and community, evidencing that healing includes liberation from evil powers. Gratitude for Christ's supremacy emboldens deliverance ministry that honors dignity, avoids sensationalism, and points to the cross as legal victory (Col 2:15).

Discerning Roots: Trauma, Habit, or Demonic Affliction?

Not every struggle is demonic; Scripture distinguishes flesh, world, and devil (Eph 2:1-3). Wise ministers seek root causes—medical factors, psychological wounds, sinful habits—before defaulting to exorcism. Gratitude for the Holy Spirit's discernment prevents harmful misdiagnosis. Comprehensive healing plans may integrate repentance, counseling, medication, and deliverance, each step bathed in prayerful thanksgiving.

Maintaining Freedom: Filling the House with the Spirit

Jesus warns that expelled spirits may return to an empty house (Mt 12:43-45). Post-deliverance discipleship—Scripture intake, worship, community—fills vacancy with Holy Spirit occupancy. Gratitude functions as guard dog; thankful hearts less hospitable to temptation. Testimonies of sustained freedom encourage others, reinforcing culture where deliverance is gateway to sanctified living, not an isolated spectacle.

8.9 Community & Social Dimensions of Healing

Reintegration of Former Outcasts into Society

Levitical law required cleansed lepers to present themselves to priests (Lev 14). Jesus follows protocol, ensuring social reintegration (Lk 17:14). Modern parallels include churches helping healed addicts find employment, housing, and supportive relationships. Gratitude fuels advocacy, for those thankful for personal healing fight stigma hindering others from full inclusion.

Justice as Preventive Medicine: Addressing Structural Harm

Prophets link sickness to injustice—oppressed laborers, polluted land, exploitative landlords (Jer 22:13-17). Public health today recognizes social determinants—poverty, racism—as disease drivers. Kingdom healing includes reforming unjust structures: fair wages, clean water, accessible healthcare. Gratitude for personal wellbeing compels believers to pursue societal conditions where all may thrive, fulfilling Isaiah's vision of repairers of broken walls (Isa 58:12).

Church as Healing Family: Support Groups & Hospitality

Early Christians shared meals and possessions, erasing loneliness and material lack (Acts 2:46-47). Contemporary churches host grief-share, recovery programs, foster-care networks—spaces where relational warmth accelerates healing trajectories. Gratitude fosters hospitality: healed people open homes, wallets, and schedules to others. Healing thus becomes contagious, spreading through the ecosystem of loving community.

8.10 Suffering, Mystery, and Unanswered Prayer

Paul's Thorn: Grace in Ongoing Weakness

Paul pleads thrice for thorn removal yet hears "My grace is sufficient" (2 Cor 12:7-10). Chronic issues can coexist with divine favor, reframing weakness as platform for power. Gratitude here is paradoxical—thanking God amid pain for sustaining grace. Acceptance without resignation emerges, trusting eventual resurrection while serving fruitfully now.

Lament Psalms: Validating Pain in Faith

Nearly a third of Psalms voice lament, proving that complaint can be faithful when addressed to God. Jesus quotes Psalm 22 on the cross, sanctifying raw anguish (Mt 27:46). Gratitude and lament are companions, not opposites; honest sorrow ultimately deepens appreciation for redemption. Churches that allow lament services, blues-style worship, and prayer for the sick, even when healing tarries, embody holistic faith.

Hope Deferred yet Alive: Holding Tension, Holding Christ

Hebrews 11 lists heroes who "died not receiving the promise" yet were commended for faith (Heb 11:13). Healing delays test endurance but can yield refined trust. Gratitude during waiting seasons focuses on God's character, not outcomes, whispering "Even if not" (Dan 3:18). Such resilience shines to skeptics, revealing treasure in jars of clay surpassing temporary wellness (2 Cor 4:7-18).

8.11 Practices that Cultivate a Healing Culture

Confession & Repentance: Clearing Blockages

James links healing to confession of sins (Jas 5:16). Hidden guilt can manifest psychosomatically; repentance releases spiritual congestion. Gratitude for forgiveness lubricates confession, transforming shame into freedom. Churches normalizing confession—liturgy, accountability groups—prepare soil where healing seeds sprout readily.

Corporate Worship & Atmosphere of Faith

Israel's psalms recount healings to bolster communal faith (Ps 107). Contemporary worship nights that exalt Jesus as healer create expectancy atmospheres. Gratitude-saturated songs shift focus from illness magnitude to God's mercy expanse, priming hearts for miracles during or after worship.

Fasting, Communion, and Scripture Declarations

Fasting humbles soul, aligning appetites with heavenly provision (Isa 58:8). Communion, as explored earlier, channels Calvary's virtue. Speaking healing promises aloud—"He sent His word and healed them" (Ps 107:20)—reprograms neural pathways toward faith. Gratitude integrates these disciplines, preventing mechanistic ritual by maintaining relational awe.

8.12 Gratitude & Testimony

Ten Lepers—Only One Returned

Luke 17 records ten cleansed, one thankful Samaritan. Gratitude proved differentiator between mere benefit and deeper wholeness—Jesus declares him "well" (sozo). The story warns against blessing amnesia. Churches that cultivate testimony nights, social media praise posts, and written journals imitate the Samaritan, amplifying glory to God.

Power of Story: Building Faith in the Hearers

Revelation 12:11 says believers overcome by "word of testimony." Hearing another's cancer remission or depression lift sparks hope for replication. Gratitude motivates storytellers; silence often stems from forgetting that miracles belong to body of Christ, not private archives. Recording testimonies also documents God's faithfulness for future generations, fueling intergenerational faith.

Thanksgiving as Seal of the Miracle

In John 6, leftover baskets gathered after the giving of thanks underscore thanksgiving's sealing function. Gratitude shifts focus from need to supply, guarding against relapse into fear. Post-healing, continual thanks maintains posture of receiving, acknowledging that sustained health remains divine gift, not autonomous ownership.

8.13 Eschatological Wholeness—The Ultimate Cure

No More Pain: New Heavens and New Earth

Revelation 21:4 promises eradication of death, mourning, crying, pain—ultimate healing beyond temporal miracles. Gratitude for future wholeness sustains present ministry, assuring caregivers their labor echoes eternity's reality. Every hospice prayer whispers "soon."

Resurrection Bodies: Incorruptible, Immortal, Glorious

Paul describes transformation from perishable to imperishable (1 Cor 15:42-44). Disabilities, scars, and chronic illnesses will vanish at the trumpet. Gratitude kindles hope in those with lifelong conditions, anchoring identity in coming glory rather than current limitations.

Perpetual Tree of Life: Leaves for the Healing of Nations

Revelation 22 pictures a river-watered tree bearing monthly fruit; its leaves heal nations, signaling communal and ecological restoration. Global conflicts, systemic racism, and environmental sickness will be resolved. Gratitude fuels advocacy now, stewarding creation and pursuing reconciliation as previews of that leafy promise.

Conclusion

Healing in the biblical sense is far more than the mending of muscles or the calming of anxious thoughts; it is the comprehensive restoration of creation to the harmony God intended from the beginning. Jesus, bearing the titles of Great Physician and Wounded Healer, has already inaugurated that restoration through His ministry, His cross, and His resurrection power active in the Church. Every testimony—from a fever broken to a decade-long depression lifted—serves as a living prophecy of the day when wheelchairs will be obsolete and pharmacies unnecessary. Gratitude keeps our eyes fixed on that horizon while energizing faith to pray, serve, and advocate here and now. May the Church never cease to echo the grateful Samaritan, announcing with every breath and every beat of newfound wholeness: "Thank You, Jesus, for healing body, mind, and spirit—both in this age and in the glorious age to come."

Chapter 9. Thank You, Jesus, for Freedom—Chains Broken

Slavery's bonds can take many forms—compulsive habits, legalistic demands, fear's prison, or the weight of shame—and each one stifles the vibrant life God intends. Yet at the heart of the gospel stands a liberation so profound that "where the Spirit of the Lord is, there is freedom" (2 Corinthians 3:17). In Christ, chains are broken: the law's condemnation gives way to grace, addiction's grip loosens, and fear's shackles fall off as perfect love casts out all terror (1 John 4:18). To thank Jesus for freedom is to celebrate His power to demolish every stronghold and to usher us into the wide-open pathways of joyful obedience. As we explore freedom from sin, legalism, fear, and even cosmic decay, may our hearts rejoice in the truth that Jesus came that we might have life—and have it abundantly (John 10:10).

9.1 Liberation From Sin's Power

Slaves No More: Union with Christ in Death and Resurrection

Union with Christ is the gospel's jailbreak key: when the Son walked out of the tomb, everyone joined to Him by faith walked out as well (Romans 6:4–5). Paul underscores this reality with stark language—our "old self was crucified with him" so that we should "no longer be slaves to sin" (Romans 6:6). Slavery here is not a mere metaphor; it is a judicial status change. A slave has no legal right to refuse a master's demand, but a freed person does, and the resurrection enacts that legal manumission. Daily temptations still whisper like former overseers, yet their authority is annulled—believers may heed, but they never have to. Gratitude keeps this difference vivid; instead of lamenting that temptation still exists, we praise God that refusal is now possible. Baptism dramatizes the union: burial beneath the water, emergence into new life, public evidence that the shackles slipped off (Colossians 2:12). Every time we recall that watery grave, we rehearse emancipation papers signed in Christ's blood and sealed by the Spirit.

Crucified Flesh: Old Self Rendered Powerless

Galatians 5:24 declares that "those who belong to Christ Jesus have crucified the flesh with its passions and desires." The tense is decisive—"have crucified"—indicating an accomplished fact, even as daily skirmishes remain. The "flesh" is that inward bent toward self-rule, and crucifixion means it lost executive power at Calvary. Much like a dethroned tyrant who still broadcasts propaganda, the flesh can shout but cannot lawfully command. Gratitude converts this theological truth into experiential liberty: instead of groaning, "I'll never change," we thank God that transformation has already begun and will be perfected (Philippians 1:6). Christian disciplines—prayer, fasting, confession—are not torture devices but tools that expedite the flesh's fading influence. Each victory, however small, is evidence that the nails held, that the cross worked, that the old regime is gasping its last.

Law of the Spirit of Life vs. Law of Sin and Death

Romans 8 opens with a courtroom drama: the "law of the Spirit of life" sets believers free from the "law of sin and death" (Romans 8:2). The term "law" functions here like "operating principle." Sin-and-death works relentlessly, dragging humanity toward disintegration; the Spirit-of-life now supersedes that gravitational pull like a stronger magnetic field. Airplanes overcome gravity not by canceling it but by employing a higher law of lift; likewise the Spirit raises us above sin's drag without denying that fallen impulses still tug. Gratitude focuses attention on the superior law, empowering us to set our minds "on the things of the Spirit" (Romans 8:5) instead of obsessing over the old gravity. When believers thank Jesus for the Spirit's indwelling power, they consciously shift cockpit controls from autopilot sin to Spirit-directed flight. Even turbulence—moments of failure—does not crash the plane; the new law keeps lifting as we repent and re-engage faith.

9.2 Deliverance From Condemnation

"No Condemnation" Verdict (Romans 8:1)

The gospel's first freedom often felt—and tragically often forgotten—is the lifting of condemnation: "There is therefore now no condemnation for those who are in Christ Jesus" (Romans 8:1). The Greek term *katakrima* denotes a judicial sentence; God's gavel has landed, and the verdict over every believer reads "not guilty." Condemnation differs from conviction: the Spirit still convicts specific sins to invite change, but He never condemns the person He indwells. Gratitude is the essential protest against lingering shame; it thanks God aloud that the courtroom is closed, the file sealed, the accuser overruled (Revelation 12:10–11). Condemnation's voice often masquerades as humility—"I'm just a failure"—but thanksgiving unmasks it: true humility exalts Christ's sufficiency, not our insufficiency. Each worship service becomes a parole-board reminder that parole is obsolete when the sentence itself has been vacated.

Justified by Faith: Legal Chains Shattered

Paul's courtroom imagery extends to justification: God declares the ungodly righteous by faith apart from works (Romans 3:28; 4:5). This is not a future possibility pending moral improvement but a present decree executed because Jesus absorbed the law's full penalty. Picture shackles of indebtedness snapping the moment the Judge pronounces acquittal; the prisoner doesn't ask the guards if he may leave—he walks out. Gratitude fuels bold departure from the cell of self-condemnation. It also nurtures compassion: those who know how undeserved their own verdict was tend to lobby for mercy on behalf of other offenders. Evangelism thus becomes one beggar telling another where the Judge is handing out pardons at His own expense.

Living From Acceptance, Not For It

Religion rooted in self-effort strives **for** divine approval; gospel freedom operates **from** approval already secured. Jesus hears the Father's "You are my beloved Son" before He performs any miracle or endures any cross (Matthew 3:17), modeling identity prior to activity. Gratitude rehearses that baptismal pronouncement over every believer: "accepted in the Beloved" (Ephesians 1:6 KJV). Living from acceptance disempowers perfectionism, workaholism, and people-pleasing—chains as binding as overt sin. It also energizes holy living: obedience becomes love's response, not fear's requirement (John 14:15). Whenever we slip back into merit-mindset, thanksgiving resets the heart, reminding us that Christ's merits already fill the account. Freedom thus matures into joyful service—not to earn adoption papers, but to explore the Father's house we already occupy.

9.3 Freedom From Legalism and Dead Religion

Burdens Too Heavy to Bear: Jesus vs. Pharisaic Yokes

Legalism promises control but delivers exhaustion. Jesus observes that religious leaders "tie up heavy, cumbersome loads and put them on other people's shoulders, but they themselves are not willing to lift a finger to move them" (Matthew 23:4). Centuries before, the Pharisees had added hundreds of oral traditions to the written Law, transforming worship into a burdensome checklist that oppressed common people. In contrast, Jesus characterizes His own yoke as "easy" and His burden as "light" (Matthew 11:28–30). This does not deny the call to obedience, but reframes it: instead of groaning under endless do's and don'ts, disciples learn to walk in freedom under God's gracious guidance. Gratitude blossoms when believers exchange the slavery of legal performance for the joy of Christ-enabled living. Where legalism says "do more to earn more," gospel freedom says "rest in what Christ has done, then do out of delight." Every time we lay down a list of demands and pick up Jesus' invitation to rest, we rebuke the phantom tyranny of dead religion and affirm the liberating power of divine grace.

Grace That Teaches, Not Chains That Choke

Paul insists that the same grace that saves us also "teaches us to say 'No' to ungodliness and worldly passions, and to live self-controlled, upright and godly lives" (Titus 2:12). True grace never abandons moral urgency; it provides the internal resources to live the abundant life Jesus promises. Unlike legalistic calls to "shape up or ship out," grace whispers, "I will empower you from within." It addresses root motives rather than merely policing behavior. When we thank Jesus for this grace-teaching, we celebrate a pedagogy that transforms rather than coerces, that shapes character through relationship rather than rules through fear. Grace-trained hearts bear fruit that outshines conformity produced by guilt. This freedom reframes discipline as discipleship—an invited journey into Christlikeness rather than a compulsory march under penalty of shame.

Sabbath Rest in Christ: Ceasing From Self-Effort

God's original pattern—six days of work followed by a day of rest (Exodus 20:8–11)—prefigures gospel rest in Christ. Religious legalism often turns Sabbath into yet another checklist: attend services, avoid work, follow porcupine-thorn regulations. Yet Jesus declares, "The Sabbath was made for man, not man for the Sabbath" (Mark 2:27), releasing His followers from bondage to self-inflicted performance rituals. The true Sabbath is found in ceasing from self-reliant striving and trusting the Father to provide. Hebrews exhorts believers to "make every effort to enter that rest" (Hebrews 4:11), portraying rest as an active trust rather than passive inertia. Gratitude for Christ's finished work frees us to experience weekly—and daily—rest that replenishes soul, mind, and body. In these rhythms, we learn that our worth precedes our work and that true productivity flows from communion with the Provider, not frantic lists.

9.4 Freedom From Fear and Shame

Perfect Love Casting Out Fear

John writes, "There is no fear in love. But perfect love drives out fear, because fear has to do with punishment. The one who fears is not made perfect in love" (1 John 4:18). Fear—of judgment, failure, or future uncertainty—paralyzes worship and mission alike. Yet as we grow in the knowledge of God's unconditional love revealed in Christ, those fears lose their grip. Gratitude for Jesus' sacrificial love becomes the antidote: the more we rehearse stories of grace extended to us, the less we tremble before condemnation. This freedom isn't horizontal bravado but vertical trust—resting in the Father's embrace so deeply that earthly anxieties slide away. Christian communities that practice speaking affirmations of God's love, sharing testimonies of mercy, and surrounding one another in supportive prayer cultivate environments where fear finds no home.

Covered, Not Hidden: The Gift of Righteous Robes

Isaiah foresaw the day when God would clothe His people in garments of salvation and arrays of righteousness (Isaiah 61:10). In Revelation, believers stand before the throne "robed in white," symbolizing Christ's righteousness covering every stain of sin (Revelation 3:5). Shame loses its dominion when we internalize that our identity is not based on moral pedigree but on the wedding robe custom-made by the Bridegroom's sacrifice. Gratitude for this covering empowers boldness—no longer hiding sins behind self-justification, but living transparently in the Father's protective love. When churches routinely affirm baptisms and celebrate communion, they visually and verbally reinforce that every participant stands fully covered. Freed from shame's isolation, believers can approach God and one another in vulnerability, knowing that the same grace that covers sin also heals its wounds.

Bold Access to the Throne of Grace

Through Jesus' torn veil, "we have confidence to enter the Most Holy Place by the blood of Jesus" (Hebrews 10:19–20). Formerly, only the high priest could cross the threshold once a year; now every believer may "approach in full assurance of faith" (Hebrews 10:22). Fear-driven religiosity once made God seem distant and strict, but the gospel proclaims a Father welcoming prodigals home with open arms (Luke 15:20). Gratitude for this access turns prayer from anxious pleading into confident conversation. Whether crying out in midnight anguish or whispering thanks at dawn, we perch at the throne knowing mercy awaits. Communities practicing open, expectant prayer times model this freedom—no longer relegating requests to formal petitions but inviting continuous dialogue with the living God.

9.5 Breaking Addictions and Strongholds

Weapons Mighty Through God: Demolishing Arguments

The apostle Paul reminds us that our battle is not primarily against flesh and blood but against "spiritual forces of evil in the heavenly realms" (Ephesians 6:12). Yet he immediately follows this diagnosis with the antidote: the "weapons of our warfare" which are "divinely powerful for the destruction of fortresses" (2 Corinthians 10:4). These are not bullets, but truth, righteousness, the gospel of peace, faith, salvation, the Word of God, and prayer—all wielded under the Spirit's empowerment (Eph 6:14–18). When strongholds of addiction, shame, and compulsive sin build concrete walls around a soul, these weapons crack open enemy territory. Gratitude fuels the wielding: we thank Jesus that the same power that raised Him from the dead is available to us to demolish every lie—"I cannot change," "I'm defined by this habit," "God is done with me." Each time we memorize a truth verse, pray urgently, or declare the gospel over our thoughts, we proclaim, "Thanks be to God, who gives us the victory through our Lord Jesus Christ" (1 Cor 15:57).

Renewed Minds, Re-patterned Habits

Paul links the demolition of strongholds to the renewal of the mind: "We take every thought captive to obey Christ" (2 Cor 10:5) and "be transformed by the renewing of your mind" (Rom 12:2). Cognitive behavioral approaches find parallels here—identifying lies, replacing them with truth, and then practicing new behaviors. But the Spirit equips this process, writing God's statutes on our hearts and giving us both the desire and the power to follow them (Ezek 36:26–27). Gratitude plays a catalytic role: when we thank Jesus for each small victory over a compulsive behavior—skipped drink, a night of sober rest, resisted temptation—we rewire our neural pathways around grace rather than guilt. Over time, those patterns form new highways of obedience, displacing the old ruts of addiction. Celebrating each marker of progress with thanksgiving gatherings—small groups, accountability meetings—

reinforces hearty confidence that Jesus is faithful to complete the good work He has begun (Phil 1:6).

Community Accountability and Spirit Empowerment

Scripture never envisions the Christian life as a solo venture. James exhorts believers to "confess your sins to one another and pray for one another, that you may be healed" (Jas 5:16), highlighting mutual support in breaking strongholds. Accountability partners, recovery groups, and soul friends all serve as contexts where grace and truth converge to expose darkness and ignite light. The Spirit uses voices of honest peers to speak convicting love and to remind us of our freedom in Christ. Gratitude here means thanking Jesus not only for personal deliverance but for the people He brings alongside us—those who refuse to rejoice when we stumble and who celebrate with us when chains fall off. Corporate prayers, testimonies shared at gatherings, and the laying on of hands (1 Tim 5:22) become catalysts for sustained liberty. In community, every "Thank You, Jesus" resonates as both personal praise and corporate anthem, echoing through the body until no stronghold stands.

9.6 Spirit of Adoption—Free to Be Children

Crying "Abba": From Orphans to Heirs

Paul marvels that God's Spirit enables us to cry "Abba! Father!" (Rom 8:15), an Aramaic term of affectionate intimacy. Under the old covenant, access to the Father's heart felt distant—like orphans peering through a window. But the Spirit dissolves that barrier: every believer becomes an heir of God and co-heir with Christ (Rom 8:17). Gratitude wells up as we practice Abba-prayer: those two syllables carry a lifetime of acceptance, security, and belonging. This relational address replaces orphan fear—of rejection, inadequacy, or abandonment—with childlike confidence that the Father delights in His sons and daughters. In moments of spiritual warfare or emotional fatigue, whispering "Abba" summons the warmth of home and steadies the soul.

Inheritance Secured, Not Earned

In many cultures, an inheritance requires meeting conditions or outliving rivals. But in the kingdom, our inheritance is "kept in heaven" for us, guarded by Christ Himself (1 Pet 1:4–5). It is imperishable, undefiled, beyond the reach of decay or theft. Gratitude for this unassailable promise anchors us in gratitude rather than performance. We live in the interim between first installment—our adoption by the Spirit—and the full release of assets at Christ's return (Eph 1:13–14). This perspective liberates us from ambition-driven anxiety, reminding that worth is not tied to bank balances, resumes, or social media metrics but to Father's unchanging decree: "You are mine."

Playing, Not Performing: Joyful Sonship

A healthy family invites both work and play—chores and celebrations. Spirit-filled freedom enables believers to approach God in worshipful play: dancing, singing, drawing, creating without the tyrant of self-imposed performance looming overhead. Jesus invites children to run into His arms (Mk 10:14), not wait in genteel posture to prove their eligibility. Gratitude encourages spontaneous expressions—clapping in Sunday services, celebrating small mercies, sharing laughter among prayer groups. When church cultures honor both solemn reverence and exuberant delight, they mirror the joyful Sonship access granted by the Spirit. This playfulness is not frivolous; it is prophetic, declaring that the kingdom of heaven is both now and not yet, a foretaste of eternal festivity.

9.7 Walking in Newfound Liberty

Standing Firm: Guarding Freedom From a Yoke of Slavery

Paul warns the Galatian believers not to submit again to a "yoke of slavery" after tasting freedom in Christ (Galatians 5:1). That yoke represents any belief system—legalism, performance-based approval, fear—that re-enslaves us under obligations we no longer owe. Standing firm, therefore, is both defensive and deliberate: we refuse to slip back into chains of guilt-driven behavior, and we actively choose the gospel's liberating message each morning. Gratitude empowers this resolve, because remembering the day we first felt sin's heavy burden lift gives us courage to resist old compulsions. We enlist the Spirit's help through prayer, Scripture meditation, and community encouragement, reminding ourselves that "Christ has set us free" and we are "free indeed" (John 8:36). When temptations whisper that we're not good enough unless we perform, thankful hearts can reply, "My worth was purchased by Jesus' perfect work, not my inadequate attempts." Maintaining freedom requires a vigilant heart—regularly renewing our minds with gospel truth (Romans 12:2) and confessing the lie when condemnation knocks. Each act of defiance against slavery becomes a song of praise, echoing the ancient shouts of liberated captives: "Thanks be to God, who gives us the victory!" (1 Corinthians 15:57).

Consciences Guided by Love, Not Rules Alone

Under the old covenant, conscience was often shaped by external codes—taboos and tablets of stone—leaving hearts ill-equipped to handle gray areas. The new covenant writes God's law on our hearts, enabling conscience to be guided by love rather than legal checklist (Jeremiah 31:33; 2 Corinthians 3:3). Love discerns how best to glorify God and serve neighbor, even when no rule explicitly addresses the situation. Gratitude for this grace-driven morality frees us from paralysis in ethical dilemmas: instead of asking, "What's permitted?" we inquire, "What best expresses Christ's love here?" A love-shaped conscience says no to exploitation and yes to generosity, no to gossip and yes to encouragement, even when the newspaper permits the former and our comfort tempts us away from the latter. The Spirit's renewing ministry gradually refines our inner compass, producing instinctive decisions that align with Jesus' heart. Every time we choose kindness over indifference, we silently thank the One who wrote love's law on our hearts.

Serving One Another Through Love: Liberty's Goal

Christ freed us not only from sin but for service: "For you were called to freedom, brothers and sisters; only do not use your freedom as an opportunity for the flesh, but through love serve one another" (Galatians 5:13). True liberty blossoms when we channel our rights into sacrificial love—washing feet, bearing burdens, sharing resources. Gratitude fuels generosity: remembering how much we've been forgiven compels us to forgive and uplift others without demanding our own way. Freedom that hoards its rights becomes a gilded cage; freedom that pours itself out becomes an open door to joy. In practical terms, this might look like choosing to babysit a stressed neighbor's children, giving up a parking spot for someone in need, or offering an encouraging word when silence would satisfy. Each act of love is a footnote to Christ's own service: the King who laid down His life for His friends (John 15:13). When church members serve one another in love, they embody freedom's highest calling—imaging the gospel in flesh and blood, and ensuring that gratitude circulates through both giving and receiving.

9.8 Societal Dimensions of Freedom

Jubilee Ethic: Economic and Social Reset

In Leviticus 25, God commands a jubilee every fiftieth year: debts are forgiven, land returns to original families, and slaves go free. This radical social reset combats the long-term inequalities that concentration of wealth and inherited poverty produce. Though the modern economy cannot simply flip a switch every half-century, the jubilary principle still applies: periodic forgiveness of debts, redistribution of resources, and restoration of rights reflect God's heart for equity (Deuteronomy 15:1-2). Gratitude for personal financial mercy informs our social conscience: those who have been bailed out—by grace, by generosity, or by good fortune—champion policies and practices that release others from bondage. Whether through debt-forgiveness ministries, community land trusts, or fair trade initiatives, the Church can model jubilee values in a broken economic landscape. Each act of economic restoration—canceling a medical bill, providing a rent holiday, offering microloans—acts as an echo of heaven's wealth distribution, prompting collective thanksgiving that God's economy is not zero-sum but perpetual abundance.

Good News to the Poor, Release to Captives

Jesus inaugurates His public ministry by reading Isaiah's prophecy: "He has sent me to proclaim good news to the poor, to proclaim liberty to the captives…" (Luke 4:18). "Poor" here includes the materially impoverished and those spiritually bankrupt; "captives" covers the oppressed, addicted, and marginalized. The gospel's socio-economic thrust demands that freedom not remain an abstraction but break chains—physical and ideological. Gratitude for personal deliverance from poverty of spirit drives believers to feed the hungry, advocate for the marginalized, and dismantle systems of oppression. Through partnerships with shelters, hospitals, and legal aid societies, the Church extends that very freedom Jesus proclaimed on the synagogue floor. Each story of a life released—from trafficking, addiction, or systemic injustice—becomes a stanza in the cosmic song of emancipation, inspiring communities to shout, "Thanks be to God who has delivered us from darkness into His marvelous light!"

Church as Embassy of Justice and Mercy

While prisons, courts, and governments bear responsibility for justice, the Church serves as a prophetic embassy—a foretaste of God's kingdom rule. Biblical justice intertwines mercy, requiring both fair verdicts and tender kindness (Micah 6:8). Gratitude for God's mercy fosters courageous advocacy: pushing for humane policies, de-escalating community conflicts, and nurturing restorative practices that heal rather than merely punish. Mercy ministries—compassionate prisons ministry, refugee resettlement teams, neighborhood reconciliation projects—allow the Church to incarnate divine freedom. In every courtroom and council meeting where believers testify with integrity, they model a higher jurisprudence that says, "We thank You, Lord, for breaking our chains, and we plead for the broken to be set free." The Church's public witness becomes a living petition for the day when justice and peace will kiss, when the cry, "For the Lord will judge His people!" (Psalm 149:9), is answered not with terror but with liberating restoration.

9.9 Spiritual Warfare and Ongoing Victory

Armor of God: Maintaining the Ground Won

Paul's metaphor of the full armor of God (Ephesians 6:10–18) underscores that freedom from sin's power brings new enemies—spiritual forces that still seek to reclaim territory. Each piece of armor corresponds to gospel realities: the belt of truth secures our identity in Christ; the breastplate of righteousness protects our renewed hearts; the gospel of peace readies our feet to proclaim freedom to others. The shield of faith extinguishes flaming darts of fear or accusation; the helmet of salvation guards our minds against lies about God's acceptance; the sword of the Spirit—God's Word—cuts through deception; and prayer in the Spirit ties it all together. Gratitude sharpens our vigilance: when we remember the cost of our redemption, we more readily equip each morning, consciously buckling on each element as a thanksgiving ritual. Neglecting armor invites compromise; embracing it brings assurance that every skirmish contributes to ultimate victory. As we stand firm, we declare by faith that no demonic power can overturn the nailed-down verdict of Calvary.

Authority to Trample Serpents and Scorpions

Jesus promised believers authority to "trample on serpents and scorpions and over all the power of the enemy," with nothing harmful touch them (Luke 10:19). This vivid language assures that the chains of demonic oppression have lost their binding power. Yet authority requires stewardship: it is meant for protecting the vulnerable and advancing the kingdom, not for personal aggrandizement or spectacle. Gratitude for Christ's superiority to every principality enables us to exercise this authority humbly—praying for breakthrough in places of deep oppression, standing with those tormented by powers beyond human comprehension. When we rebuke fear, despair, or spiritual bondage in Jesus' name, we are invoking the high priestly intercession of the One who disarmed the powers at His resurrection (Colossians 2:15). Each deliverance, whether dramatic or quiet, echoes our original emancipation, compelling hearts to thank Jesus for breaking every chain, natural and supernatural.

Overcoming by the Blood and the Word of Testimony

Revelation's martyrs conquer "by the blood of the Lamb and by the word of their testimony" (Rev 12:11). Their witness combines the objective efficacy of Christ's sacrifice with the subjective power of personal story. The blood speaks first—Christ's atonement has legally undone every claim of the evil one—and our testimony affirms that truth in experiential reality. Gratitude underpins both dimensions: we thank Jesus for His once-for-all sacrifice and for carrying us through trials so that we now have narratives of His faithfulness. In revival meetings, healing services, or quiet living rooms, believers sharing their testimonies reinforce the church's collective armor, reminding one another that victory is already won. This two-fold strategy—grounded in ancient blood, advanced by modern stories—ensures that spiritual warfare ends in praise rather than defeat.

9.10 Worship as an Act of Freedom

Paul and Silas in Chains: Praise That Opens Doors

Imprisoned in Philippi for preaching Christ, Paul and Silas prayed and sang hymns at midnight—and the earth shook, prison doors flew open, chains fell off (Acts 16:25–26). Their spontaneous worship transcended circumstances, demonstrating that freedom is not merely a future promise but a present reality accessible through praise. Gratitude fuels such worship: when last-season's mercies stir our hearts, we break into song even in metaphorical dungeons—be they labs, boardrooms, hospital wards, or personal crises. That praise testifies that no jailer or judicial order can silence the gospel song of redeemed souls. When communities join in thanksgiving, corporate faith surges, unlocking doors of ministry and bending resistant hearts toward mercy.

Dancing Like David: Dignity Laid Down in Delight

King David's ecstatic dance before the Ark (2 Samuel 6:14–16) exemplifies worship unshackled by decorum. He cast off royal robes, risking reproach to express unguarded joy in the Lord. Such vulnerability models freedom from concern about appearances—a recognition that divine acceptance is not contingent on social grace but rooted in covenant love. Gratitude releases inhibition; when we thank Jesus wholeheartedly, our bodies, voices, and spirits join in unrestrained adoration. Whether clapping hands, lifting banners, or simply smiling through tears, liberated worship renews our sense of identity as treasured children, unafraid to celebrate before our King.

Song, Lament, and Prophetic Declarations

True freedom in worship embraces the full spectrum of expression: triumphant songs of deliverance, honest laments in seasons of confusion, and prophetic declarations of God's coming reign. The psalmists model this range, pivoting from "Shout for joy in the Lord" (Ps 100:1) to "How long, O Lord?" (Ps 13:1) to "The Lord will reign forever" (Ps 10:16). Gratitude animates even our laments, for we lament under the shelter of God's faithfulness, confident that our tears are not wasted. Prophetic worship—declaring present and future freedom—sharpens hope and activates faith in congregations. In liberated worship, every utterance rings with "Thanks be to God, who gives us the victory through our Lord Jesus Christ" (1 Cor 15:57).

9.11 Mission of Liberty—Proclaiming Freedom

Great Commission Through a Freedom Lens

The Great Commission—"make disciples of all nations" (Mt 28:19)—becomes especially compelling when filtered through the lens of freedom. Evangelism is not salesmanship but emancipation, inviting captives of sin, fear, and injustice into the open air of grace. Gratitude for our own deliverance compels urgency: those who know how bitter was the slavery of sin are most passionate to spread the word of freedom. Mission strategies therefore integrate conversion, discipleship, and social engagement, reflecting holistic liberation. As we teach obedience, we emphasize freedom: freedom to love, to serve, to worship without fear.

Evangelism as Emancipation

Philip's encounter with the Ethiopian eunuch—Spirit-directed and Word-fed—illustrates evangelism as emancipation (Acts 8:26–39). The eunuch, bound by social and spiritual barriers, found release in the gospel and baptism. Gratitude-driven evangelism identifies with those on society's margins—immigrants, addicts, ex-offenders—and offers them the gospel's liberating power. Each conversion, each public reading of Scripture, each baptistery in a river, proclaims that Jesus "came to set the captive free" (Luke 4:18).

Making Disciples Who Walk Unfettered

True discipleship nurtures freedom, not new forms of bondage. Jesus said, "If the Son makes you free, you will be free indeed" (Jn 8:36). Discipleship pathways focus on identity formation—helping believers internalize their status as forgiven, adopted children—rather than on rigid programs of do's and don'ts. Gratitude teaches the heart to migrate from rule-obsession to relationship-orientation. Small groups that begin with testimonies of freedom, prayer for breakthroughs, and study of liberation texts create cultures where new believers learn to walk in liberty from day one.

9.12 Eschatological Freedom—Glorious Liberty of the Children of God

Creation's Future Release From Corruption

Romans 8 foretells that "the creation itself will be liberated from its bondage to decay and brought into the freedom and glory of the children of God" (Rom 8:21). This cosmic emancipation parallels our personal freedom—it extends Jesus' chains-breaking work to mountains, seas, and skies groaning for renewal. Gratitude for this eschatological hope sustains us through ecological crises, reminding us that planet-wide healing is ordained. Each tree planted, each reef restored, each conservation effort participates in God's original healing agenda.

Resurrection Bodies: Final Emancipation

Believers anticipate bodies no longer subject to disease, disability, or death: "It does not yet appear what we shall be, but we know that when He appears we shall be like Him" (1 Jn 3:2). This is the ultimate personal freedom—flesh made imperishable, minds unclouded, eyes unweary. Gratitude for this future reality transforms our pain-filled present with glimmers of glory. Every advance in medicine or rehab becomes a foreshadowing of that final cure.

Eternal Celebration: No More Night, No More Chains

Revelation's culmination depicts a New Jerusalem where "the servants of God will worship Him; they will see His face, and His name will be on their foreheads" (Rev 22:3–4). There is no temple because God and the Lamb are its temple—provision and presence complete (Rev 21:22). No sun or moon is needed, for Christ's glory provides endless light. And "there shall be no more curse" (Rev 22:3) —the last chain removed at last. Gratitude for this consummation ripples backward into every present celebration, infusing daily freedoms with anticipation of eternal liberty.

Conclusion

Freedom in Christ is far more than the alleviation of guilt; it is the comprehensive undoing of every chain sin, fear, legalism, shame, addiction, and even physical decay may forge. Jesus, through His life, death, and resurrection, has unlatched the gates of every prison—from the most intimate stronghold of the human heart to the cosmic shackles binding creation itself. As the Church embraces this freedom, worship transforms into liberation festivals, discipleship into emancipation journeys, and mission into acts of deliverance echoing across the globe. Gratitude punctuates each step forward: each sinner set free, each community restored, each prophecy of new creation edged closer, we cry anew, "Thank You, Jesus, for freedom—chains broken!" May our lives continually testify to the glorious liberty secured by the Lamb, until every captive stands repaid in the splendor of His unending reign.

Chapter 10. Thank You, Jesus, for Peace in Storms—Comfort and Assurance

In life's most turbulent moments—when grief strips us of security, illness clouds our minds, or storms of uncertainty rage—the human heart cries out for a steadfast anchor. The Christian narrative answers that cry in the person of Jesus Christ, who not only calms literal seas with a word but also speaks peace into our inner chaos. From the first breath that hovered over primordial waters (Gen 1:2) to the final vision of a river of life flowing in the new creation (Rev 22:1–2), Scripture frames divine peace as both the original intention for creation and the ultimate promise for redeemed humanity. To thank Jesus for peace in storms is to celebrate His sovereignty over external turmoil and His comforting presence amid internal battles. In the following sections, we explore the rich biblical portrait of divine shalom, prophetic promises that herald Christ's calming role, the Gospels' dramatic storm-silencing episodes, and the Spirit's ministry of inner quiet. May each reflection deepen your confidence that the Prince of

Peace dwells with you—and in you—no matter how fierce the gale.

10.1 Portrait of Divine Peace

Eternal Calm in the Trinity

Long before creation's first dawn, peace was intrinsic to the divine life shared between Father, Son, and Holy Spirit. Jesus prays that believers might share in "the fellowship of the Father and of his Son, Jesus Christ" (1 John 1:3), implying that communion with God invites participation in eternal harmony. In the Trinity, there is no discord; each Person delights in perfect unity of will and glory. When we marvel at the Trinity, we see that peace is not merely the absence of conflict but a positive fullness of relational joy. Gratitude for this eternal calm shapes our worship: we bow not to a solitary monarch but to a loving community whose unity overflows into creation. The peace that weds justice and mercy at God's heart becomes the pattern for human relationships, calling us to mirror divine synergy. As we contemplate the Trinity's internal peace, our souls begin to reflect that same serenity, liberated from the tyranny of isolation and fear.

Shalom in Creation's Original Order

Genesis 1 portrays a universe in which land, sea, sky, vegetation, animals, and humans each flourish in a choreographed dance of shalom. The Hebrew word shalom encompasses wholeness, well-being, and mutual flourishing—a state far deeper than mere absence of war. In Eden, human work required neither anxiety nor toil (Gen 2:15); relationships required neither jealousy nor mistrust; the land required neither exploitation nor lament. Creation's "very good" verdict (Gen 1:31) celebrates cosmic peace that sustains both physical and relational life. Gratitude for this original order invites environmental stewardship, as caring for ecosystems echoes God's own regard for harmonious balance. When we thank Jesus for restoring peace, we do so with hope that the redeemed cosmos will once again embody

Eden's radiance, and we commit ourselves to practices—sustainability, reconciliation, justice—that anticipate creation's ultimate healing.

Peace Lost: Discord After the Fall

Sin's entry disrupted Eden's calm: Cain's murderous jealousy (Gen 4), Adam and Eve's hiding in shame (Gen 3), and creation's groan for liberation (Rom 8:22) narrate peace's fracture. The serpent's whisper sowed fear, Eve's disobedience birthed distrust, and Adam's blame-shifting inaugurated conflict. Physical decay, emotional turmoil, social alienation, and cosmic unrest all issue from that primal rupture. Gratitude for Jesus' reconciling work emerges most poignantly against this backdrop of brokenness; only a Savior who carries every discord can fully restore. Yet even amid present strife—political polarization, family feuds, personal anxieties—Christ's presence offers foretaste of reclaimed harmony. When storms of regret or societal division howl, we cling to the promise that the cross and resurrection dismantle the roots of every rebellion, knitting creation back toward the unity for which it was first designed.

10.2 Prophetic Promises of Calming Presence

"He Will Be Our Peace" (Micah 5)

In the prophet Micah's oracle, the Messiah born in Bethlehem is called "our peace" (Mic 5:4, ESV). This title transcends political peace treaties or national security; it signifies an inner tranquility rooted in divine presence. Israel's repeated failures and surrounding threats left the nation longing for a peace more enduring than any armistice. By identifying the coming ruler as "the LORD is our peace" (Mic 5:5, NASB), God assures His people that the Messiah will establish a shalom that neither sword nor siege can unsettle. Gratitude for this prophecy fuels trust amid personal battles: when fear or grief threatens to overrun us, we remember that Jesus' very name embodies the peace we seek. Preaching Micah's words in Advent and beyond reminds congregations that prophetic hope always centers on the One who stills storms both external and internal.

Prince of Peace Foretold (Isaiah 9)

Isaiah's majestic vision of the Messiah describes Him as "Wonderful Counselor, Mighty God, Everlasting Father, Prince of Peace" (Isa 9:6). The fourth title, Prince of Peace, crowns a cascade of divine attributes, signaling that peace flows from wisdom, power, and paternal care. Unlike worldly princes who maintain order through force, this Prince makes peace by reconciling enemies, forgiving sin, and transforming hearts. Gratitude intensifies as we ponder the fullness of His reign: every fearful heart addressed by His counsel, every powerless soul strengthened by His might, every orphan embraced by His fatherly love. In the church's liturgy and hymnody—"Hark! The Herald Angels Sing," "Come Thou Long-Expected Jesus"—Isaiah's promise resounds, inviting renewed thanksgiving that Jesus inaugurates a kingdom where swords are beaten into plowshares, and peace flows like a river (Isa 2:4; 66:12).

Covenant of Peace in Ezekiel's Shepherd Oracle

Ezekiel's vision of the Good Shepherd portrays Jesus as one who seeks and carries the lost, binding up wounds and providing pasture (Ezek 34:11–16). In a later prophecy, God pledges a new covenant of peace: "I will make with them a covenant of peace... I will rid the land of savage beasts, and they will live securely in the wilderness... and they will lie down in the woods and sleep in peaceful rest" (Ezek 34:25–26). Under this covenant, peace extends beyond human relationships to security in every environment—wilderness, forest, or battlefield. Gratitude for Christ's shepherding care grows when believers experience this promise personally: safe rest amid trials, protection in hostility, restoration after exile. Churches reflecting this shepherd-heart offer safe spaces for the hurting—healing groups, prayer rooms, shelter ministries—manifesting Ezekiel's vision today. Each testimony of found rest becomes a note in God's ongoing covenant song, inspiring hearts to echo, "Thank You, Jesus, for being our Shepherd and our peace."

10.3 Jesus, the Storm-Silencer

Sea of Galilee: "Peace, Be Still!"

In Mark 4:35–41 we find Jesus and His disciples crossing the Sea of Galilee when a furious squall threatens to swamp their boat. Though seasoned fishermen accustomed to sudden storms, even they panic at the waves crashing over the gunwale. In the midst of their terror, Jesus sleeps on a cushion—absolute calm amid chaos. When they awake Him, He stands, rebukes the wind and waves with a single command—"Peace! Be still!"—and instantly the gale subsides into glass-like calm. The disciples, awestruck, ask one another, "Who then is this, that even wind and sea obey him?" Their awe turns into awakening: Jesus is not merely a Rabbi but Lord over creation. Gratitude pours out when we recall that the same voice that stilled Galilee still speaks peace over our inner storms—anxiety, grief, or crisis—and brings quiet where once was commotion. Every time we pray for ease amid overwhelm, we echo that command, trusting that He who sculpted waves can steady the tumult within us.

Walking on Water: Courage in the Wind

A night later, the disciples see Jesus approaching on the water—another demonstration of His mastery over nature (Matt 14:22–33). Peter's faith flares: he steps out of the boat and walks toward Jesus, only to sink when his focus shifts from the Master to the swirling sea. Jesus immediately reaches out, grasping Peter's hand and saying, "O you of little faith, why did you doubt?" Then they both climb into the boat, and the wind ceases. This encounter teaches that trust in Jesus invites us to step into the impossible; our faltering steps remind us that faith is risky but resuscitated by the Savior's touch. Gratitude deepens when we reflect on times we've walked toward Christ in uncertainty, felt ourselves start to sink, and then experienced His hand lifting us back. Storm-time courage is birthed in such moments, and thanksgiving cements our identity as both learners and recipients of His sustaining power.

From Fear to Worship: Disciples' Awe-Filled Response

Following both miracles—calming the sea and walking on it—the disciples' response is the same: "Truly you are the Son of God" (Matt 14:33; Mk 4:41). Their confession arises not from intellectual deduction but from raw awe: witnessing supernatural authority evokes worship. Fear is transformed from paralysis into adoration: what once threatened them becomes the occasion for praise. Gratitude for these Gospel narratives inspires our own worship gatherings: when we recall personal storms stilled—health scare averted, relationship mended, fear overcome—our hearts move from dread to adoration. The liturgy of thanksgiving echoes the disciples' confession, reinforcing that Jesus' identity is inseparable from His power to bring peace. Each testimony "He calmed my storm!" becomes both a sermon in a song and an invitation for others to join in worshipful trust.

10.4 Peace for Troubled Minds

"Let Not Your Heart Be Troubled" (John 14)

On the night of His betrayal, Jesus comforts His disciples with words that still resonate: "Let not your hearts be troubled. Believe in God; believe also in me" (John 14:1). He anticipates their grief at His departure and anticipates ours amid life's losses. Rather than offering a panacea for circumstances, He redirects their trust to His person and His promise of an eternal home. Gratitude arises when we heed this invitation: instead of letting circumstances drive our emotions, we let the certainty of Christ's love ground our souls. Personal practices—repeating this verse in prayer, meditating on its truth—help rewire anxious thought patterns toward peace anchored in relationship rather than in changing conditions. Every time life's betrayals threaten to unmoor us, we remember His voice inviting us back to the Father's peace.

Spirit of Peace: Paraclete's Inner Witness

Jesus promises that the Holy Spirit will be another Counselor, "the Spirit of truth, whom the world cannot receive, because it neither sees him nor knows him. You know him, for he dwells with you and will be in you" (John 14:17). This indwelling presence brings inner peace by testifying to our spirit that we are God's children and heirs of His kingdom (Romans 8:16–17). The Spirit convicts us of sin but also reassures us of God's unchanging love, replacing self-condemnation with restful certainty. Gratitude for this inner witness transforms prayer: we no longer grope for reassurance in circumstances but lean into the Spirit's unspoken affirmations. In moments of doubt, we pause and listen for that still, small voice reminding us, "You belong; you are secure."

Casting Anxiety: Learning the Unforced Rhythms of Grace

Jesus instructs His followers, "Do not be anxious about your life… but seek first the kingdom of God… and all these things will be added to you" (Matthew 6:25–33). He characterizes anxious striving as futile—like addled birds preening their feathers—yet promises that gracious attention to God's priorities aligns our needs under His provision. Gratitude accelerates this alignment: counting daily blessings shifts focus from deficits to gifts, from dread to wonder. Practices such as gratitude journaling, breath prayers ("Jesus, grant me peace"), and corporate testimonies of provision cultivate unforced rhythms of grace. Over time, worry loses its instinctive claim on the heart, while trust becomes our default response to uncertainty. In this gracious pattern, we learn not only to weather storms but to welcome them as opportunities to rehearse thanksgiving and to deepen our dependence on the Prince of Peace.

10.5 Peace That Surpasses Understanding

Philippians 4 Rx: Prayer, Thanksgiving, Guarded Hearts

Paul's prescription for anxious minds is remarkably simple yet profoundly countercultural: "Do not be anxious about anything, but in everything by prayer and supplication with thanksgiving let your requests be made known to God. And the peace of God, which surpasses all understanding, will guard your hearts and your minds in Christ Jesus" (Philippians 4:6–7). Here "with thanksgiving" is not a tacked-on afterthought but the key that unlocks divine peace. In practice this means turning every worry into a prayer request framed by gratitude—thanking God in advance for His faithful provision. Scientific studies show that gratitude exercises reduce anxiety, but Paul roots it in divine promise: a peace so deep that it defies logical explanation. Thankful prayer shifts our posture from frantic striving to calm dependency, inviting God's own shalom to stand sentinel over our emotions. Over time, this rhythm rewires our reflexes—when tension rises, we pause to pray and to remember past mercies. In small groups and personal devotions, rehearsing answered prayers fosters collective trust, so that corporate prayer times feel less like obligation and more like gatherings of grateful children. By embracing this "Philippians Rx," we cultivate a mindscape where peace guards us like a fortress, impervious to life's turbulent currents.

Isaiah 26:3: The Stayed Mind

Isaiah 26:3 promises, "You keep him in perfect peace whose mind is stayed on you, because he trusts in you." The Hebrew word for "stayed" conveys the image of a mast securely braced on a ship—firmly fixed despite stormy seas. Such mental anchoring arises through focused meditation on God's character, promises, and past faithfulness. Gratitude serves as the windlass that hoists our thoughts back to His unchanging nature: recalling sunrises we did not deserve, healing we did not earn, relationships restored by grace. Spiritual disciplines—centering prayer, breath prayers, repeated Scripture memorization—help believers rehearse divine truths until their minds instinctively return to God when fears surface. Over time, our cognitive "mast" grows reinforced by repeated thanksgiving experiences, enabling us to maintain inward calm amid outward chaos. Communities that practice collective lectio divina or guided gratitude meditations help participants learn how to fix their minds on Christ rather than churn through worst-case scenarios. In this way, perfect peace is not an elusive ideal, but the byproduct of a mind habitually anchored in gratitude-fueled trust.

Colossians 3:15: Peace as Umpire in Community Decisions

Paul directs the Colossians: "Let the peace of Christ rule (Greek: umpire) in your hearts, to which indeed you were called in one body. And be thankful" (Colossians 3:15). In ancient athletic contests, an umpire (or referee) had the authority to settle disputes and maintain order; likewise, Christ's peace is meant to arbitrate conflicts within the church. When decisions on worship style, resource allocation, or interpersonal boundaries spark disagreement, grateful hearts defer to the inner assurance Christ provides rather than hardening positions. Gratitude for Christ's reconciliatory work on the cross cultivates humility, reminding believers that each person stands equally pardoned and valued in His sight. In practice, teams and leadership bodies that begin meetings with a brief gratitude round—sharing personal or communal blessings—notice a shift from debate to collaboration. When conflicts arise, invoking, "What does the Prince of Peace's peace guide us to do?" reorients the discussion toward unity rather than victory. As gratitude and peace take joint dominion, community life becomes a foretaste of the new creation, where "there shall be no more death, mourning, crying, or pain" (Rev 21:4) and relationships flow in unhindered harmony.

10.6 Songs in the Night—Worship as Storm Shelter

Paul & Silas at Midnight

In Philippi, Paul and Silas are beaten, stripped, and cast into an inner prison with their feet secured in stocks (Acts 16:25). Yet instead of despair, they "prayed and sang hymns to God, and the prisoners listened to them." Their midnight worship shook the foundations, opened the prison doors, and loosened every chain (Acts 16:26). This narrative teaches that praise in crisis is not naiveté but a strategic declaration of faith that summons divine intervention. Gratitude fuels such worship: pausing amid pain to recall God's past deliverances transforms lament into anthems of trust. Churches and small groups that host "Songs in the Night" services—playing gentle lamps, offering acoustic worship, inviting testimonies—create sacred spaces where the Holy Spirit can broach breakthrough. The legacy of Paul and Silas echoes in every sanctuary candlelit at midnight, every hushed chord rising above fear, reminding us that worship is as much a pathway to peace as prayer or proclamation.

Psalms of Lament Turning to Praise

The biblical Psalter devotes nearly one-third of its chapters to lament—raw cries of "How long, O Lord?"—yet each lament often pivots into praise. Psalm 42 exemplifies this movement: "Why are you cast down, O my soul?... Hope in God; for I shall again praise him" (Ps 42:5, 11). Lament validates anguish as honest worship, refusing to short-circuit grief, while thanksgiving readies the soul to celebrate hope. In lament workshops or guided liturgies, congregations learn to express sorrow with honesty and then to transition into gratitude-driven adoration. Over time, this practice trains worshipers to navigate spiritual storms, allowing pain to surface without getting buried under despair. When lament turns to praise, hearts experience a tangible shift: the same tears become seeds for joy, and uncertainty yields to remembrance of God's unshakable character.

Modern Hymns Born from Hardship

The history of Christian hymnody brims with songs penned in the furnace of trial. Charles Wesley's "And Can It Be" blossomed from his own struggle with assurance; Horatio Spafford wrote "It Is Well with My Soul" after personal tragedy struck his family; Mary Bowley Peters sang "Great Is Thy Faithfulness" amid economic depression and global conflict. These anthems, soaked in tears yet anchored in gratitude, become framers for communal worship, teaching new generations how to praise in storm. Gratitude for these historic voices encourages modern songwriters and worship leaders to craft fresh texts and melodies that capture today's struggles—pandemics, social upheaval, mental health crises—while pointing to the unchanging Lord. When congregations sing these hymns, they enter a multi-century fellowship of sufferers-turned-singers, renewing faith that storms are neither final nor fatal. Thus worship becomes a storm shelter: a place where lyrics and melodies join hearts in thankful resilience until the tempest passes.

10.7 Spiritual Warfare and the Shoes of Peace

Armor of God: Readiness from the Gospel of Peace

Paul's call to "put on the whole armor of God" begins with the "belt of truth" and the "breastplate of righteousness," but quickly highlights the "shoes of the readiness given by the gospel of peace" (Ephesians 6:14–15). The imagery of sturdy footwear reminds us that peace equips us to traverse hostile terrain—be it internal doubt or external opposition—without stumbling. While the belt and breastplate protect our core convictions, the gospel-shod feet propel us into mission fields and personal conflicts with confidence rather than fear. Gratitude for Jesus' peace transforms preparation into worship: as we tighten our sandals each morning in prayer, we rehearse thankfulness that His reconciliation secures us to stand firm against every assault. Churches practicing "armor-up" liturgies—brief communal prayers over each piece—cultivate a corporate readiness rooted not in human strategy but in Christ's finished work. In moments of spiritual attack, remembering the shoes of peace shifts our posture from defensive retreat to purposeful advance, declaring that the gospel's peace outruns every lie the enemy hurls.

Crushing the Accuser Under Our Feet (Romans 16:20)

Romans 16:20 offers a stark promise: "The God of peace will soon crush Satan under your feet." This victory is not achieved by human might but guaranteed by divine faithfulness. Underfoot imagery conveys decisive authority: the accuser who once kept us bound now lies defeated in the dust. Gratitude for this promise ignites boldness in prayer and proclamation. When feelings of condemnation or fear resurface, believers can recall this pounding prophecy—Satan has already been trampled at the cross and resurrection. Worship songs that declare "Satan, you have lost" join a long line of rejoicing in victory, shifting the church's focus from defensive crouch to triumphant anthem. Each testimony of breakthrough—fears dissipated, accusations silenced, peace restored—becomes a demonstration of this promise, urging us to lift our feet in praise rather than shrink in shame.

Peaceful Authority over Chaos and Darkness

Jesus' first recorded miracle, turning water into wine, foreshadows a larger theme: the inauguration of order over chaos (John 2:1–11). As the Creator spoke light into darkness in Genesis, so the Son brings order into spiritual confusion. Believers share in His peaceful authority when they stand against demonic oppression—not through shouting or sensationalism, but by speaking Christ's name and praising His lordship. Gratitude for our position "in Christ" (Ephesians 2:6) propels us to exercise this authority with humility: we dwell in peace even as we proclaim it. In spiritual deliverance ministries, focusing first on thanksgiving for Christ's victory sets a tone of respectful confidence rather than combative aggression. Testimonies of lives freed from occult bondage, depression, or fear underscore that peace is more than absence of conflict; it is active dominion over every form of darkness.

10.8 Community Carriers of Christ's Calm

Bearing One Another's Burdens

Galatians 6:2 instructs believers to "bear one another's burdens, and so fulfill the law of Christ." Storm-time peace often arrives through the care of fellow disciples carrying each other's heavy loads—grief, anxiety, financial desperation, or relational strife. Gratitude for such community helpers fuels our own willingness to step in: driving to appointments, sitting in waiting rooms, cooking meals, or simply listening without offering solutions. Churches that structure "care teams" or prayer partners translate Christ's shalom into tangible relief, demonstrating that peace is communal as well as personal. Each act of compassionate presence becomes both a balm to the afflicted and a thanksgiving offering to Jesus who says, "Inasmuch as you did it to one of the least of these… you did it to me" (Matt 25:40).

Gentle Answers that Turn Away Wrath

Proverbs extols "a soft answer [that] turns away wrath" (Prov 15:1), illustrating how calm words defuse escalations and restore relational harmony. In heated conversations—whether at home, work, or online—choosing measured, peace-filled responses reflects Christ's own ethos. Gratitude for the Spirit's fruit of gentleness (Gal 5:23) empowers us to pause before firing back, asking instead, "How can my words reflect the peace I've received?" Role-playing workshops, communication training, and sermon series on conflict resolution equip congregants to practice this biblical principle. When churches preach and model gentle speech, they become havens where truth is spoken without fear of verbal retaliation, advancing shalom in families, neighborhoods, and digital forums.

Hospitality that Heals the Anxious Soul

Ancient Near Eastern culture prized hospitality as more than etiquette: it was an art of cultivating peace. Inviting weary travelers into one's home for food, rest, and social warmth mirrored the Creator's own welcoming nature. The New Testament church embraced this practice (Rom 12:13; Heb 13:2), offering strangers a place at the table in Jesus' name. Gratitude for God's generosity—"I was a stranger and you welcomed me" (Matt 25:35)—drives believers to open their homes, creating sacred spaces where anxious hearts find rest. Small gatherings around shared meals, prayer lodges with comfortable seating, and coffee fellowship after services all become incarnations of divine hospitality. In such environments, newcomers discover that Christ's peace is not only preached but also tasted in the aroma of fresh bread and the warmth of kind conversation.

10.9 Peace amid Suffering and Persecution

Beatitudes: Blessed Are the Peacemakers in a Hostile World

In the Sermon on the Mount, Jesus blesses peacemakers—those who actively pursue reconciliation amid conflict (Matt 5:9). This teaching comes to followers who already face persecution for righteousness' sake. Yet instead of retreating, they become artisans of peace, building bridges across divides. Gratitude for this calling transcends comfort theology; it honors the paradox of suffering to serve as shalom-makers. Historical examples—from the early martyrs singing in the arena to modern Christians advocating for persecuted minorities—demonstrate that peace can thrive amid hostility. The church that celebrates peacemaking as a virtue empowers members to engage cultural, political, and personal conflicts with grace-wielding courage rather than retreat or aggression.

Early-Church Martyrs' Serenity

Acts 7 records Stephen facing death with "the face of an angel," praying for his killers even as stones pelted him (Acts 7:55–60). His serenity in persecution testifies that peace springs from vision of God enthroned and from forgiveness born of gratitude. Later martyrs—Polycarp, Perpetua, and so many unnamed—echoed this calm witness, singing hymns as they marched to their deaths. Gratitude for their legacy emboldens modern believers to stand faithful under threat, anchoring courage not in personal strength but in remembrance of the One who defeated death itself. Martyr commemorations in churches around the world keep this legacy alive, encouraging present generations to uphold peace in the darkest circumstances.

Petrine Exhortation: Quiet Hope That Provokes Questions

Peter urges suffering Christians to "always be prepared to make a defense to anyone who asks you for a reason for the hope that is in you; yet do it with gentleness and respect" (1 Pet 3:15). Quiet, confident hope rooted in Christ's peace provokes genuine curiosity rather than hostility. Gratitude for our unshakable hope drives respectful conversations rather than argumentative debates. Communities that train members in personal testimony—sharing stories of comfort received—equip them to answer questions about suffering and peace with authenticity and love. Such encounters often become seeds for deeper dialogue, revealing that the peace we bear is not a flimsy veneer but a robust foundation that withstands the fiercest storms.

10.10 Practical Practices for Storm-Time Peace

Breath Prayer & Meditative Scripture

Breath prayers—simple two-phrase prayers synchronized with inhales and exhales, such as "Jesus, Prince of Peace" inhale; "Calm my anxious heart" exhale—ground us in the present and connect body, mind, and spirit. Meditating on key passages like Psalm 46:10 ("Be still, and know that I am God") or Isaiah 26:3 transforms them from ink on a page into living realities. Gratitude amplifies these practices: as we breathe out thanks for a specific mercy—health restored, a supportive friend, a slice of beauty in nature—the practice becomes a sacred pause that dissolves turmoil. Mobile apps and guided prayer groups can help congregants integrate breath prayers and Scripture meditation into daily routines, creating unforced rhythms of grace. Over time, these simple practices accumulate into a reservoir of peace upon which we draw in crises.

Gratitude Journaling in Distress

Writing down three things we are grateful for each day—even amid hardship—trains our brains to seek the "grain of grace" in every situation. Psychological research links gratitude journaling to reduced anxiety and improved resilience. Biblically, Daniel and his friends resolved to seek God's mercies even in exile (Dan 1:8–16), illustrating that thankfulness transcends circumstances. Churches can facilitate gratitude journaling by providing journals at retreat centers or hosting "grace reflection" events where members share entries. During times of communal crisis—natural disaster, economic downturn, or health epidemic—a collective gratitude journal offers tangible proof of God's sustaining presence.

Sabbath Rhythms and Digital Detox

Uninterrupted rest is a powerful antidote to informational overload—the modern storm that dims Sabbath. Instituting regular digital-free periods—an afternoon, a sunset-to-sunset cycle—reconnects us with creation (Psalm 104), community, and prayer. Gratitude for Christ's invitation to rest (Matthew 11:28–29) motivates us to resist the tyranny of "always-on" culture. Worship services incorporating candlelit vespers, labyrinth walks, or silent retreats provide frameworks for sabbath celebration. Families and small groups that practice collective screen-free sabbaths discover renewed relational rhythms and deeper awareness of God's daily provision.

10.11 Eschatological Assurance—The Final Calm

New Heaven & Earth: No More Sea of Chaos

Revelation concludes with a vision of the river of life flowing from God's throne and no sea—a symbol of chaos—anywhere in the new creation (Rev 21:1–2). The removal of the sea signifies the final eradication of disorder, matrix of storms, and forces that once threatened. Gratitude for this permanent peace sharpens our perspective: current tempests are but preludes to the city where no hurricane, no tsunami, and no whirlwind can ever arise. Christian environmentalism, social justice, and peacemaking ministries all labor in light of this covenant promise, offering tangible glimpses of Eden restored.

Lion & Lamb: Cosmic Reconciliation

Isaiah 11 portrays a scene of perfect harmony: "The wolf shall dwell with the lamb... the lion shall eat straw like the ox" (Isa 11:6–9). These poetic images convey not only human peace but cosmic reconciliation—hostile species living in peace before the LORD's majestic reign. Gratitude for this vision inspires cross-cultural and multi-ethnic unity, as we anticipate a kingdom where former enemies—Jew and Gentile, male and female, gay and straight—dwell together in harmony under Christ's banner of peace. When congregations celebrate this prophetic hope, they rehearse a foretaste of unbroken peace that transcends all current divisions.

Eternal Light, No Night There—Rest Unbroken

Revelation 22 promises, "There will be no more night" (Rev 22:5)—no more darkness to obscure divine presence, no more loneliness that invites fear. In that eternal day, sleep and shadows fade before unbroken communion with the Lamb. Gratitude for this final calm empowers us to persevere through present clouds, knowing that the end of longing is secured. Daily devotions that focus on "that great day" fuel joy in trials, as we echo the heavenly refrain: "Worthy is the Lamb who was slain, to receive power and wealth and wisdom and might and honor and glory and blessing!" (Rev 5:12). In that consummated peace, every tear is wiped away (Rev 21:4), uniting our voices in endless praise for the Comforter who promised—and guaranteed—calm for every storm.

Conclusion

Throughout Scripture—from Eden's original shalom to the new creation's unending day—the Lord weaves a sovereign promise of peace into every narrative thread. Jesus Christ, the Prince of Peace, fulfills that promise not only in spectacular storm-silencing miracles but also in the quiet assurances of His presence, the whisper of the Spirit's indwelling calm, and the community of believers called to bear one another's burdens. Practical rhythms—prayer with thanksgiving, Sabbath rest, breath prayer—equip us to taste this peace amid life's fiercest gales. In every wartime hospital room, broken family gathering, or sleepless night, the same peace that trounced Galilean tempests awaits us. One day, storms themselves will vanish in the eternal light of the Lamb, and the sea—symbol of chaos—will be remembered only as a precursor to God's final calm. Until that dawn, our hearts join the ancient song: Thank You, Jesus, for peace in storms—your comfort is our anchor, your assurance our song.

Chapter 11. Thank You, Jesus, for the Fellowship of Believers—Community in Christ

From its first breath at Pentecost through every generation that has gathered in His name, the Church has been God's vessel for manifesting the love, joy, and unity of Christ to a watching world. Fellowship among believers is more than social interaction; it is a foretaste of the eternal communion we will one day share with the triune God and with one another in the New Jerusalem (Rev 21:3–4). In this space of shared grace, hearts learn forgiveness as they are forgiven (Col 3:13), burdens are borne as if they were one's own (Gal 6:2), and gifts flourish for mutual strengthening (1 Cor 12:7). To say "Thank You, Jesus" for these communities is to honor the spiritual DNA encoded in the Scriptures—where the Body of Christ, like a living organism, grows through interdependence, sacrificial service, and joyful celebration. Over the course of this chapter, we will trace the biblical foundations of Christian community, survey the vibrant life of the early Church, explore the means of grace that bind us, and glimpse the eternal banquet for which our fellowship now prepares us. May each reflection deepen our gratitude for the "fellowship of the Spirit" (Phil 2:1) that knits believers into a family transcending every barrier.

11.1 Biblical Foundations of Christian Community

The Upper Room Covenant: Church Born in Unity (Acts 1–2)

In those ten days between Christ's ascension and Pentecost, the Eleven and a faithful band of about 120 gathered in the Upper Room with one accord (Acts 1:13–15). United by prayer and expectation, they embodied the New Covenant fellowship Jesus promised—a community empowered and guided by the Spirit (John 14:16–17). When the Spirit arrived in tongues of fire, their unity exploded into bold proclamation, transforming fear into fearless mission (Acts 2:1–4). Their shared experience of Christ's promises fulfilled birthed a new family whose life together revolved around apostolic teaching, fellowship, breaking of bread, and prayer (Acts 2:42). Gratitude for this foundational moment reminds us that Christian community is not a man-made club but a covenant congregation sealed by divine presence. Every church gathering today echoes the Upper Room's energy, as we pray, praise, and await fresh Spirit outpourings together.

"One Body" Imagery: Mystical Union in Scripture (1 Corinthians 12; Romans 12)

Paul's epistles to the Corinthians and Romans unfold the rich metaphor of the Church as a single body with many members (1 Cor 12:12–27; Rom 12:4–5). In this organic union, diversity of gifts—apostles, prophets, teachers, healers—serves the common good, just as hands, feet, and eyes serve the body (1 Cor 12:7–11). No member can boast over another, for each is integral and indispensable to the whole (1 Cor 12:18–20). Gratitude for our inclusion in this body reshapes identity: we are never lone individuals but branches grafted into the vine of Christ (John 15:5). Mutual interdependence becomes a practical reality when congregations honor each gifting, offer space for participation, and pray for one another's flourishing.

New Covenant Table: Communion as Family Meal (1 Corinthians 11; Luke 22)

On the night He was betrayed, Jesus reframed the Passover Seder into a meal pointing to His body broken and blood shed for many (Luke 22:19–20). Paul admonishes believers to "discern the body" when gathering at the Lord's Supper, highlighting that communion is countercultural family dinner where social status, ethnicity, and gender distinctions fall away (1 Cor 11:17–34). Participation in the Supper binds us in a tangible covenant meal—symbols of forgiveness and unity (1 Cor 10:16–17). Gratitude transforms each celebration from rote ritual into heartfelt remembrance, as we proclaim Christ's death until He comes. In homes and halls around the globe, the shared loaf and cup become the tablecloth upon which fellowship's fullest expression is served.

11.2 The Early Church Model

Shared Goods and Radical Generosity (Acts 2:44–45; 4:32–37)

In Jerusalem's newborn congregation, no one claimed personal ownership of possessions; rather, members "had all things in common" and sold property to distribute proceeds to anyone in need (Acts 2:44–45). This radical sharing fulfilled Jesus' command that His followers love one another as He loved them (John 13:34–35). When Barnabas sold a field and laid proceeds at the apostles' feet, he exemplified the grace-driven generosity that overcame scarcity mindsets (Acts 4:36–37). Gratitude for our own spiritual inheritance—rich beyond measure—compels similar sacrificial giving today. Churches that develop benevolence funds, microloan programs, or community gardening projects reenact this early-model generosity, becoming living testimonies that God's economy operates on trust, not hoarding.

Prayerful Gatherings: Power in Corporate Petition (Acts 4:23–31)

After Peter and John were released from the Sanhedrin, the believers gathered to pray for boldness and unity. They lifted voices in one accord, confessing fearlessly, "Lord, look on their threats and grant to your servants to continue to speak your word with all boldness" (Acts 4:29). The place shook, and they were all filled with the Holy Spirit, emboldened to witness despite renewed opposition (Acts 4:31). This narrative underscores that corporate prayer is not religious formality but strategic, Spirit-ignited enterprise. Gratitude for answered prayers fosters a culture of expectation and dependence on God. Modern churches that dedicate weekly prayer evenings—cradles of intercession—draw upon the same well of power that propelled the early Church from hidden gatherings into public witness.

Mission in Pairs and Teams: Apostolic Sending (Acts 13; 16)

The early Church's multiplication strategy prioritized teamwork: Barnabas and Saul were commissioned by the Holy Spirit and the church in Antioch (Acts 13:1–3), and Paul and Silas departed in tandem, covering wider territory (Acts 16:1–5). This model honored the biblical pattern of mutual encouragement (Ecclesiastes 4:9–12) and combined complementary gifts for mission effectiveness. Gratitude for Christ's sending of His disciples (John 20:21) propels contemporary partnerships—cross-cultural missions, campus ministries, local outreach teams—where no one labors alone. Such collaboration showcases unity-in-diversity, enabling the fellowship to bear coherent witness across linguistic, cultural, and geographical divides.

11.3 Means of Grace in Fellowship

Word Proclaimed and Interpreted: Sound Doctrine in Community

The foundation of every healthy fellowship is the faithful proclamation of God's Word, for "all Scripture is breathed out by God and profitable for teaching" (2 Tim 3:16). In community, hearing the Word together multiplies its impact: sermons, Bible studies, and small-group discussions allow believers to ask questions, wrestle with difficult passages, and apply truth to everyday life. Paul charges Timothy to "preach the word; be ready in season and out of season" (2 Tim 4:2), underscoring that corporate proclamation is a primary means of grace. In Colossians, Paul describes his ministry as "presenting everyone mature in Christ" through "warning everyone and teaching everyone with all wisdom" (Col 1:28), highlighting both exhortation and instruction. When congregations practice exegetical preaching—careful exposition of the biblical text—they guard against doctrinal drift and cultivate spiritual depth. Gratitude for this means of grace arises as we recognize that community interpretation prevents isolationist misreadings and fosters collective discernment. Discussion groups, lecture series, and collaborative journaling around key doctrines become venues where the Spirit illuminates Scripture in relational context. Thus the Word not only educates minds but shapes hearts and binds the body together in truth.

Sacraments Administered Together: Baptism and Eucharist

Jesus instituted two enduring signs of covenant fellowship: baptism, signaling entrance into the family of God, and the Lord's Supper, sustaining ongoing remembrance of His sacrifice. He commanded, "Go therefore and make disciples of all nations, baptizing them… teaching them to observe all that I have commanded you" (Matt 28:19–20), linking initiation with ongoing obedience. In 1 Corinthians 11:23–26, Paul recounts Jesus' words at the Last Supper—"Do this in remembrance of me"—reminding the church that every communal meal proclaims His death until He returns. When churches gather around the font, they celebrate new birth by water and Spirit, rejoicing as each believer publicly identifies with Christ's death and resurrection. At the table, the shared bread and cup unite diverse participants in a foretaste of the heavenly banquet. Gratitude for these sacraments emerges in the sense of holy communion—a profound, tactile reminder that salvation is both once-for-all event (baptism) and continuous reliance (Eucharist). Training children, catechumens, and new believers in the meaning of these rites deepens their appreciation for community's formative power.

Mutual Prayer and Laying on of Hands

The early church embraced collective intercession and the laying on of hands as pivotal to spiritual and physical well-being. James instructs, "Is anyone among you sick? Let him call for the elders of the church, and let them pray over him, anointing him with oil in the name of the Lord. And the prayer of faith will save the one who is sick" (Jas 5:14–15). In Acts, Peter and John laid hands on Samaritan believers, resulting in the reception of the Holy Spirit (Acts 8:14–17). These practices demonstrate that grace often flows through communal touch and united prayer. When a congregation gathers around someone in need—whether of healing, calling, or commissioning—the tangible act of laying hands conveys God's personal care. Gratitude arises as participants witness answers to prayer and sense the Spirit's power in touch-centered ministry. Prayer chains, care teams, and commissioning services all echo this apostolic pattern, reinforcing that faith is not a solo endeavor but a shared journey.

11.4 Spiritual Gifts and Roles

Gifts Distributed for Edification (1 Cor 12:4–11; Eph 4:11–13)

Paul teaches that "there are varieties of gifts, but the same Spirit… to each is given the manifestation of the Spirit for the common good" (1 Cor 12:4, 7). These gifts—wisdom, knowledge, faith, healing, miracles, prophecy, discernment, tongues, interpretation—are not bestowed for personal prestige but to build up the body (1 Cor 12:27). Ephesians expands the metaphor by describing Christ's gifts of apostles, prophets, evangelists, pastors, and teachers "to equip the saints for the work of ministry, for building up the body of Christ" (Eph 4:11–12). Healthy fellowships actively identify, affirm, and deploy these diverse gifts, ensuring that no essential ministry is neglected. Gratitude for gift variety fosters humility and interdependence as members celebrate one another's contributions. Structured gift inventories, mentoring relationships, and rotating service opportunities help believers discover and exercise their charisms. In doing so, communities reflect the dynamic unity and maturity of Christ's body, moving "from faith to maturity, to the measure of the stature of the fullness of Christ" (Eph 4:13).

Elders, Deacons, and Shepherds: Oversight and Care (1 Tim 3; Titus 1)

Scripture outlines leadership roles—elders/overseers and deacons—as essential to church health. Paul instructs Timothy on qualifications: elders must be "above reproach, the husband of one wife, sober-minded, self-controlled… able to teach" (1 Tim 3:2–7), while deacons must be "worthy of respect, sincere, not indulging in much wine… hold the mystery of the faith with a clear conscience" (1 Tim 3:8–10). Titus receives similar guidelines for Crete, paired with the admonition to "refute… the older men… older women… young women" (Titus 2:1–5), emphasizing discipleship and character formation. These offices provide structure for pastoral care, sound teaching, and sacramental oversight. Gratitude for spiritual leadership prompts active prayer for elders and deacons and gracious accountability. Leadership development pathways—internships, formal training, pastoral residencies—ensure succession and resilience. When overseers shepherd the flock "not under compulsion, but willingly… eagerly" (1 Pet 5:2), the whole community thrives in Christlike care.

Every-Member Ministry: Priesthood of All Believers (1 Pet 2:9; Rom 12:6–8)

The New Covenant democratizes ministry: "You are a chosen race, a royal priesthood" (1 Pet 2:9), empowering every believer to offer spiritual sacrifices of praise, service, and testimony. Romans 12 urges each to "use whatever gift you have received to serve one another, as good stewards of God's varied grace" (Rom 12:6). This priesthood rejects professional–laity divides; deacons and pastors equip rather than monopolize ministry (Eph 4:12). Gratitude for universal calling propels laypeople into classrooms as teachers, neighborhoods as evangelists, marketplaces as witnesses. Congregations flourish when Sunday's un-churched world sees a mosaic of believers—teachers, bus drivers, nurses, retirees—each ministering out of thankfulness for Christ's transforming grace. Mobilizing every member fosters a vibrant, resilient community where gifts multiply and service becomes a lifestyle.

11.5 Discipline, Restoration, and Forgiveness

Church Discipline as Love (Matthew 18:15–17; Galatians 6:1)

Jesus' instruction in Matthew 18 for confronting a sinning brother—first privately, then with witnesses, and finally before the church—reflects a pastoral process rooted in love and restoration rather than punishment (Matt 18:15–17). Its aim is to reconcile the offender, not to shame permanently. Paul echoes this restorative spirit when he urges, "If anyone is caught in any transgression, you who are spiritual should restore him in a spirit of gentleness" (Gal 6:1). Genuine church discipline acknowledges the seriousness of sin's harm to individuals and community, yet proceeds from a posture of humility: those who correct must first examine themselves (Matt 7:5). Gratitude for Christ's own merciful discipline—He "disciplines the one he loves" (Rev 3:19)—enables the church to enact correction with compassion. Accountability structures (elders' oversight, reconciliation groups) ensure fairness and protect dignity. When discipline succeeds, a truly repentant member rejoices in restored fellowship, often leading to deeper gratitude and commitment. Thus, church discipline, properly applied, becomes a grace-filled means of healing rather than exclusion.

Forgiveness Network: Sevenfold Grace (Matthew 18:21–35)

Peter asks Jesus how many times he must forgive—up to seven?—anticipating generosity (Matt 18:21). Jesus answers not "seven times" but "seventy-seven times," teaching unceasing forgiveness (Matt 18:22). He illustrates with the parable of the unmerciful servant, whose own debt is forgiven "ten thousand talents" (an unimaginable sum), yet he refuses to forgive a fellow servant's humble debt of "a hundred denarii" (Matt 18:24–28). The king's subsequent wrath underscores that those who receive boundless mercy must also extend it. Gratitude for our own immeasurable pardon (Eph 1:7) fuels willingness to forgive repeated offenses. Churches can foster this culture through teaching series on grace, small-group exercises in confession and forgiveness, and corporate absolution rites. Practically, this might involve mediated reconciliation sessions, periodic "forgiveness Sundays," or testimonies of restored relationships. In a fellowship shaped by sevenfold grace, bitterness dissolves, unity deepens, and hearts echo the grateful refrain: "Thank You, Jesus, for forgiving me—let me forgive as I've been forgiven."

Reconciliation Rituals: Restoring Broken Relationships (2 Corinthians 2:5–11)

Paul instructs the Corinthians to forgive and comfort a repentant offender "so that such a one might not be overwhelmed by excessive sorrow" (2 Cor 2:7). He warns that unforgiveness allows Satan "to outwit us" (2 Cor 2:11). Reconciliation involves both confession and welcome—rituals that mark forgiveness as public and communal (2 Cor 2:10). These rituals can include shared meals, prayer circles around the reconciled couple, or laying on of hands, symbolizing the body's reunification. Gratitude for Christ's reconciling work— "He himself is our peace… reconciling us to God" (Eph 2:14–

16)—underpins our own reconciliation efforts. Churches can equip members with peacemaking training (Matt 5:9), conflict mediation teams, and "restoration days" when those estranged are invited back into community life. When broken relationships are healed in Christ's name, the entire fellowship experiences a surge of love and unity, reinforcing our collective witness.

11.6 Corporate Worship and Liturgical Rhythms

Sabbath Gatherings and the Lord's Day (Hebrews 10:24–25; Acts 20:7)

The early church's pattern of gathering "on the Lord's Day" (Sunday) for breaking bread and teaching (Acts 20:7) echoes the Sabbath principle of communal rest and worship (Heb 10:24–25). This weekly rhythm honors God's creative rest (Gen 2:2–3) and celebrates Jesus' resurrection, the "first day of the week" (John 20:1). Corporate worship provides a spiritual reset: believers encourage one another, remind each other of gospel truths, and renew commitments. Gratitude for this rhythm transforms attendance from ritual duty into joyful reunion. Churches that integrate liturgical elements—responsive readings, confessions, benedictions—help worshipers experience continuity with centuries of faith. Practical features like designated children's moments, hospitality zones, and clear liturgical flow ensure that each gathering feels like a foretaste of the eternal feast. Consistent Lord's Day observance embeds the gospel more deeply into daily life, making Sabbath rest both a gift and discipline.

Hymns, Psalms, and Spiritual Songs (Colossians 3:16; Ephesians 5:19)

Paul exhorts believers to let "the word of Christ dwell in you richly… teaching and admonishing one another in all wisdom, singing psalms and hymns and spiritual songs, with thankfulness in your hearts to God" (Col 3:16). Singing together embeds doctrine in memory, shapes affections, and unites voices across demographics. The Psalms offer a model for corporate lament, praise, and petition, while hymns born from church history connect present worshipers with generations past. Spiritual songs—spontaneous or prophetic—invite the Spirit's fresh breath in gatherings. Gratitude for this rich repertoire inspires congregations to invest in both tradition (ancient chants, gospel standards) and innovation (new compositions reflecting contemporary contexts). Choirs, bands, congregational sing-alongs, and small-group worship teams all contribute to a robust song culture. When unified singing lifts voices in thanksgiving, the church becomes a living doxology, offering up prayers in melody.

Fasting, Feasting, and Festival Observances (Acts 13:2–3; 1 Corinthians 5:8)

Fasting and feasting serve as bookends in the gospel story: seasons of fasting prepare hearts (Acts 13:2–3), while "with the unleavened bread of sincerity and truth" Paul urges a festival mindset (1 Cor 5:8). Church calendars built around spiritual rhythms—Advent, Lent, Easter, Pentecost—shape communal devotion and celebration. Fasts foster humility and dependence, creating space for deeper prayer; feasts express joy in salvation and community. Gratitude for redemption fuels festival cheer—Christmas pageants, Easter sunrise services, harvest celebrations. Small groups might observe a Daniel fast followed by a communal meal, linking spiritual discipline with relational bonding. Cultural adaptations—food banks at Thanksgiving, liturgical arts festivals—translate ancient rhythms into local contexts. In these liturgical seasons, corporate worship transcends Sunday morning, becoming a daily pilgrimage marked by both penitence and praise.

11.7 Mission, Witness, and Unity

Great Commission as Communal Calling (Matthew 28:18–20)

Jesus' final command unites every believer in shared mission: "All authority in heaven and on earth has been given to me. Go therefore and make disciples of all nations…" (Matt 28:18–

19). This mandate is inherently communal—Jesus sends the collective "you" into the world, not lone individuals. When churches approach evangelism as a family endeavor, each member contributes according to gifting: some preach, others pray, still others host newcomers. Gratitude for Christ's authority undergirds our obedience; we march out of pews with heartfelt thanks that the risen Lord commissions and empowers us. Discipleship flows from relationship, as mentor–mentee pairs multiply the gospel in homes, offices, and marketplaces. Training programs that pair new believers with seasoned disciples echo barn-raising models: everyone pitches in, everyone learns, and everyone rejoices when another faith takes root. In this fellowship-shaped implementation of the Great Commission, unity and mission become two sides of the same coin, reflecting the one body called to bear Christ's name.

Cross-Cultural Partnerships: Jew and Gentile United (Ephesians 2:14–22; Galatians 3:28)

Paul celebrates the gospel's power to break down dividing walls—ethnic, social, gender—so that "there is neither Jew nor Greek" but one new humanity in Christ (Galatians 3:28). Ephesians 2 portrays Christ as our peace, who "has broken down in his flesh the dividing wall of hostility" and "created in himself one new man in place of the two" (Eph 2:14–15). The early church's inclusion of Gentiles shattered the synagogue–temple exclusivity and birthed churches in Antioch, Ephesus, and Rome that embodied radical unity. Gratitude for this cross-cultural reconciliation spurs partnerships between majority- and minority-ethnic congregations, missionary networks, and sister-church relationships across continents. Joint worship services that blend languages, music styles, and traditions concretize Paul's vision of a multi-ethnic temple where Christ dwells through the Spirit (Eph 2:22). In such settings, the diversity of gifts, accents, and stories illustrates the manifold wisdom of God (Eph 3:10). Every shared meal and joint outreach project becomes both a celebration of reconciliation and a foretaste of the heavenly multitude gathered around the throne (Rev 7:9).

Social Witness: Justice, Mercy, and Advocacy (Isaiah 1:17; Micah 6:8)

Biblical fellowship extends beyond walls to address systemic injustices that harm the vulnerable. Isaiah commands, "Learn to do good; seek justice, correct oppression; bring justice to the fatherless…" (Isa 1:17). Micah condenses God's requirement: "to act justly and to love mercy and to walk humbly with your God" (Mic 6:8). The early Church embodied these values by caring for widows, feeding the poor, and advocating for marginalized groups (Acts 6:1–6). Gratitude for Christ's sacrificial love compels us to pursue modern justice initiatives—anti-trafficking efforts, refugee resettlement, prison reform—viewing them as mission fields rather than secular activism. Partnerships with NGOs and faith-based coalitions amplify impact while maintaining gospel distinctiveness. When congregations host forums on racial reconciliation, sponsor community health fairs, or advocate for living wages, they reflect the integrated mercy and justice Jesus modeled. Each act of advocacy, born of thankful hearts, proclaims that the fellowship of believers is a living laboratory for the kingdom's restorative work.

11.8 Hospitality and Practical Care

Open Homes as Gospel Outposts (Romans 12:13; 1 Peter 4:9)

Paul exhorts, "Contribute to the needs of the saints and seek to show hospitality" (Rom 12:13), while Peter adds, "Show hospitality to one another without grumbling" (1 Pet 4:9). In the ancient world, an open door signified a safe haven; in the New Covenant, open homes become extensions of the Upper Room, where strangers become family. Gratitude for our welcome into God's household motivates us to replicate that welcome, offering couches for college students, spare rooms for visitors, or simple dinners for newcomers. Regular "home church" gatherings break down barriers of performance, allowing authentic sharing of life's joys and struggles. Cooking teams, rotating host schedules, and hospitality training equip congregants to receive guests with warmth and dignity. Each meal shared in grace-filled fellowship broadcasts the gospel's hospitality more convincingly than tracts or sermons. As believers thank Jesus for His open invitation to feasts of grace, they become living invitations for seekers to taste Christ's welcome firsthand.

Visiting the Sick and Imprisoned (Matthew 25:36; James 1:27)

Jesus identifies personal ministry to those in need as service to Himself: "I was sick and you visited me... I was in prison and you came to me" (Matt 25:36). James links "visiting orphans and widows" with "keeping oneself unstained" by the world (Jas 1:27). Visiting the sick and incarcerated requires intentional effort—learning visitation protocols, safeguarding confidentiality, and cultivating compassionate listening. Gratitude for Christ's own solidarity with the suffering, as He touched lepers and wept at tombs (Mk 1:41; Jn 11:35), compels modern believers to mirror that presence. Hospital chaplaincy teams, prison ministry cohorts, and pastoral visitation committees bring the Body's tangible care to those often forgotten. Small gestures—cards, phone calls, prayer shawls—validate the worth of the vulnerable and remind them they remain part of the fellowship. Through these ministries, churches incarnate Christ's compassion, and every shared sorrow becomes a shared thanksgiving when recovery, reconciliation, or peace eventually emerges.

Resource Sharing: Benevolence Funds and Community Kitchens (Acts 6:1–7)

When Hellenistic widows complained of neglect, the Apostles established deacons to ensure equitable distribution of food (Acts 6:1–7). This early benevolence fund model informs today's mercy ministries: benevolence funds that pay utility bills, community kitchens that feed the hungry, clothing closets that serve low-income families. Gratitude for God's abundant provision stirs churches to allocate budget lines for direct aid and to mobilize volunteers for distribution. Partnerships with social services ensure that aid includes case management, preventing dependency and promoting dignity. "Soup kitchen Sundays," mobile pantries, and holiday gift drives become community landmarks where the Body's generosity shines. Each meal served and bill paid echoes the apostles' conviction that practical care is integral to gospel proclamation. As believers thank Jesus for His provision, they extend that provision through organized compassion to neighbors in need.

11.9 Intergenerational and Multicultural Fellowship

Elders, Adults, Youth, and Children Together (Deuteronomy 6:7; Psalm 78:4–6)

From the dawn of covenant life, God envisioned faith transmitted across generations. Deuteronomy 6 exhorts parents to teach God's commandments "when you sit in your house, and when you walk by the way, and when you lie down, and when you rise" (Deut 6:7), embedding spiritual formation in every family rhythm. Psalm 78 recounts how one generation shares God's deeds and statutes with the next, so that sons yet unborn might set their hope in God (Ps 78:4–6). In Christ's Body, this translates into congregations intentionally weaving elders, adults, youth, and children into shared worship and service. When grandparents pray aloud for toddlers, teenagers see faith's continuity; when children join praise teams, adults taste fresh awe. Gratitude for childhood prayers that shaped us motivates seasoned believers to invest in young lives today. Intergenerational events—worship services with multigenerational choirs, mission trips where teens serve alongside retirees, church picnics where stories of God's faithfulness flow as freely as lemonade—embody the truth that no age has a monopoly on God's insight. In such gatherings, diversity of experience becomes a tapestry of testimony, and each generation offers unique gifts to the Body.

Cross-Generational Mentoring and Discipleship (Titus 2:3–5; 2 Timothy 2:2)

Paul charges older women and men to teach younger counterparts in gospel virtues—"train the young women… and… exhort the young men" (Titus 2:3–5)—so that Christ's character ripens across ages. Likewise, he instructs Timothy to entrust teaching to "faithful men who will be able to teach others also" (2 Tim 2:2), establishing a chain of discipleship. Cross-generational mentoring pairs seasoned saints with emerging leaders, enabling wisdom to flow down and innovation to bubble up. Gratitude for mentors who guided our earliest faith steps compels us to pay it forward, investing time in regular coffee conversations, prayer phone calls, and life-on-life apprenticeships. Structured programs—"Adopt-a-Student," "Grandfriends," "Mentor-Mentee" cohorts—provide frameworks, but the core is relational presence: sharing highs, lows, and the Jesus who sustains both. When a teenager trusts a septuagenarian with doubts about God's plan, or a young pastor receives counsel on pastoral care from an elder, the church's apostolic roots deepen. Such intentional discipleship ensures that spiritual DNA is faithfully transmitted and adapted to each cultural moment.

Embracing Ethnic and Cultural Diversity in Christ (Revelation 7:9; Acts 10)

John's vision of a great multitude "from every nation, tribe, people, and language" standing before the Lamb (Rev 7:9) portrays the church as the most diverse family ever gathered. Peter's vision and subsequent baptism of Cornelius (Acts 10) shattered ethnic barriers, confirming that the gospel crosses all cultural thresholds. Churches that celebrate this diversity—through multilingual liturgies, cultural fairs, and shared meals—reflect heaven's panorama. Gratitude for early breakthroughs that welcomed Gentiles compels modern congregations to break down enclaves of sameness. Intentional steps—diverse worship teams, translation services, cultural competency workshops—ensure that everyone finds "a seat at the table." When children hear hymns in several languages, when adults pray alongside refugees and exchange stories of homeland, unity in Christ transcends national and ethnic identities. In these shared experiences, believers practice Revelation's vision, offering the world a living preview of a reconciled humanity praising the Lamb in glorious unity.

11.10 Digital and Distance Community

Online Gatherings and Zoom Communion

In an age when geographical barriers no longer confine fellowship, online gatherings have become vital extensions of church life. Video platforms like Zoom allow congregations to worship, pray, and even celebrate communion together across cities and continents, embodying Jesus' promise, "For where two or three are gathered in my name, there am I among them" (Matt 18:20). Gratitude for technological provision arises as homebound, traveling, or otherwise isolated believers join corporate worship, ensuring no one misses the means of grace. Establishing virtual communion protocols—sending elements ahead and sharing Christ's words simultaneously—reaffirms that the Lord's table transcends physical proximity. Churches leveraging tech invest in tutorials, technical support teams, and high-quality streaming to maintain excellence in digital worship. In these online sanctuaries, chat prayers, breakout rooms for fellowship, and live chats during sermons foster intimacy. Each pixelated face on-screen becomes a reminder that Christ's Body extends beyond brick and mortar, uniting all who thank Him for the gift of fellowship.

Virtual Small Groups and Prayer Chains

Small groups are the bloodstream of the church, and virtual versions ensure pulsations continue unabated. Through weekly video calls, members share life updates, pray over emerging needs, and study Scripture together, practicing "bearing one another's burdens" (Gal 6:2) even when thousands of miles apart. Gratitude for digital connectivity inspires creativity: themed prayer zooms, online book clubs, and text-based "prayer chains" where urgent needs cascade through phones. Leaders are trained in facilitating digital group dynamics—monitoring chat, encouraging muted microphones, and using online whiteboards for interactive Bible study. These gatherings often become lifelines for parents juggling childcare, professionals with irregular hours, or expatriates longing for spiritual home. Each virtual high-five, each screen-shared testimony, and each group "amen" testifies that distance cannot dilute the gospel's power to bind hearts.

Digital Discipleship: Apps, Podcasts, and Social Media

The smartphone has become the pew pocket of the 21st century, holding apps that remind us to pray, podcasts that feed us biblical teaching, and social media groups that sustain daily encouragement. Gratitude for these digital discipleship tools translates into church-endorsed recommendations, app-based Bible reading plans, and weekly podcast discussion groups. Pastors launch sermon–note apps where listeners can submit prayer requests, while Bible teachers host live Q&A on social platforms. Online mentorship platforms connect mature believers with seekers for one-on-one discipleship via video chat. Social media pages become daily devotion hubs, posting short reflections, gratitude prompts, and micro-sermons that caption daily struggles with gospel hope. When digital discipleship is integrated with in-person community—linking online prayer threads with Sunday prayer walls—the church maximizes its reach and nurtures continuous growth. Each download, stream, and share becomes an act of thanksgiving, leveraging modern channels to fulfill the timeless call: "teach them to observe all that I have commanded you" (Matt 28:20).

11.11 Overcoming Conflict and Building Reconciliation

Biblical Peacemaking Principles (Matthew 5:9; Romans 12:18)

Jesus opens the Sermon on the Mount by declaring, "Blessed are the peacemakers, for they shall be called sons of God" (Matt 5:9). Peacemaking here is active, not passive; it involves pursuing reconciliation amid broken relationships, injustices, and misunderstandings. Paul echoes this ethos when he urges believers, "If possible, so far as it depends on you, live peaceably with all" (Rom 12:18). These twin exhortations form the bedrock of Christian conflict resolution: peacemakers step into tension with humility, gentleness, and a posture of grace rather than pride. Gratitude for the Prince of Peace instills courage to initiate dialogue, listen without defensiveness, and seek mutual understanding. Practically, this means replacing harsh words with soft answers (Prov 15:1), choosing to forgive quickly (Eph 4:26–27), and offering blessing instead of retaliation (Rom 12:14). Churches that embed peacemaking in their culture train members in Matthew 18's four-step process, cultivate regular "peace labs" for role-playing reconciliation, and celebrate stories of restored relationships. Every forgiven slight and repented offense becomes a fresh opportunity to thank Jesus for His reconciling work and to mirror His mercy in human community.

Apology, Repentance, and Restitution Rituals

True reconciliation often requires ritualized steps that move hearts beyond mere words. Jesus outlines a restorative sequence: private confrontation, enlistment of witnesses, and—if necessary—public admonition (Matt 18:15–17). This pattern safeguards against gossip and ensures fairness. Beyond confrontation, genuine apology involves acknowledging specific wrongs, expressing sorrow, and requesting forgiveness—mirroring David's confession in Psalm 51. When relationships involve material harm, restitution becomes crucial: Zacchaeus pledged to repay fourfold what he had extorted (Luke 19:8), demonstrating that reconciliation often entails tangible repair. Gratitude for Christ's sacrificial atonement frees us to repent without fear, knowing our own debts are canceled (Col 2:13–14). Churches can facilitate these rituals through guided reconciliation services: trained mediators lead confessing parties through structured dialogue, prayer prayers, and symbolic acts such as returning an item or writing a letter of forgiveness. In these sacred spaces, apology transitions from awkward formality to a profound witness of gospel grace, prompting both reconciler and reconciled to exclaim, "Thank You, Jesus, for restoring what was broken."

Peacemaker Ministries and Reconciliation Workshops

Given conflict's inevitability in fallen societies, many denominations now sponsor specialized peacemaker ministries and reconciliation workshops. Organizations like Peacemaker Ministries and the Mennonite Central Committee train facilitators in biblical conflict resolution, active listening, and restorative justice. Workshops often combine teaching on Scripture's peacemaking mandates (Isa 1:17; James 3:17–18) with experiential exercises: role-play, case studies, and forgiveness ceremonies. Gratitude for these resources translates into church partnerships—hosting public seminars, equipping small-group leaders, and embedding reconciliation modules into membership classes. Certified peacemakers then serve as on-call mediators for congregational disputes, family estrangements, or community tensions. Churches report that when trained peacemakers intervene early, potential conflicts defuse before escalating into schisms. The ripple effect strengthens overall fellowship, as members learn not only to avoid harm but to actively pursue the peace Jesus promised. In this way, professionalized peacemaking ministries become extensions of the Church's call to proclaim good news to the afflicted and to bind up broken hearts (Isa 61:1).

11.12 Eschatological Fellowship—The Banquet of the Lamb

Anticipating the Marriage Supper (Revelation 19:6–9; 22:17)

John's vision of heaven crescendos in a great multitude crying, "Praise our God, all you his servants, you who fear him, small and great" (Rev 19:5). Then the heavenly host proclaims the marriage of the Lamb and His Bride, inviting all redeemed to the wedding feast (Rev 19:6–9). Later, the Spirit and the Bride jointly say, "Come!" offering the water of life to the thirsty (Rev 22:17). These passages weave a tapestry where fellowship culminates as intimate union and lavish celebration. Gratitude for our small foretaste—communion, fellowship meals, congregational feasts—stirs eager longing for the full banquet. Churches can rehearse this eschatological hope by crafting wedding-feast themed services, blessing marriages as signposts of Christ's union with the Church, and using celebratory liturgies that point beyond Sunday morning. Each shared loaf and cup anticipates the moment when sorrow and separation vanish, and the Bridegroom leads His guests into unending festivity. In this warm glow of future joy, present fellowship gains a horizon that transforms routine gatherings into sacred anticipation.

No More Tears, No More Partings (Revelation 21:3–4)

Revelation 21 unveils the New Creation where God dwells with His people and "wipes away every tear" (Rev 21:3–4). No longer will death, mourning, or separation mar relationships; the pain of loss yields to unbroken communion. Gratitude for this promise sustains fellowship through present grief—honoring those who have gone before at all-saints services, lighting candles in memory, and affirming the reunion hope. Churches that integrate "eternal life ceremonies" into funerals remind mourners that farewells are temporary. In small groups, reading Revelation 21 together and sharing testimonies of loved ones lost inspires both lament and celebration. Every tear shed in community becomes a seed of worship, as hearts cry out, "Thank You, Jesus, for the day when death itself will die." This eschatological perspective recasts loss not as final exile but as a brief interlude before the "great welcome home."

All Nations Gathered in Unity and Praise (Psalm 133; Isaiah 2:2–4)

Psalm 133 celebrates the beauty of brothers dwelling in unity: "how good and pleasant it is when God's people live together in unity!" (Ps 133:1). Isaiah prophesies a day when "many peoples shall come, and say, 'Come, let us go up to the mountain of the LORD'... and they shall beat their swords into plowshares" (Isa 2:2–4). Revelation echoes these themes—every tribe, tongue, and nation gathered around the throne (Rev 7:9). Gratitude for such diverse unity informs present mission: inviting refugees, engaging indigenous voices, and celebrating multi-ethnic worship. Worship services featuring global songs, communal prayers for world peace, and educational events on cultural reconciliation bring heaven's dinner table into earthly fellowship. Each embraced stranger, each translated hymn, and each cross-cultural collaboration becomes a brick in God's reconciled temple. When churches labor toward unity, they write thank-you notes to Jesus for inaugurating a fellowship that transcends every earthly barrier, pointing ahead to the day when every knee will bow and every voice shout praise to the Lamb.

Conclusion

Christian fellowship is no mere social club but the living embodiment of the gospel's power to unite sinners, heal divisions, and rehearse the eternal banquet prepared by Christ. From the Upper Room's first gathering to online small groups spanning continents, the Body of Christ grows through shared Word, sacraments, service, and song. Conflict-resolution frameworks, intergenerational mentoring, and digital ministries all serve one purpose: manifesting the love, grace, and unity Jesus purchased with His life. As we thank Him for the fellowship of believers, we acknowledge that our strength, joy, and spiritual growth flow inseparably from relationships knit by the Spirit. Every act of hospitality, every forgiven offense, every gift exercised in love stands as a note in the grand symphony of redemption. Until the day when every tear is wiped away and every tribe stands reconciled around the throne, may gratitude pulse through our communal life, echoing each moment: Thank You, Jesus, for the fellowship of believers—our family in You and for You, now and forever.

Chapter 12. Thank You, Jesus, for Purpose—Calling and Service

Every human heart longs to know that it matters—to understand that our days are not aimless wanderings but steps on a divinely charted path. In Christ, that longing finds its answer: we are not only forgiven sinners but also commissioned servants, "created in Christ Jesus for good works" which our Father prepared in advance for us to walk in (Ephesians 2:10). Our adoption into God's family secures our identity, and our assignment in His kingdom gives our lives meaning. To thank Jesus for purpose is to celebrate the dual gift of belonging and becoming—knowing that He has placed each of us where we can bear lasting fruit.

Across Scripture we see this calling unfold: Moses learns that leading God's people is more than a job, it is an encounter with the living God (Exodus 3); the prophets discover that speaking justice and mercy echoes heaven's heartbeat (Micah 6:8); and the Apostle Paul finds that tentmaking becomes an altar of witness to the gospel (Acts 18:3–4). Even now, the Spirit whispers direction through prayer, Scripture, and the counsel of godly friends (John 10:27; Proverbs 15:22).

As we explore the manifold dimensions of calling and service—from daily discipleship to global mission, from stewardship of time and talent to the grand vision of eternity—we will trace how Jesus shapes our ordinary tasks into kingdom impact.

12.1 Divine Calling and Commission

Chosen for Good Works (Ephesians 2 : 10)

From eternity the Father crafted a blueprint for each redeemed life, declaring that we are "his workmanship, created in Christ Jesus for good works, which God prepared beforehand" (Eph 2 : 10). The Greek term *poiēma*—work of art—means our very existence is a display piece of divine creativity. Salvation therefore is never an endpoint but a launching pad into pre-arranged pathways of service that reveal God's beauty to the world. Every assignment—whether composing symphonies, designing software, or tutoring a neighbor's child—becomes a brushstroke in the Artist's larger masterpiece. Gratitude awakens when we realize purpose is not something we must invent under pressure but a gift to be discovered in relationship with Christ. Daily prayer that whispers, "Thank You, Jesus, that my day is already filled with prepared works," turns commutes into commissions and laundry into liturgy. Even setbacks fit the design; God repurposes detours into testimonies that amplify His grace (Rom 8 : 28). As we walk in these works, we embody the gospel's claim that grace not only saves but also deploys.

From Adoption to Assignment — Our Dual Calling

Scripture presents a twofold summons: first *to belong* as beloved children, then *to be sent* as faithful servants. Paul reminds the Galatians that the Spirit cries "Abba, Father" in our hearts (Gal 4 : 6), grounding identity in adoption before activity. Yet the same Abba instantly involves His kids in family business: "As the Father has sent me, even so I am sending you" (John 20 : 21). This sequence prevents both performance-driven religion and passive complacency. Gratitude for adoption nurtures secure servants who labor from acceptance, not for it. Ministries that begin team meetings with five minutes of "identity declarations"—statements like *I am chosen, redeemed, empowered*—teach volunteers to serve from overflow. Conversely, meditating on our missional assignment intensifies appreciation for adoption; who are we that the King entrusts us with kingdom errands? Holding both truths in tension keeps purpose vibrant: sons and daughters who joyfully shoulder royal responsibilities.

Hearing God's Voice — Prayer, Scripture, and Counsel

Discovering concrete direction within God's overarching purpose involves tuning our ears to His multifaceted voice. Jesus promises that His sheep *hear* His voice and *follow* (John 10 : 27), implying relational attentiveness rather than mystical elitism. Primary guidance comes through Scripture, "a lamp to my feet" (Ps 119 : 105); verses leap alive, highlighting passions or warning against missteps. Prayer translates those impressions into dialogue: we lay plans before the Lord and sense either peace that surpasses understanding (Phil 4 : 7) or unrest that signals a red light. Wise counsel completes the triad; Proverbs insists plans succeed with many advisors (Prov 15 : 22). Gratitude for mentors, pastors, and discerning friends reminds us calling is discerned in community, not isolation. Keeping a journal of scriptural insights, prayer nudges, and counsel received becomes a chronicle of divine breadcrumbs, stirring thanksgiving each time patterns clarify. Over years these pages reveal a coherent story only the Author could script.

12.2 Spiritual Gifts and Vocation

Varieties of Gifts, Same Spirit (1 Corinthians 12)

Paul lists wisdom, knowledge, faith, healing, miracles, prophecy, discernment, tongues, and interpretation, insisting "one and the same Spirit" empowers all (1 Cor 12 : 4-11). This kaleidoscope of charisms ensures no believer is gift-less and no gift is superfluous. Gratitude blossoms when we stop comparing and start celebrating the Spirit's diverse artistry.

Like instruments in an orchestra, gifts achieve symphonic beauty only when played together under the Spirit's baton. Simple exercises—gift assessments, affirmation circles where peers name strengths they observe—help believers identify and embrace their God-given tools. Leaders then map ministries to gifts: administrators organize outreaches, mercy-givers run benevolence funds, teachers craft discipleship courses. Such alignment converts Sunday spectators into weekday ministers, proving that the pew is as strategic as the pulpit. Every time a hidden gift surfaces, the community echoes, "Thank You, Jesus, for equipping Your body so completely."

Aligning Gifts with God's Kingdom Goals

Spiritual gifts realize full impact when yoked to kingdom priorities: evangelism, edification, and societal renewal. Acts 6 models this alignment—administrative deacons ensure equitable food distribution, freeing apostles for prayer and the Word; the result is gospel expansion (Acts 6 : 1-7). Churches today replicate this by drafting "mission matrices" that list core objectives down one axis and member gifts across another, visually matching people to purposes. Gratitude fuels willingness to deploy gifts outside comfort zones, trusting that the Spirit who empowers also sustains (1 Pet 4 : 11). Annual "dream-with-God" workshops invite members to envision how their passions—coding, cooking, counseling—could solve local problems. Stories of alignment—an accountant revolutionizing church budgeting, a gardener launching a community plot—reinforce that vocation and kingdom need are not competing forces but converging callings.

Marketplace as Mission Field

Paul made tents in Corinth while reasoning in synagogues (Acts 18 : 3-4), exemplifying how secular work can advance sacred mission. Colossians 3 : 23 commands, "Whatever you do, work heartily, as for the Lord," converting cubicles and classrooms into pulpits. Christians in medicine see each patient as an image-bearer; engineers design with stewardship in mind; baristas offer listening ears with lattes.

Gratitude for God's placement—*Thank You, Jesus, for sending me to this office*—transforms Monday blues into kingdom opportunities. Workplace prayer huddles, lunchtime Bible studies, and ethical excellence evangelize peers long before formal sermons. Marketplace apostles build bridges to church, inviting colleagues to explore faith through alpha courses or service projects. Thus, vocation and ministry intertwine like warp and weft, weaving witnesses into every sector of society.

12.3. Discipleship as Daily Calling

Deny Self and Take Up the Cross (Mark 8:34)

Jesus issued a startling charge to His followers: "If anyone would come after me, let him deny himself and take up his cross and follow me" (Mark 8:34). To deny self is to refuse the tyranny of comfort, ambition, or personal preference when they conflict with Christ's will. Yet the cross was a symbol not only of death but of obedience and ultimate service, showing that discipleship carries both cost and dignity. Gratitude for the Savior's own self-denial—His "emptying" of divine privilege for our sake (Phil 2:7)—makes our willingness to bear lesser burdens a joyful honor. In practical terms, daily cross-bearing can look like choosing prayer over panic, sacrificial time spent with family over personal leisure, or truth-telling in love instead of convenient silence. Spiritual rhythms—morning examen, prayer walks, confession journals—help us recognize cross-bearing moments and offer them back to Jesus in thanksgiving. Each small refusal of impulse, each embrace of sacrificial service, becomes a living echo of the Master's own path, and stirs the heart to exclaim, "Thank You, Jesus, for calling me to follow You—even to the cross."

Abide in Christ for Fruitfulness (John 15)

In John 15, Jesus depicts Himself as the true vine and His disciples as branches: "Abide in me, and I in you. As the branch cannot bear fruit by itself, unless it abides in the vine, neither can you, unless you abide in me" (John 15:4). Abiding is not a one-time event but a continual, moment-by-moment communion—praying, meditating on Scripture, and practicing gratitude. When we rest in His love ("As the Father has loved me, so have I loved you," John 15:9), our lives naturally blossom in ways that honor Him. Gratitude fuels our abiding: remembering past answered prayers or mercies received draws our hearts back to the vine whenever they wander. Spiritual practices such as breath prayers ("Jesus, I trust You") or simple morning worship playlists become lifelines connecting us to Christ throughout busy days. Fruit of the Spirit—love, joy, peace—then emerges not from human effort but from organic life in the vine (Gal 5:22–23). Each kindness shown, each moment of self-control, and each word of encouragement testifies that we have indeed remained in the fruitful vine, prompting the church to rejoice and say, "Thank You, Jesus, for producing Your good fruit in us."

Counting the Cost: Commitment Over Comfort

Jesus warned that following Him could cost families, fortunes, even lives: "Whoever does not bear his own cross and come after me cannot be my disciple" (Luke 14:27). Yet He also illustrated that any worthwhile endeavor requires calculation: a builder estimates cost before laying a foundation (Luke 14:28–30). Discipleship is thus a deliberate covenant, not a casual club. Gratitude for Jesus' lavish commitment—leaving glory, enduring shame, conquering death—empowers us to count costs without flinching. Church communities can assist this countdown by offering "discipleship retreats" where participants prayerfully assess their commitments and receive counsel. When believers publicly pledge time, talents, and resources in covenant services, they celebrate commitment over comfort and encourage one another to press on. Each renewal of vows—whether at a church anniversary or personal milestone—becomes a sacrament of dedication, and inspires collective thanksgiving: "Thank You, Jesus, for calling me to walk the hard yet most rewarding path."

12.4 Models of Service in Scripture

Moses and Tabernacle Ministry

Moses' calling began with a burning bush but found its fullest expression in leading Israel and overseeing Tabernacle worship (Exodus 3; 35–40). Though initially reluctant, Moses embraced God's commission to mediate between a stubborn people and holy God. He organized skilled artisans, instituted sacrificial rites, and maintained the congregation's spiritual life through wilderness decades. Gratitude for Moses' obedience stirs appreciation for the unseen, administrative facets of ministry—logistics, conflict resolution, worship planning—that are vital for God's purposes. Modern "Moses types" include church administrators, operations directors, and lay leaders whose service undergirds every pulpit moment. Recognizing and thanking these servants—through public affirmation, paid stipends, or simple "thank you" notes—honors the biblical pattern that every act of organization is an act of worship.

Prophets' Prophetic Service

Prophets in Israel—Elijah, Isaiah, Amos—served God by calling the nation back to covenant faithfulness, often at great personal cost. Their ministry involved speaking hard truths, foretelling judgment, yet also proclaiming hope of restoration. Gratitude for their courage reminds us that prophetic service remains essential in the church: confronting injustice, upholding biblical ethics, and envisioning God's future. Today's prophetic ministers may emerge as social justice advocates, authors, or outspoken pastors who call both church and culture to righteousness. Equipping prophetic voices through training in biblical preaching and pastoral sensitivity ensures their messages build up rather than tear down (1 Cor 14:3). When congregations receive prophetic insight in prayer nights or public forums—with humility and discernment—they participate in the timeless call to "declare to his people their transgression" and offer "the way of peace" (Isa 57:19). Every spoken word that convicts, corrects, and consoles becomes a conduit of God's prophetic service, inspiring hearts to say, "Thank You, Jesus, for calling us to speak Your truth in love."

Jesus, the Servant–King Washing Feet (John 13)

On the eve of His passion, Jesus took on the towel of a slave, washing the disciples' feet and commanding, "You also ought to wash one another's feet" (John 13:14). This radical inversion—Lord as servant—redefined greatness in God's kingdom as humble service. Gratitude for Jesus' example empowers believers to embrace lowly tasks—parking cars, scrubbing dishes, mentoring the troubled—as sacred ministry. Churches can ritualize foot-washing services to reenact this lesson, inviting members to both serve and be served. In everyday life, recognizing foot-washing opportunities means noticing unnoticed needs: a hospital corridor, a school hallway, a corporate office. Each gesture of humble care echoes the King's own fleshly humility and prompts mutual thanksgiving: "Thank You, Jesus, for teaching us that true leadership is found in serving." Through such incarnational acts, Jesus' servant-king rule continues to overturn power structures and bind His Body in bonds of love and gratitude.

12.5 Servant Leadership and Church Roles

Elders and Deacons: Shepherds and Servants (1 Timothy 3; Titus 1)

Scripture appoints elders (also called overseers or pastors) and deacons as formal leaders to shepherd the flock and manage practical needs. Paul's qualifications for elders stress character and competence: "able to teach," "self-controlled," "respectable," and "manages his own household well" (1 Tim 3:2–5). Deacons, though often serving behind the scenes, must be "worthy of respect, sincere, not indulging in much wine… holding the mystery of the faith with a clear conscience" (1 Tim 3:8–9). Gratitude for these servant-leaders arises when we recognize that their oversight and care flow from Christ, the Good Shepherd (John 10:11). Through elders' teaching, counseling, and pastoral visits, the church experiences the hands of Jesus extending healing and guidance. Deacons ensure that practical ministry—hospitality, benevolence, facility care—operates smoothly, reflecting God's provision. Churches that publicly affirm and pray for their leaders foster a culture of appreciation, reminding elected servants that their labor is seen by the Lord (Heb 13:17). Each qualification fulfilled and task carried out becomes an occasion to say, "Thank You, Jesus, for raising up leaders who model Your heart."

The Priesthood of All Believers (1 Peter 2:9)

Peter proclaims, "You are a chosen race, a royal priesthood, a holy nation," declaring that all Christians share in priestly ministry (1 Pet 2:9). This priesthood means every believer can approach God directly "by one Spirit" (Eph 2:18), offering spiritual sacrifices of praise, service, and witness (Heb 13:15–16). Gratitude for this universal access breaks down laity-clergy barriers, empowering every disciple to intercede, teach, and serve in the community. In practice, churches uphold this truth by providing training for lay ministry—hospitality teams, neighborhood outreach, children's teaching—recognizing each act of service as priestly worship. Celebrating testimonies from non-staff members highlights the Body's corporate priesthood. When congregations cover one another in prayer, share communion responsibilities, and mentor emerging leaders, they live out the truth that no part of the Body is redundant. Each baptized member thus celebrates the privilege of priesthood, responding to Christ's call with thanksgiving for the gift of ministry to others.

Mentoring the Next Generation of Leaders

Paul's instruction to Timothy—"What you have heard from me in the presence of many witnesses entrust to faithful men who will be able to teach others also" (2 Tim 2:2)—establishes mentoring as a key leadership pipeline. This multigenerational relay ensures the gospel's transmission and the church's enduring health. Gratitude for mentors from our own journeys compels seasoned believers to invest time and wisdom in younger disciples. Effective mentoring relationships blend formal apprenticeship—in preaching, pastoral care, administration—with informal support: coffee dates, crisis counseling, and prayer partnerships. Churches can structure "mentor cohorts" pairing established elders or ministry heads with aspiring leaders, including regular feedback loops and observation opportunities. Celebrating milestones—first sermon delivered, first outreach led—acknowledges progress and spurs further growth. As mentors and mentees rejoice in shared victories and labor through challenges together, the fellowship witnesses the living out of Christ's promise that He remains with His church "to the end of the age" (Matt 28:20).

12.6 Mission and the Great Commission

Go, Make Disciples of All Nations (Matthew 28:18–20)

With resurrection authority, Jesus commissions the church: "Go therefore and make disciples of all nations, baptizing them... teaching them to observe all that I have commanded you" (Matt 28:19–20). This mandate carries urgency and scope—from local streets to global unreached people groups. Gratitude for the risen Lord's presence ("I am with you always") fuels courage to cross cultural and comfort boundaries. Discipleship begins with invitation—sharing personal stories of Christ's work—and flows into intentional teaching, mentoring, and community integration. Churches respond by supporting missionaries, hosting cross-cultural teams, and integrating global vision into Sunday services. Training in gospel presentation, cultural sensitivity, and contextual theology ensures that "making disciples" respects diverse backgrounds while maintaining doctrinal fidelity. As congregations commission and send out workers—praying over them and tracking progress—they embody a grateful obedience to the Great Commission's call.

Contextualizing the Gospel in Culture

Paul became "all things to all people" to win some for Christ (1 Cor 9:22), demonstrating gospel flexibility without theological compromise. Contextualization means understanding local customs, languages, and worldviews to present the gospel in intelligible, relevant forms. Gratitude for the Spirit's guidance in missions encourages cross-cultural training, language learning programs, and partnerships with indigenous churches. Modern missionaries leverage ethnographic research, local artistic expressions, and technology—radio, apps, social media—to bridge cultural divides. Domestic churches likewise contextualize: worship songs in diverse musical styles, youth ministries that engage contemporary issues, and outreach methods tailored to urban or rural settings. Each well-crafted translation of Scripture or culturally appropriate ministry model becomes an act of thanksgiving for Christ's universal lordship over all nations.

Partnering in Global and Local Mission

Effective mission involves collaboration between sending churches, NGOs, and local believers. Acts 13:2–3 models this synergy—Antioch's church worships and fasts together before sending Barnabas and Paul on their first journey. Gratitude for cooperative mission stirs churches to form networks—citywide alliances, cross-denominational task forces, international partner summits. Shared resources—funds, personnel, training facilities—maximize impact and prevent duplication. Local congregations engage in "short-term" trips that equip rather than consume, under the mentorship of local leaders. Reciprocal visits, video conferences, and joint projects sustain relationships beyond the initial launch. Each fruit of partnership—new church plants, relief distributions, theological education centers—rises as collective thanksgiving to Jesus, who designed His Body to serve and witness together across the globe and around the corner.

12.7 Stewardship of Time, Talent, and Treasure

Talents as Trusts (Parable of the Talents)

Jesus told the parable of a master who entrusted his servants with his wealth "each according to his ability" (Matt 25:15). One received five talents, another two, and another one; the first two invested and doubled their amounts, while the third hid his in the ground and returned only the original (Matt 25:16–18). When the master returned, he commended the faithful stewards—"Well done, good and faithful servant. You have been faithful over a little; I will set you over much" (Matt 25:21). This story reframes talents—originally coins—as metaphors for every gift and opportunity God entrusts us with, from waking hours to spiritual abilities. Gratitude for Jesus' commendation motivates us to invest every resource he gives—our time, abilities, and finances—into kingdom expansion. Each morning we ask, "Lord, how shall I multiply what You've given me today?" Practically, this can look like scheduling solid blocks for prayer, offering mentoring hours, or using personal skills to serve local ministries. As we steward these trusts faithfully, we echo the master's joy in seeing fruit born from our grateful obedience.

Budgeting for Kingdom Impact

Biblical stewardship involves intentional planning of our finances so that generosity toward God's purposes is not an afterthought but a priority. Paul instructs the Corinthians to set aside "on the first day of every week" a sum in keeping with one's prosperity (1 Cor 16:2), modeling a disciplined, proportional approach. Proverbs commends the diligent planner: "The plans of the diligent lead surely to abundance, but everyone who is hasty comes only to poverty" (Prov 21:5). Gratitude for Christ's provision propels us to create budgets that allocate a percentage for giving—tithes, benevolence, missionary support—alongside savings and essential expenses. Faithful budgeting can involve church-led workshops teaching envelope systems or digital apps that track "kingdom accounts." Churches that publish annual impact reports showing how collective giving advances justice projects, church plants, or relief efforts foster a culture of transparent stewardship. When members see the fruit of pooled resources—clean water wells sunk, refugees housed—they rejoice together, affirming, "Thank You, Jesus, for providing through our generosity."

Volunteering: Sacrificial Service in Community

Mark reminds us that Jesus came "not to be served but to serve, and to give his life as a ransom for many" (Mark 10:45). Volunteering echoes this servant heart, as believers offer time and effort without expectation of pay or acclaim. Gratitude for Christ's sacrificial service fuels our willingness to roll up sleeves—teaching Sunday school, serving meals at shelters, painting community centers. Volunteer programs that match individual passions—culinary skills in community kitchens, counseling expertise in crisis hotlines—ensure that service is both effective and fulfilling. Churches can host annual "service fairs" where nonprofits present volunteer opportunities, inspiring members to commit hours for local impact. Each act of sacrificial service becomes an embodied prayer: "Lord, I thank You for saving me; let me serve others in Your name." Over time, a robust volunteer culture weaves the church into the fabric of its community, demonstrating that Jesus' love never remained theoretical but overflowed in tangible deeds.

12.8 Perseverance and Renewal in Service

Running with Endurance (Hebrews 12:1–3)

Hebrews exhorts believers to "run with endurance the race that is set before us" and to "look to Jesus, the founder and perfecter of our faith" (Heb 12:1–2). Service, like a long-distance race, requires stamina, proper pacing, and focus on the finish line rather than the weariness of the moment. Gratitude for Jesus' own endurance—"enduring the cross… for the joy that was set before him" (Heb 12:2)—motivates us to press on through fatigue, discouragement, or opposition. Spiritual practices such as communal encouragement, periodic goal-setting reviews, and "perseverance prayer circles" sustain servants' resolve. Sharing stories of past faithfulness helps refill our "joy reservoirs," enabling us to run the next lap. When church volunteers weary or staff feel burnout, recalling the race's eternal prize—crowns of righteousness—rekindles commitment. Each step taken in steadfast service becomes an affirmation: "Thank You, Jesus, for modeling patient endurance and empowering me to finish well."

Rest and Sabbath Rhythms for Servants

Even servants need rest: God instituted Sabbath rest for creation's good (Exod 20:8–11) and beckoned Jesus' weary disciples to "come away... and rest a while" (Mark 6:31). Regular rhythms of rest protect servants from burnout and keep hearts fresh for ministry. Gratitude for God's own rest (Gen 2:2) encourages us to carve out weekly sabbaths or monthly retreats where no ministry tasks are performed. Churches can model this by ensuring ministers take sabbaticals, by organizing "rest retreats" for volunteers, and by teaching the theology of rest in congregational workshops. Practical measures—sabbatical policies, volunteer rotation, sabbath-themed services—emphasize rest as divine gift rather than optional extra. When servants return from rest enriched, their renewed passion and creativity bless the entire community, prompting collective thanksgiving for rhythms that mirror Creator and Redeemer.

Rekindling Passion Through Retreat and Renewal

Throughout His ministry, Jesus withdrew periodically—to solitary hills (Mark 6:46), to desert places (Luke 5:16)—to pray and recharge. Similarly, intentional retreats for service leaders and volunteers foster spiritual renewal and vision recasting. Gratitude for these sabbatical moments leads churches to offer annual "retreat grants" or host regional renewal conferences featuring worship, teaching, and solitude. Structured retreat agendas include guided reflections on call, times of silence for listening to God's voice, and creative workshops for ministry innovation. Participants often return with rekindled passion, fresh insights into community needs, and renewed commitment to sacrificial service. When testimonies of changed perspectives and revitalized ministries fill post-retreat gatherings, the Body celebrates what the Spirit accomplishes when servants pause to be refilled. Each retreat becomes a living testimonial: "Thank You, Jesus, for leading me into seasons of renewal that sustain a lifetime of service."

12.9 Community Engagement and Social Witness

Doing Justice and Loving Mercy (Micah 6:8)

Micah's succinct summons—"to do justice, and to love kindness, and to walk humbly with your God" (Mic 6:8)—captures the heart of gospel-driven social engagement. Justice here extends beyond charity to systemic fairness: advocating for the oppressed, challenging exploitation, and ensuring that laws and practices protect the vulnerable. Loving mercy personalizes justice by emphasizing compassion: feeding the hungry, visiting the lonely, and extending grace to those society shuns. Walking humbly undergirds both, reminding us that our own deliverance came by grace, not merit. Congregations express this triad through community legal clinics, restorative justice programs, and partnerships with fair-trade enterprises. Gratitude for Jesus' own commitment to the marginalized—He preached good news to the poor and set captives free (Luke 4:18)—animates participation. As members witness refugees welcomed, ex-offenders rehabilitated, and children mentored, they join Micah's chorus: "Thank You, Jesus, for calling us to justice and mercy as integral to our faith."

Hospitality to the Stranger and Poor (Matthew 25:35)

In the judgment scene of Matthew 25, Jesus equates caring for "the least of these" with serving Himself: "I was a stranger and you welcomed me, I was hungry and you fed me" (Matt 25:35). Hospitality here transcends hospitality as we know it; it is a sacramental practice, embodying Christ's own welcome. Churches that turn open doors into gospel outposts equip members to host homeless families, intern volunteers from other countries, and build community through shared meals. Gratitude for our own reception into God's family inspires radical generosity: spare rooms become guest quarters, tables extend for neighborhood feasts, and kitchens become places of belonging. Threefold training in cultural sensitivity, safety protocols, and reverent service ensures that hospitality is both warm and wise. When a newcomer finds sanctuary in a stranger's home and meets Jesus in human kindness, the community rejoices, echoing the welcome of our heavenly Father.

Advocacy, Relief, and Development

Biblical fellowship calls believers into advocacy not only for individuals but also for societal structures. The prophets denounced exploitative practices; Jesus healed systemic ailments of religious hypocrisy; the early church redistributed wealth for communal flourishing. Modern churches express this prophetic impulse through campaigns against human trafficking, coalitions lobbying for criminal-justice reform, and relief efforts in disaster zones. Development work—microfinance, clean-water projects, mentorship in entrepreneurship—addresses root causes of poverty. Gratitude for Christ's redemptive work impels churches to invest resources and prayer into long-term community transformation, not only quick fixes. By collaborating with NGOs, government agencies, and local leaders, believers ensure sustainable impact. Each policy shift influenced, each community rebuilt, and each life lifted from despair stands as thanksgiving incarnate to the One who came to proclaim liberty to captives (Luke 4:18).

12.10 Collaboration, Teams, and Networks

The Body of Christ in Action (1 Corinthians 12:12–27)

Paul's "one body" metaphor underscores that the church's mission requires coordinated action: "If one member suffers, all suffer together; if one member is honored, all rejoice together" (1 Cor 12:26). Teams within the church mirror biological organs, each performing unique but interdependent functions. Outreach teams, worship bands, children's ministries, and administrative groups collaborate under the Spirit's governance to advance the gospel. Regular "team huddles" and joint planning retreats foster mutual understanding and shared vision. Gratitude for this interconnection leads members to honor unseen roles—sound technicians, greeters, prayer intercessors—as vital to the Body's health. When one team celebrates a breakthrough, others join in, reflecting the gospel's communal heartbeat.

Inter-Church Partnerships and Missions

No congregation exists in isolation; New Testament churches supported one another across regions (Philippi sent gifts to Paul, 2 Cor 8–9). Today, healthy network churches pool resources for church planting, mission trips, and theological education. Such partnerships—between suburban and urban, majority-world and Western congregations—mobilize broader expertise and foster cross-pollination of ideas. Gratitude for the global Body spurs these alliances, transforming competition into cooperation. Joint conferences, shared online platforms, and reciprocal pastor exchanges deepen unity. When churches co-sponsor relief efforts or community centers, they model the universal fellowship Jesus prayed for (John 17:21), magnifying thanksgiving across cultural and geographic divides.

Bridge-Building Across Denominations

Ecclesial unity, though tested by doctrinal differences, finds expression in collaborative endeavors—worship festivals, service projects, public prayer gatherings—where believers from varied traditions serve side by side. Acts of service and witness under shared banners of compassion often pave the way for theological dialogue. Gratitude for the common ground of Christ's lordship (Phil 2:10–11) motivates denominations to recognize each other's strengths and learn from distinct emphases. Formal ecumenical bodies, pastoral councils, and city-wide coalitions institutionalize this bridge-building. As churches from different backgrounds join hands to combat poverty or host prayer at city hall, they give the world a powerful sign of the reconciled fellowship Jesus purchased, prompting collective praise: "Thank You, Jesus, for knitting Your Body into one family."

12.11 Vision Casting and Discipleship Pathways

Articulating a Compelling Vision

Healthy fellowships are propelled by a clear, inspiring vision of what God is calling them to become and to do. Nehemiah galvanized rebuilding by sharing a vivid blueprint and inviting volunteers to "come and let us rebuild" (Neh 2:18). Similarly, church leaders must cast visions rooted in Scripture—planting 100 churches, feeding a million meals, raising up disciples who multiply spiritual families. Gratitude for Jesus' ultimate vision—the consummation of all things—grounds local dreams in eternal perspective. Voting on mission statements, creating visual mission walls, and rehearsing testimonies of vision-led miracles keep the fellowship's goals fresh in members' minds. When congregations collectively dream under God's leading, each department—from children's ministry to global mission—finds coherence, and hearts echo, "Thank You, Jesus, for the adventure of advancing Your kingdom."

Small-Group and One-on-One Discipleship

Vision without pathways stagnates. Paul's model—"the things you have heard from me… entrust to faithful men who will teach others also" (2 Tim 2:2)—translates into layered discipleship: large-group worship stirring vision, small groups contextualizing it, and one-on-one mentoring internalizing it. Gratitude for mentors and peers who invested time ensures that every believer can engage in growth relationships. Churches resource small-group coaches, train discussion facilitators, and match mentors with mentees based on gifts and season of life. Curriculum leverages Bible-based studies, spiritual disciplines, and mission projects to move from head knowledge to heart transformation. When small groups celebrate baptisms, new ministries launched, or lives rescued from bondage, they manifest effective pathways and give thanks to Jesus who multiplies disciples through relational chains.

Measuring Fruit: Growth and Multiplication

Jesus tracked apostolic fruit by how many disciples a ministry produced—"you will be my witnesses" (Acts 1:8), not by program attendance. Similarly, churches assess health by lives transformed, small groups multiplied, new churches planted, and communities served. Gratitude for every incremental breakthrough—an unbeliever converted, a mentor commissioned, a program launched—shifts focus from budgets to kingdom outcomes. Data dashboards showcasing worship attendance, outreach contacts, and spiritual-growth metrics help members see gospel impact. Annual reports that spotlight stories and statistics together foster transparency and thanksgiving. When leaders review metrics in prayer, they celebrate God's faithfulness and recalibrate strategies under the Spirit's guidance. This balanced approach ensures vision remains rooted in both faith and fruit.

12.12 Eschatological Purpose and Eternal Rewards

Living with the End in Mind (2 Corinthians 4:18)

Paul urges believers to fix their gaze "not on what is seen…but on what is unseen. For what is seen is transient, but what is unseen is eternal" (2 Cor 4:18). This eternal perspective anchors purpose in God's unchanging kingdom rather than in shifting cultural values. Gratitude for future glory fuels present endurance: service fatigue bows before the promise of "an eternal weight of glory" (2 Cor 4:17). Churches embed this vision through sermon series on hope, art installations depicting new-creation imagery, and liturgies that recount the ultimate victory. When congregants rehearse eternity in worship, they gain fresh resolve to invest in temporal tasks with eternal significance.

Crowns of Service (1 Peter 5:4; 2 Timothy 4:8)

Scripture speaks of "the crown of glory that never fades" for faithful shepherds (1 Pet 5:4) and "the crown of righteousness" for those longing for Christ's appearing (2 Tim 4:8). These metaphoric rewards honor sacrificial service and steadfast faith. Gratitude for such promises incentivizes perseverance: pastors lead without craving accolades, knowing that heavenly commendation outweighs earthly approval. Lay leaders serve kitchens, classrooms, and counseling rooms with the same diligence, motivated by reward that "fadeth not away." Churches can celebrate retirements and farewells by reading these texts, blessing outgoing servants with prayer and symbolic crowns, reinforcing that every act of faithfulness contributes to eternal reward.

The Marriage Supper and the Servants' Inheritance (Revelation 19:9)

Revelation's "marriage supper of the Lamb" (Rev 19:9) portrays the ultimate fellowship, where servants of God partake in the consummation of redemption. The Book of Revelation proclaims that those who "keep the commandments of God and the faith of Jesus" will dine at this heavenly feast (Rev 22:14). Gratitude for this eternal banquet reshapes earthly service into rehearsal dinners, anticipating the final celebration. Communion services and Lord's Day meals thus become appetizers to the grand feast, filling hearts with joy beyond present trials. When churches craft liturgies that weave in this eschatological hope—candles, festal garments, celebratory hymns—they help congregants live in the tension of "already, but not yet." Each shared meal, each act of service, becomes a down payment on the inheritance awaiting God's faithful servants.

Conclusion

Purpose in Christ transcends mere ambition; it is a gracious invitation to co-labor with the living Lord who gifted us new life for the sake of others. From the inauguration of our divine calling to the consummation of eternal feasts, every step of service reflects Christ's handiwork. Spiritual gifts, vocational roles, sacrificial offerings of time and treasure, and collaborative networks all testify that God's grand design unfolds through communal obedience. As we steward resources, endure trials, and cast vision for future generations, gratitude remains the wellspring of our motivation: thanking Jesus for assigning us tasks that uncover His glory, strengthen His Body, and bless a broken world. May each chapter of service we write be an offering of praise, resonating with the eternal chorus of redeemed souls who ever declare, "Worthy is the Lamb, for You were slain, and by Your service we live."

Chapter 13. Thank You, Jesus, for Your Kingdom—Reign of Justice and Mercy

From Genesis' first promise of a seed to crush the serpent (Gen 3:15) to Revelation's vision of a throne where justice and mercy reign side by side (Rev 21:3–4), the Bible unfolds one grand story: the coming and consummation of God's kingdom. This kingdom is neither foreign nor future alone—it broke into history in Jesus of Nazareth, whose life, death, and resurrection inaugurated a rule characterized by righteousness and compassion. Yet the kingdom is also "already and not yet": its values and power are present through the Spirit even as we await full expression at Christ's return. To thank Jesus for Your kingdom is to praise Him for this reign of justice that rights wrongs, the mercy that forgives sins, and the hope that sustains us amid present brokenness. As we explore prophetic promises, gospel proclamations, ethical demands, community expressions, and eschatological visions, may our hearts grow in gratitude for the King whose scepter brings healing, whose throne upholds the lowly, and whose table welcomes all.

13.1 Kingdom in Prophecy and Promise

Ancient Promises of a Davidic King (2 Samuel 7; Isaiah 9)

God's covenant with David established that his offspring would sit upon an unending throne: "Your house and your kingdom shall be made sure forever before me. Your throne shall be established forever" (2 Sam 7:16). Centuries later, Isaiah elaborated that this heir would be called "Wonderful Counselor, Mighty God, Everlasting Father, Prince of Peace" (Isa 9:6), assuring Israel that political stability would flow from divine personhood. These ancient promises intertwined royalty with deity, foreshadowing a Messiah who would extend God's reign beyond territory into every human heart. Gratitude for Jesus as the fulfillment of David's line and Isaiah's vision surfaces in worship that blends royal acclamation with humble adoration. When we sing "All hail King Jesus," we echo the same wonder that amazed Israel's prophets: the transcendent God bringing His kingdom to earth. The Davidic covenant's permanence reminds us that even when earthly regimes falter, Christ's kingdom stands immutable, prompting thankful trust amid political upheaval.

Suffering Servant as Kingdom Bringer (Isaiah 53)

Isaiah's portrait of the Suffering Servant—in verses that Matthew applies to Jesus (Matt 8:17)—reveals unexpected kingdom dynamics: the King triumphs by bearing griefs and carrying sorrows (Isa 53:4). Instead of a conquering general, God's ruler appears as a rejected man acquainted with suffering (Isa 53:3), whose wounds purchase our healing and whose scourging restores our peace. This paradox links justice and mercy: the Servant bears divine wrath against sin so that sinners receive mercy instead of judgment. Gratitude deepens as we contemplate the cross not merely as a tragic event but as the very moment the kingdom's power redeemed creation's curse. Every time we reflect on Christ's silent submission "like a lamb that is led to the slaughter" (Isa 53:7), our hearts respond with awe and thanksgiving that through suffering, the King has made a way for us to enter His rule of grace.

The New Covenant and Everlasting Throne (Jeremiah 31; Ezekiel 37)

Jeremiah foretold a new covenant: "I will put my law within them, and I will write it on their hearts. And I will be their God, and they shall be my people" (Jer 31:33). Ezekiel envisioned dry bones revived and united by the Spirit (Ezek 37:1–14), symbolizing a people restored under one shepherd and one king (Ezek 37:24–25). These prophecies promise not only a Davidic ruler but an indwelling rule—God's justice and mercy internalized rather than merely legislated. Gratitude for this internal kingdom surges when we sense the Spirit convicting of sin and empowering obedience, testifying that Christ now reigns within us. Communion itself enacts this promise: as we eat bread and drink cup, we welcome Christ's reign into our bodies and communities. Ultimately, these new covenant assurances remind us that the King's throne endures forever because it rests on the immovable foundation of God's own faithfulness rather than human performance.

13.2 Jesus' Kingdom: Inauguration and Invitation

"The Time Is Fulfilled..."—Proclaiming the Kingdom (Mark 1:15)

When Jesus opened His public ministry, He declared, "The time is fulfilled, and the kingdom of God is at hand; repent and believe in the gospel" (Mark 1:15). This ushers in a decisive kairos moment—God's appointed hour—when heaven's rule breaks into human history. Rather than a distant future hope, the kingdom arrives in the person of the Messiah, demanding a response of repentance. Gratitude wells up at the thought that Jesus not only announced the kingdom but embodied it, calling us into dynamic relationship rather than passive observation. His call to repent—change one's mind and direction—signals that participation in the kingdom involves a daily turning toward God's reign. Believing the gospel means trusting that evil's hold is broken and that Jesus' authority overflows into every corner of our lives. As crowds flocked to hear Him, we too "flock" to His word with thankful hearts, knowing that the kingdom's inauguration promises restoration for all creation.

Parables of the Hidden Treasure and Pearl (Matthew 13:44–46)

To illustrate the inestimable value of God's kingdom, Jesus likens it first to a hidden treasure in a field, then to a pearl of great price (Matt 13:44–46). In both parables, the seeker sells all to possess what was worth infinitely more than any earthly gain. Gratitude saturates these images: once we "find" the kingdom—Christ Himself—we gladly surrender lesser pursuits without regret. The hidden-treasure motif reminds us that the kingdom often lies beneath mundane routines and unpromising ground, discovered by those who diligently search Scripture and prayer. The pearl teaches that aesthetic beauty and moral goodness in God's reign surpass every human-crafted treasure. Our thankfulness should move us to forsake distractions—status, wealth, comfort—to claim the kingdom's full joy. Ministry efforts that invite seekers to taste small "pearl" experiences—like authentic community or answered prayer—echo these parables, urging all to count the cost and follow Jesus wholeheartedly.

Miracles as Kingdom Breakthroughs (Luke 11:20; Matthew 12:28)

Jesus' miracles were not mere wonders but signs that heaven's reign was invading earth's realm. He proclaimed, "If I cast out demons by the finger of God, then the kingdom of God has come upon you" (Luke 11:20), and Matthew adds that His exorcisms demonstrated "the Spirit of God" breaking sin's power (Matt 12:28). Each healing—restored sight, cleansed leper, raised dead—displayed kingdom justice (victory over disease) and mercy (compassion for sufferers). Gratitude for these displays of divine authority inspires us to pray for kingdom breakthroughs today—physical healings, deliverance from oppression, and social transformation. When communities witness food multiplied or clean water flowing, they glimpse the same kingdom power at work. Our own stories of rescue from addiction or despair become modern-day miracles, fueling thankfulness and bold testimony. As we pray and serve, we stand on the foundation of Christ's miraculous inauguration, trusting that His kingdom continues to expand by Spirit-wrought power.

13.3 Kingdom Ethics: Justice, Mercy, and Humility

Sermon on the Mount as Kingdom Constitution (Matthew 5–7)

Jesus' Sermon on the Mount reads like a constitution for kingdom citizens, defining the character and conduct expected under His rule. Blessed are the poor in spirit, the merciful, the peacemakers (Matt 5:3–9)—not the powerful or self-sufficient. He raises the moral bar above external conformity to internal transformation: anger equates to murder, lust to adultery (Matt 5:21–28). Gratitude for these standards grows as we recognize they do not enslave but secure our flourishing under a just and loving King. The Lord's Prayer (Matt 6:9–13) situates us daily before our Father's throne, pleading for kingdom will and daily provision together. "Seek first the kingdom... and all these things will be added" (Matt 6:33) reorients ambition from self-promotion to divine purposes. Practicing these ethics—purity, generosity, non-retaliation—cultivates a community that lives as heaven's embassy on earth, prompting collective thanksgiving for a constitution that both challenges and liberates.

Love of Neighbor and Enemies (Matthew 22:37–40; Luke 6:27–36)

When asked for the greatest commandment, Jesus distilled all law into love of God and neighbor (Matt 22:37–40). Yet He goes further: "Love your enemies... do good to those who hate you" (Luke 6:27), modeling a mercy that reflects the Father's impartial kindness (Luke 6:35). Such radical love shatters human norms of reciprocity, embodying kingdom mercy in personal relationships. Gratitude for Jesus' enemy-embracing mercy—He died for His persecutors (Rom 5:8)—empowers us to forgive deep hurts and extend goodwill where pain once reigned. Practical applications include welcoming refugees, praying for political opponents, and offering aid to those who oppose us. Churches that implement "enemy lists" in prayer gatherings, interceding for personal antagonists, translate command into compassion. As communities practice this hard love, they testify to a reign where mercy outstrips justice, and rivers of grace flow even to the unlovable.

Economic Justice in Jubilee Vision (Leviticus 25; Luke 4:18–19)

God's law for Jubilee—every fifty years debts forgiven, land returned, slaves freed—reveals an economy undergirded by divine justice and mercy (Lev 25:8–17). Jesus announces this jubilee vision in Nazareth: "He has sent me to... proclaim liberty to the captives, to set at liberty those who are oppressed" (Luke 4:18–19). Jubilee principles confront wealth hoarding, unbridled interest, and perpetual poverty by resetting social and economic balances. Gratitude for the ultimate Jubilee—the release from sin's debt through Christ—compels believers to champion debt relief initiatives, community land trusts, and living wages. Churches can host "Jubilee Sabbaths" where no collections are taken, and ministries focus on forgiveness of small debts and mutual aid. When congregations simulate Jubilee resets, they give tangible foretaste of kingdom fairness, prompting praises for a reign that transforms economies rather than exploiting them.

13.4 Kingdom Community: People of the King

Citizenship in Heaven (Philippians 3:20; Ephesians 2:19)

Paul reminds believers that our true citizenship is not anchored in earth's shifting nations but in heaven itself: "But our citizenship is in heaven, and from it we await a Savior" (Phil 3:20). Citizens of an eternal realm share a common passport stamped by grace, giving us identity and rights that transcend cultural or political change. Gratitude for this heavenly status wells up when we realize no border control can revoke Christ's claim on our lives. As "members of the household of God" (Eph 2:19), we belong to a family whose values—compassion, justice, unity—supersede any earthly program. In practical terms, heavenly citizenship shapes our priorities: we invest energy in eternal relationships rather than temporal accolades, and we advocate for policies that reflect kingdom principles of mercy. Churches reinforce this identity by incorporating liturgical prayers that acknowledge God's reign over all nations and by celebrating global prayer weeks that unite believers across continents. Whenever political turmoil tempts us toward despair, we remember whose embassy we represent, and our hearts respond in thankful worship that Jesus has seated us at His right hand (Eph 2:6), secure beyond all earthly conflict.

The Bride, the Body, and the Temple (Revelation 19–21; 1 Corinthians 12)

John's apocalyptic vision portrays the Church as the spotless Bride adorned for her Husband, the Lamb (Rev 19:7–8), and as the living Temple where God dwells with humanity (Rev 21:3). Simultaneously, Paul describes believers corporately as one Body with many parts, each necessary for the whole (1 Cor 12:12–27). These complementary images underscore both intimacy—with Christ—and interdependence—with one another. Gratitude for our bridal relationship emerges in the joy of spiritual union: each communion service rehearses the wedding feast to come. Equally, thankfulness for the Body metaphor compels us to honor every member's gift—no eye envies the hand, no foot resents the ear. Churches that celebrate "Body Sunday" spotlight ministries often overlooked—cleaning crews, prayer teams—to remind all that each function contributes to the health of the Temple. When believers gather for prayer meetings in worship centers, lay hands on new members, and intercede for distant congregations, they enact Revelation's vision of a unified Bride and living Temple, provoking chorus after chorus of gratitude to Jesus for making us His cherished community.

Signs of Kingdom Unity across Diversity (John 17; Galatians 3:28)

On the night before His crucifixion, Jesus prayed "that they may all be one... so that the world may believe" (John 17:21). That unity is not uniformity but a kaleidoscope of cultures, ages, and gifts harmonized under Christ's lordship. Paul affirms this in Galatians: "There is neither Jew nor Greek... for you are all one in Christ Jesus" (Gal 3:28), announcing a kingdom where ethnic, social, and gender divisions dissolve. Gratitude for this reconciliatory power fuels cross-cultural outreach, where multiethnic worship teams and joint-service projects model heaven's diversity. When a Sudanese refugee shares testimony alongside a third-generation congregant, the accents of praise converge into one symphony. Church festivals that celebrate international foods, music, and testimonies give tangible foretaste of John's vision. Every handshake between former rivals, every shared meal bridging linguistic divides, prompts believers to exclaim, "Thank You, Jesus, for forging our unity amid diversity and letting the world see Your kingdom in our fellowship."

13.5 Servant–King: Leadership in the Kingdom

Jesus' Example—Foot Washing and Lasting Authority (John 13)

In the Upper Room, Jesus performed the lowliest of tasks—washing His disciples' feet—and then instructed, "You also ought to wash one another's feet" (John 13:14). This act inverted every worldly notion of authority, showing that kingdom leadership flows from humble service rather than coercive power. Gratitude for this model reshapes church governance: elders lead by listening, pastors guide by empowering, and every leader evaluates success not by status but by sacrificial care. When congregations hold "foot-washing services," they reenact the gospel's most vivid lesson: the King of glory stoops to bless the lowly. In everyday ministry contexts—mentoring youth, hospital visitation, meal delivery—leaders adopt Jesus' posture, bending rather than beckoning, ministering rather than commanding. Each towel wrapped around servant-hearts becomes a symbol of Christ's ongoing reign, and every humbled leader hears the echo of Jesus' words, "If I then, your Lord and Teacher, have washed your feet, you also ought to wash one another's feet" (John 13:14), stirring worshipful thanks for a kingdom where greatness is defined by love in action.

The Twelve as Kingdom Ambassadors (Matthew 10; Luke 9)

Jesus selected twelve disciples and sent them out two by two with authority to heal and proclaim the kingdom (Matt 10:1–8; Luke 9:1–6). These apostles functioned as ambassadors—official representatives—of the King, empowered to extend His reign into new territories. Gratitude arises for their obedience despite danger, as they preached in synagogues, cast out demons, and shared Christ's mercy with marginalized communities. Churches often replicate this pattern through short-term mission teams, campus ministries, and local outreach pairs, reinforcing that every believer carries kingdom credentials. Training sessions for ambassadors emphasize clear communication of the gospel, cultural sensitivity, and reliance on the Spirit for signs and wonders. When teams return with stories of lives transformed, their reports fuel congregational praise for a King whose authority transcends human boundaries. In every passport stamp and every shared meal with strangers, we see the kingdom's advance—thanking Jesus that He commissions us just as He did the Twelve, to bring justice and mercy to a world in need.

Patterns of Servant Leadership in the Church (Philippians 2:5–11; 1 Peter 5:2–3)

Paul's Christ-hymn exhorts believers to adopt Jesus' mindset: "Though he was in the form of God, he… emptied himself, by taking the form of a servant" (Phil 2:5–7). Peter instructs elders to shepherd "not under compulsion, but willingly, as God would have you; not for shameful gain, but eagerly" (1 Pet 5:2). Together these passages sketch a template for church leadership that blends humility with zeal, authority with affection. Gratitude for this dual standard—Christ's self-emptying and elders' willing care—inspires leadership development programs that emphasize character as well as competence. Workshops on servant leadership teach conflict resolution, financial stewardship, and pastoral empathy, ensuring that those who lead also serve. Congregations affirm these patterns by publicizing leaders' acts of service—home visits, personal donations, prayer nights—highlighting that Christlike authority flows from loving sacrifice. Every consecration of a new elder or deacon thus becomes an act of worship, as the Body says together, "Thank You, Jesus, for defining leadership by the towel, the cross, and the washing of feet."

13.6 Kingdom Mission: Extending Justice and Mercy

"Seek First the Kingdom…"—Priority of God's Rule (Matthew 6:33)

Jesus taught His followers to orient every concern around God's reign: "But seek first the kingdom of God and his righteousness, and all these things will be added to you" (Matt 6:33). By placing God's justice and mercy at the top of our agenda—above food, shelter, and personal security—we acknowledge that His purposes are primary and everything else is secondary. Gratitude for Jesus' invitation to participate in His kingdom shifts our priorities: budget lines are adjusted, schedules are reordered, and prayer lives refocused on kingdom-advancing petitions. When congregations dedicate the first portion of every service—time and offering—to kingdom causes, they embody this teaching. Personal practices such as daily "kingdom check-ins" in prayer journals remind us that every decision—career choice, family budget, volunteer opportunity—ought to answer one question: "Does this advance God's reign?" As we cultivate this posture, our trust in His provision grows, and our gratitude deepens, for we see that aligning with His rule always results in life-abundant flourishing.

Great Commission as Kingdom Mandate (Matthew 28:18–20)

Jesus' final earthly words spelled out the scope of kingdom expansion: "All authority in heaven and on earth has been given to me. Go therefore and make disciples of all nations…" (Matt 28:18–20). This Great Commission is both an invitation and a mandate: every believer is enlisted as an ambassador of God's justice and mercy. Gratitude for Christ's universal authority—over every power and principality—imbues our mission efforts with confidence. Local churches partner with global agencies, send short-term teams, and support missionaries to unreached peoples, knowing they carry the King's credentials. Training in cross-cultural communication, biblical contextualization, and holistic ministry ensures that disciple-making reflects both the message and the character of the kingdom. When new believers are baptized and integrated into community, each one testifies to the living reality of Jesus' mandate—worth a thousand sermons. Every fellowship foots the cost of gospel advance amid hardship out of grateful obedience to the King who said, "Lo, I am with you always."

Mercy Ministries and Justice Initiatives (Isaiah 58; James 1:27)

The book of Isaiah pairs true fasting with acts of justice: "Is not this the fast that I choose… to loose the bonds of wickedness… to set the oppressed free?" (Isa 58:6). James similarly defines pure religion as "visiting orphans and widows in their affliction" (Jas 1:27). Kingdom mission thus integrates both relief for immediate needs and advocacy for systemic change. Gratitude for Christ's compassion compels churches to run food banks, shelter programs, and legal-aid clinics alongside campaigns for living wages, fair housing, and human rights. By combining soup kitchens with policy-advocacy workshops, believers embody the twin reign of justice and mercy. Collaborating with local nonprofits and government bodies, congregations extend the kingdom's footprint into every social sphere. When lives are restored—body, mind, and dignity reclaimed—communities of faith burst forth in collective thanksgiving, exalting Jesus whose kingdom brings both mercy and equity.

13.7 Kingdom Conflict and Victory

Spiritual Warfare and Christ's Triumph (Colossians 2:15; Ephesians 6:10–18)

Though the kingdom advances, it encounters fierce resistance: "For we do not wrestle against flesh and blood, but against... spiritual hosts of wickedness" (Eph 6:12). Yet Colossians proclaims that Christ "disarmed the rulers and authorities" and "triumphed over them" (Col 2:15). Gratitude for Jesus' victory on the cross and resurrection assures us that any spiritual opposition is already defeated. Our calling is to stand firm in the full armor of God—truth, righteousness, the gospel of peace, faith, salvation, the Word, and prayer (Eph 6:14–18)—knowing that each piece is a gift from the King. When believers pray under these protections and witness breakthrough—addictions shattered, deceptions exposed, demonic strongholds broken—they celebrate not their cleverness but Christ's conquest. Every answered battle cry, every storm calmed within, stirs hearts to thanksgiving: "Thank You, Jesus, for securing our victory and equipping us for spiritual conflict."

Persecution as Kingdom Refining (Acts 14; 1 Peter 4:12–19)

From the first gospel proclamation, Jesus warned that following Him would provoke hatred: "They will deliver you up to tribulation... but the one who endures to the end will be saved" (Mark 13:9,13). Paul and Barnabas experienced this firsthand—stoned at Lystra before rising again to advance the Word (Acts 14:19–20). Peter exhorts believers not to be surprised at suffering as though it were strange, but to rejoice insofar as they share Christ's sufferings (1 Pet 4:12–13). Gratitude for this refining fire flips our perspective: persecution becomes a means of deepening faith, sharpening witness, and conforming us to Christ's own pattern. Testimonies from persecuted churches around the world fuel our prayers and inspire solidarity. When congregations dedicate services to pray for the persecuted, they unite global Body in worship under duress. Each badge of suffering—scars, arrests, social ostracism—becomes, paradoxically, a crown of testimonies that provoke praise: "Thank You, Jesus, for counting us worthy to suffer for Your kingdom."

Anticipating the Final Judgment (Revelation 20; Matthew 25:31–46)

Scripture reveals that the kingdom's consummation includes final judgment when Christ returns "in his glory" to separate "the sheep" from "the goats" (Matt 25:31–33). Revelation 20 describes the Great White Throne, where books are opened and every deed is judged (Rev 20:11–13). Gratitude for the King's righteous verdict—He who endured unjust judgment on our behalf—energizes us to proclaim mercy now, offering rescue before the final reckoning. The judgment parable's criteria—feeding the hungry, welcoming the stranger, clothing the naked—underscore that kingdom allegiance is visible in works of compassion (Matt 25:35–40). Churches that invest in social ministries do so in light of eternity, knowing that deeds done in love last beyond the grave. Preaching on the judgment scenes balances grace with sober warning, motivating holy living. And when communities unite in mercy initiatives, they provide living previews of the coming kingdom court, prompting corporate exclamation: "Thank You, Jesus, for justly reigning and mercifully saving us before the end."

13.8 Kingdom Living: Present and Future

Kingdom Values in Daily Life (Romans 14:17; Galatians 5:22–23)

The apostle Paul declares that "the kingdom of God is…righteousness and peace and joy in the Holy Spirit" (Rom 14:17). These transcendent qualities are meant to shape every choice—from how we speak to how we spend our money. Love, joy, peace, patience, kindness, goodness, faithfulness, gentleness, and self-control blossom in everyday contexts when the Spirit reigns within us (Gal 5:22–23). Gratitude for this internal reign fuels our desire to manifest kingdom virtues at home, work, and in public life. A simple act—offering a kind word to a stressed coworker, exercising patience in traffic, giving generously to a stranger's need—becomes a declaration that Christ's rule governs our actions. Small-group discussions and personal devotions centered on one fruit of the Spirit per week help believers integrate these values into their routines. Over time, habits anchored in gratitude replace old patterns, and daily life becomes a living sermon of kingdom transformation rather than mere ethical striving.

Eschatological Hope—New Heavens and New Earth (2 Peter 3; Revelation 21)

Peter reminds us that, though the world now suffers decay, God has promised "a new heaven and a new earth in which righteousness dwells" (2 Pet 3:13). John's vision in Revelation 21 amplifies this hope: a city with no temple because "the Lord God the Almighty and the Lamb are its temple" (Rev 21:22). Gratitude for this future reality fuels perseverance amid present trials—environmental crises, social breakdown, personal suffering—by anchoring our hope in a consummated kingdom. Worship services that read these chapters aloud and use art installations to depict the New Jerusalem deepen congregants' sense of mission as they labor toward that day. Practical stewardship of creation—tree planting, sustainable building, clean-up campaigns—becomes a rehearsing of new-creation values. Each act of care for planet and people testifies to a kingdom that will one day eliminate every tear, curse, and death (Rev 21:4), igniting fresh praise for the King who prepares a forever home for His redeemed.

"Thy Kingdom Come"—Praying and Proclaiming (Matthew 6:10; Luke 11:2)

When Jesus taught His disciples to pray, the second petition was "Your kingdom come" (Matt 6:10; Luke 11:2), placing advance of God's reign at the heart of our spiritual agenda.

This petition is both request and proclamation, acknowledging present lack and proclaiming future reality. Gratitude for present-kingdom experiences—answered prayers, community breakthroughs, personal transformation—gives substance to our longing for fullness. Prayer groups that focus entire sessions on "Thy kingdom come" intercede for justice reform, global missions, and spiritual awakening, weaving spoken petitions with silent expectancy. Likewise, personal prayers that blend thanksgiving for past mercies with hopes for kingdom expansion cultivate a posture of confident anticipation. When we say "Your will be done" in unison with "Thy kingdom come," our corporate voice becomes a trumpet blast announcing the King's approach. Such praying and proclaiming align our hearts with heaven's priorities and evoke continuous gratitude that Jesus has entrusted us with the privilege of advancing His reign.

13.9 Songs and Symbols of the Kingdom

Hymns of Zion and Hosanna Shouts (Psalm 118; Matthew 21:9)

Psalm 118:25–26 bursts into the New Testament narrative when crowds wave palm branches and shout "Hosanna!" to welcome Jesus into Jerusalem as King (Matt 21:9). These ancient hymns of Zion celebrated God's reign over Israel and now echo centuries later in congregational hymns like "All Glory, Laud, and Honor." Gratitude for this musical heritage inspires churches to teach psalms and hymns of the kingdom, connecting modern worshipers with the biblical story. Incorporating palm-processions on Palm Sunday or singing Psalm 118 in services reminds us that history's grandest concert celebrated the arrival of the eternal King. Contemporary composers draw on these motifs, crafting new anthems that blend ancient texts with modern melodies. Each shout of "Blessed is he who comes in the name of the Lord!" becomes both praise and prophetic declaration that Jesus still reigns. Through song, we embody our gratitude, proclaiming the kingdom to one another and to the watching world.

Symbols—Crown, Scepter, and Throne (Revelation 4–5; Zechariah 9:9)

Scripture abounds with regal imagery: Zechariah foretold a King riding on a colt, "lowly and riding on a donkey" (Zech 9:9), while Revelation's Lamb receives a crown of many diadems and a scroll containing all authority (Rev 5:12–13). Crowns signify honor; scepters denote rule; thrones embody governance. Gratitude for these symbols surfaces when churches incorporate visual elements—crowns above sanctuaries, scepter motifs in communion tables, throne-like chairs for worship leaders—to remind believers of Christ's sovereignty. Art installations, stained glass, and liturgical vestments draw from these images, sparking reflection: Who is worthy to open the scroll? Only the Lamb. In personal devotion, wearing a simple ring or medallion embroidered with crown imagery can prompt daily thanksgiving for our King. Each symbol becomes a sacramental portal: a glance at a crown on the wall redirects our gaze to heaven, renewing gratitude that Jesus holds all rule and power in His pierced hands.

The Wedding Feast and the Marriage Supper (Revelation 19:6–9; Isaiah 25:6)

John's vision of heaven climaxes in the marriage supper of the Lamb—an invitation to "those invited to the marriage supper of the Lamb" (Rev 19:9). Isaiah earlier painted a feast on the mountain with rich foods and aged wine, "to swallow up death forever" (Isa 25:6–8). These vivid feasts symbolize the union between Christ and His Bride, the Church, under a reign of justice and mercy. Gratitude for these banquet images infuses communion services with festive joy, reminding us that each Eucharistic gathering is a rehearsal for the eternal feast. Church potlucks, wedding-themed celebrations, and art-driven meditations on banquet scenes help believers anticipate the fullness of fellowship in the kingdom. When congregations partake in shared meals—breaking bread and blessing the cup—they enact Revelation's supreme celebration, their voices rising in thanksgiving for a King who invites us forever to His table.

13.10 Living in Kingdom Citizenship

Obedience as Kingdom Loyalty (John 14:15; 1 John 2:3–6)

Jesus ties love and loyalty to obedience: "If you love me, you will keep my commandments" (John 14:15). John echoes, "By this we know that we have come to know him, if we keep his commandments" (1 John 2:3). Such obedience is not burdensome rule-keeping but demonstration of allegiance to the King. Gratitude for Christ's perfect obedience on our behalf motivates us to align our choices with His will—from ethical business practices to compassionate speech. Churches cultivate this loyalty by teaching practical applications of Christ's commands—hospitality, honesty, generosity—and celebrating testimonies of changed lives. When believers make decisions guided by kingdom priorities, they wear obedience like a royal insignia, proclaiming loyalty through both action and attitude. Each faithful step fosters unity under Christ's reign and elicits communal thanksgiving: "Thank You, Jesus, for giving us commands that lead to abundant life and demonstrate our devotion."

Witness in Culture—Salt and Light (Matthew 5:13–16)

Jesus likens His followers to salt—preventing decay—and light—illuminating darkness—in the world (Matt 5:13–16). These metaphors underscore kingdom citizenship lived outwardly: preserving moral integrity, exposing injustice, and showcasing God's glory through good works. Gratitude for our saltiness and brightness stirs creative cultural engagement: artists produce films that reflect kingdom values, journalists highlight stories of mercy, and entrepreneurs innovate sustainable solutions. Churches can host "salt-and-light" forums where congregants brainstorm cultural initiatives—community gardens, mentorship programs, ethical business incubators. When neighbors see Christ's light in grit rather than glamour—a kind deed in a parking lot, an honest price in a marketplace—they glorify the Father in heaven. Each public act of witness thus becomes a prism refracting the King's justice and mercy, drawing appreciative hearts to the source of our salt and shine.

Kingdom Economy—Generosity and Stewardship (2 Corinthians 9; Luke 16:10–13)

Paul's teaching on giving highlights kingdom economics: "Whoever sows sparingly will also reap sparingly, and whoever sows bountifully will reap bountifully" (2 Cor 9:6). Jesus warns that one cannot serve both God and money, calling us to faithfulness in little things—small financial decisions—before entrusting greater riches (Luke 16:10–13). Gratitude for God's provision leads us to generosity as a lifestyle: tithing, sacrificial offerings, and strategic investing in missions and mercy ministries. Churches support this ethos through stewardship campaigns, transparent reporting of funds used for kingdom work, and testimonies of lives transformed by generous giving. Practical workshops on budgeting, microfinance, and ethical investments equip members to steward resources wisely. When congregations witness collective generosity—new churches planted, schools built, hunger alleviated—the Body celebrates the kingdom's upside-down economy, praising Jesus for a reign where mercy is the currency and generosity the privilege of every citizen.

13.11 Kingdom Fellowship: Celebrating Together

Communion as Kingdom Meal (1 Corinthians 10:16–17; Luke 22:19–20)

Paul describes the cup and bread as participation in Christ's body and blood, proclaiming community across time and space (1 Cor 10:16–17). Luke's account links the bread to Jesus' body given for us and the cup to His blood of the new covenant (Luke 22:19–20). As a kingdom meal, communion transcends walls and time: each participant, from every tribe and tongue, eats of the same loaf. Gratitude for this shared feast draws congregations into deeper unity—laying aside personal preferences to focus on the one Table where all are welcome. Periodic all-church celebrations, home-based communion kits for shut-ins, and one-anothers' memories of first communions reinforce the meal's unifying power. When believers approach the Table with hearts full of thanksgiving, they affirm the kingdom's hospitality and the King's invitation to fellowship without end.

Feasts and Festivals—Easter, Pentecost, Jubilee

The early church inherited Jewish festivals—Passover, Pentecost—and reinterpreted them around Christ's life. Easter proclaims resurrection victory; Pentecost celebrates Spirit-empowerment; Jubilee envisions economic and social renewal (Acts 2:1–4; Lev 25). Gratitude for these feasts inspires vibrant church calendars: drama and candles at Easter, red banners and corporate prayer at Pentecost, Jubilee sermons and mercy-project launches. Seasonal observances root believers in salvation history, aligning communal joy with cosmic milestones. Intergenerational celebrations—children's pageants, youth service projects, seniors' testimony nights—reveal the kingdom's multigenerational scope. As each festival unfolds, congregations step into a living tapestry where past, present, and future converge in thanksgiving for Jesus' reign over time itself.

Community Rhythms—Worship, Prayer, and Service

Kingdom fellowship thrives on shared rhythms: weekly worship gatherings, daily prayer habits, and ongoing service partnerships. These patterns—temporal sacraments—shape the community's identity and mission, echoing heaven's ceaseless praise (Rev 4:8–11). Gratitude for these rhythms leads churches to craft liturgies that balance reverence and creativity, to host 24-hour prayer rooms, and to sustain year-round volunteer teams. Positioning these rhythms publicly—posting prayer schedules, service opportunities, and worship themes—invites participation and accountability. When community life pulsates with predictable yet vibrant patterns, members find spiritual stability and mutual encouragement. Each repetition of worship, each shared hour of prayer, each act of service becomes a heartbeat of the kingdom, prompting voices to rise in kebful thankfulness for life together under Christ's reign.

13.12 Eschatological Consummation of the Kingdom

The Lamb's Reign and the Defeat of Death (Revelation 21–22; 1 Corinthians 15:54–57)

Revelation's closing vision depicts the Lamb seated on the throne, pouring life into the river of the water of life (Rev 22:1–3). Paul proclaims that death is swallowed up in victory—"Death is swallowed up in victory… Thanks be to God, who gives us the victory through our Lord Jesus Christ" (1 Cor 15:54–57). Gratitude for this final triumph fuels Christian hope, transforming fear of mortality into anticipation of unending communion with the King. Funerals become celebrations of transition rather than lament alone, filled with hymns that affirm resurrection. Every baptism also rehearses this victory, as believers pass from death into life. By preaching and rejoicing in the Lamb's eternal reign, churches prepare hearts for the day when time gives way to eternity and every tear is wiped away.

No More Curse, No More Tears (Revelation 22:3–4; Romans 8:21)

The New Creation erases the curse unleashed at Eden's fall: "No longer will there be any curse" (Rev 22:3), and "the creation itself will be set free… to the freedom of the glory of the children of God" (Rom 8:21). Gratitude for this cosmic liberation shapes our engagement with creation today—motivating environmental care, social restoration, and healing ministries as foretaste of unbroken wholeness. Churches integrate creation care into worship through eco-themed sermons, planting trees in community, and creation-focused prayer. Small groups read Romans 8 together, tracing groaning creation to assured glory. Each ecological or social initiative thus becomes an act of eschatological gratitude, advancing freedom's footprint. When congregations celebrate Earth Day with worship outdoors, they testify that the curse's end is certain under the King who makes all things new.

Forever with the King—Eternal Praise (Revelation 5:13; Psalm 145:10)

In heaven's grand chorus, every creature in heaven and on earth declares, "Worthy is the Lamb who was slain" (Rev 5:13). Psalm 145 amplifies this, affirming that "all your works shall give thanks to you, O Lord, and all your saints shall bless you!" (Ps 145:10). Gratitude for the prospect of eternal praise motivates worship that anticipates unending doxologies. Churches can incorporate songs from Revelation into liturgy, host "heavenly worship nights" envisioning eternal service, and encourage artistic expressions—dance, painting, poetry—that reflect endless adoration. Personal devotions might include journaling "eternal thanks," envisioning the scenes to come. By living in light of forever, believers lift each act of service and every hymn of praise as foretaste of the age to come. This eschatological orientation grounds present worship in the surety that Jesus' kingdom will never end and that our gratitude will flow ceaselessly around His throne.

Conclusion

Christ's kingdom stands as history's ultimate redemption narrative—a realm where the raw demands of justice meet the unbounded embrace of mercy. From prophetic promises through Jesus' inaugural miracles, from ethical teachings to communal celebrations, the kingdom threads God's steadfast reign through every page of Scripture and every chapter of the Church's story. Our daily lives—rooted in values of righteousness and joy, shaped by rhythms of worship and service—become vessels of that reign. As we steward resources, engage culture, wage spiritual warfare, and suffer for righteousness' sake, we anticipate the kingdom's full arrival when the Lamb sits on the eternal throne. To thank Jesus for Your kingdom is to embrace both its present power and its coming glory—to serve now with eyes fixed on the New

Heavens and New Earth. May every heartbeat echo the refrain of Revelation's multitude: "Worthy is the Lamb, for You have wrought justice and mercy in triumph, and to You be glory forever!"

Chapter 14. Thank You, Jesus, for Eternal Glory—Hope Unfading

From the first glimmer of God's presence in the Tabernacle to John's final vision of a new heaven and new earth, Scripture unveils a tapestry of divine radiance that transcends time and trials. Yet the brightest of these glimpses finds its fullest expression in Jesus Christ, whose resurrection ignited an unfading hope and secured our share in eternal glory. To say "Thank You, Jesus" for eternal glory is to celebrate more than future bliss—it is to affirm that every promise of God's dwelling with His people, every victory over death's sting, and every crown of righteousness awaits us because of Him.

In our present pilgrimage—marked by joy and sorrow, triumph and struggle—this hope becomes an anchor for the soul (Heb 6:19), sustaining us through life's fiercest storms. We look forward to bodies transformed, an inheritance kept in heaven (1 Pet 1:3–4), and a wedding feast where the Lamb Himself presides (Rev 19:9). Yet even now, the Spirit infuses our worship with foretaste of that glory, guiding us to live and serve in light of eternity.

14.1 Biblical Glimpses of Glory

The Shekinah in the Tabernacle (Exodus 40:34–38)

When Moses completed construction of the Tabernacle, Scripture records that "the cloud covered the tent of meeting, and the glory of the LORD filled the tabernacle" (Ex 40:34). This luminous presence—later called the Shekinah—manifested God's royal residence among His people, a visible banner of divine approval and protection. For forty years, Israel followed the pillar of cloud by day and the pillar of fire by night, trusting that the same glory that rested on the Tabernacle would guide their wilderness journey (Ex 13:21–22). Gratitude wells up when we consider that the Creator chose to dwell in a tent amid a nomadic people, endorsing their frailty with His transcendent light. The Tabernacle's glory was not static; it "would lift up and the people of Israel would set out. And if the cloud did not lift, they did not set out" (Num 9:22–23), illustrating that every step of faith was under God's radiant command. As the Temple later housed that glory with greater splendor, the message remained: the King's presence accompanies His subjects wherever they go. Today, we remember the Shekinah as a foretaste of Christ's incarnational glory—God dwelling among us (John 1:14)—and thank Jesus that His Spirit now tabernacles within every believer (2 Cor 6:16).

"They Shall See My Glory" Promise (Isaiah 40:5; 60:1–3)

Isaiah prophesied that when the Lord revealed Himself, "the glory of the LORD shall be revealed, and all flesh shall see it together" (Isa 40:5). This universal unveiling signaled not only judgment but the dawning of salvation: a light rising on those in darkness (Isa 60:1–3). The prophet's words anticipate the Messiah's ministry, when crowds would witness healings, exorcisms, and the transfiguration—tangible signs of God's glory breaking into human history (Matt 17:1–5). Gratitude for these promises deepens as we consider the inclusivity of the vision: people from distant lands and varied backgrounds are drawn to the radiance of the King. When Jesus walked Galilee, the amazed onlookers declared, "Never has anything like this been seen in Israel" (Matt 9:33), affirming Isaiah's forecast. The New Testament proclaims that through Christ's work on the cross and His resurrection, the fullness of divine glory is now available to all who call on His name (2 Cor 4:6). As we gather in worship, each glimpse of beauty—sunrise, sacramental light, communal praise—echoes Isaiah's invitation to lift our eyes and rejoice at the unveiling of God's presence.

Heaven as God's Dwelling Place (Psalm 11:4; 145:13)

The psalmists lift a hymn of exaltation to the One who sits enthroned above the circle of the earth: "The LORD is in his holy temple; the LORD's throne is in heaven" (Ps 11:4). Heaven is depicted as the eternal palace of divine sovereignty, where justice and mercy flow from the throne in unbroken harmony (Ps 145:13). Gratitude for this heavenly dwelling shapes our perspective on earthly trials: though we live in frail tents, we belong to a household whose true walls cannot be shaken (2 Cor 5:1). The imagery of God's throne also reminds us that every ruler and regime on earth is ultimately subordinate to the King of kings (Rev 4:2–3). In moments of political uncertainty or personal upheaval, believers draw strength by envisioning the unassailable court of heaven, where petitions are received and answered according to perfect wisdom. Modern worship spaces that incorporate high ceilings, stained glass, or aerial art seek to evoke that transcendence, inviting congregants to lift their hearts beyond the temporal. Each note of corporate song becomes a celestial echo of Psalm 145's doxology, giving "thanks to the LORD" whose "kingdom is an everlasting kingdom" (Ps 145:10,13).

14.2 Resurrection and the Firstfruits

Christ the Firstfruits of Those Who Sleep (1 Corinthians 15:20–23)

Paul celebrates Jesus as the "firstfruits" of those who have fallen asleep, meaning His resurrection is the guarantee of ours (1 Cor 15:20–23). In Jewish harvest imagery, the firstfruits are a pledge of the full harvest to come, and Christ's rising is God's down payment on our eternal life. Gratitude wells up when we grasp that Jesus did not merely conquer death in principle but personally broke its grip, assuring every believer of a future bodily resurrection. His victory transforms our mourning into hope: we grieve, but "not as those who have no hope" (1 Thess 4:13). The early church preached this truth amid hostile persecutions, knowing that tombs could not hold the King (Acts 2:24). Today, every Easter sunrise service and every testimony of a believer's passing becomes a celebration that the Firstfruits lives forever. In our own moments of grief—loss of loved ones, fading health—we thank Jesus for rising first, that we might follow Him into unending glory.

Victory Over Death's Sting (1 Corinthians 15:54–57; Revelation 1:17–18)

Paul triumphantly declares, "Death is swallowed up in victory… Thanks be to God, who gives us the victory through our Lord Jesus Christ" (1 Cor 15:54–57). The sting of death—sin's penalty and our fear—has been neutralized by Christ's atoning work. Revelation's vision adds personal reassurance: the risen Lord says, "I am the Living One; I was dead, and behold I am alive for evermore, and I hold the keys of Death and Hades" (Rev 1:17–18). Gratitude for this potent reality emboldens us to face mortality without dread. Rather than avoiding funerals, we attend with thanksgiving, proclaiming the gospel before grieving hearts. Each funeral sermon that centers on resurrection hope becomes a proclamation of Christ's mastery over the last enemy. In our own dying moments, the believer's confidence rests not on our merit but on the One who unlocked death's prison and invited us into His eternal life.

Our Hope Laid Up in Heaven (Philippians 3:20–21; Colossians 3:1–4)

Paul reminds believers that "our citizenship is in heaven" and that we eagerly await a Savior "who will transform our lowly body to be like his glorious body" (Phil 3:20–21). Similarly, Colossians exhorts us to "set our minds on things above… where Christ is, seated at the right hand of God. For you have died, and your life is hidden with Christ in God. When Christ who is your life appears, then you also will appear with him in glory" (Col 3:1–4). Gratitude surges as we recognize that the trials and labors of this life are temporary scaffolding for an eternal building. Our possessions, ambitions, and even our earthly identities are shadows compared to the weight of our heavenly inheritance. Regularly rehearsing this hope—through creedal recitations, heaven-themed hymns, and personal meditation—guards our hearts against despair. When temptations whisper that this world is all there is, we reply, "Thank You, Jesus, that my true home and hope are secured in You."

14.3 New Resurrection Bodies

Imperishable, Glorious, Powerful, Spiritual (1 Corinthians 15:42–44)

Paul contrasts our present bodies—"perishable, dishonorable, weak, natural" (1 Cor 15:42–44)—with the resurrection body: "imperishable, glorious, powerful, spiritual." Grave clothes will give way to garments woven of eternal substance. Gratitude for this transformation emerges when we contemplate disabilities and diseases laid aside, replaced by bodies unbound by decay. The adjective "glorious" reminds us that our renewed form will radiate God's light, reflecting the Creator's glory in every cell. "Powerful" signals freedom from fatigue, frailty, and limitation, while "spiritual" indicates a body animated by the Spirit, responsive to divine will. When we pray for healing today, we do so in faith that our ultimate healing is already secured. Each glimpse of restored mobility or renewed health foreshadows the fullness of body life to come.

Transformation at the Last Trumpet (1 Corinthians 15:51–52; 1 John 3:2)

Paul reveals a mystery: "We shall not all sleep, but we shall all be changed… at the last trumpet… the dead will be raised imperishable, and we shall be changed" (1 Cor 15:51–52). John adds, "we shall be like him, for we shall see him as he is" (1 Jn 3:2). This sudden metamorphosis will occur in an instant—no gradual process—uniting living and dead in the same glorious condition. Gratitude ignites when we consider that even those alive at Christ's return need not fear death but will participate directly in the climactic resurrection. This truth transforms eschatological anxiety into eager anticipation: the trumpet's blast becomes the sweetest sound we will ever hear. Churches that preach the "blessed hope" and that incorporate trumpet motifs in art remind congregations of this promised moment. Each Advent reading and each rousing doxology fosters thankfulness that Jesus will complete the work He began in us.

Co-Heirs with Christ in Resurrection Splendor (Romans 8:17; Titus 2:13)

Paul teaches that as children of God we are "heirs of God and fellow heirs with Christ" (Rom 8:17), a status that extends beyond redemption to participation in His glory. Titus describes "waiting for our blessed hope, the appearing of the glory of our great God and Savior Jesus Christ" (Titus 2:13). Gratitude for co-heirship with the King shifts our identity: we are not subjects in a distant realm but privileged beneficiaries of every blessing reserved in heaven. This noble inheritance draws us into worship and motivates holy living as we aim to honor our royal status. The church's liturgical calendar, highlighting "hope Sunday" or "glory Sunday," encourages reflection on our future adoptions. When we speak of heavenly rewards—not as bribes but as loving recompense—we celebrate the stupendous grace that invites us into eternal family wealth and glory.

14.4 Eternal Inheritance

An Inheritance That Never Fades (1 Peter 1:3–4)

Peter bursts into praise with a doxology: "According to his great mercy, he has caused us to be born again... to an inheritance that is imperishable, undefiled, and unfading, kept in heaven for you" (1 Pet 1:3–4). Unlike earthly inheritances that depreciate or decay, ours is secure beyond any market crash, political upheaval, or physical decay. Gratitude floods our hearts as we realize that God Himself serves as the Trustee, guarding our portion until the appointed time. This inheritance includes not only eternal life but also every blessing of sonship—co-heirship with Christ, access to the Father's throne, and reign alongside the King (Rom 8:17). In practical terms, this assurance frees us from anxiety over retirement funds or legacy concerns. We can invest in kingdom causes without fear of loss, knowing our "storehouse" is in heaven (Matt 6:20). When passing the peace or celebrating baptisms, we remind one another that these moments testify to a birthright that no adversary can strip away. Thus every "Amen" and every "Alleluia" echoes Peter's firstfruits of praise for a heritage woven into the very fabric of heaven.

Many Mansions in the Father's House (John 14:2; Hebrews 11:16)

Jesus comforts His disciples with an astonishing promise: "In my Father's house are many rooms. If it were not so, would I have told you that I go to prepare a place for you?" (John 14:2). The original Greek term *monai* evokes guest quarters—places of welcome and rest for each believer. Similarly, Hebrews praises those of faith who "desire a better country, that is, a heavenly one. Therefore God is not ashamed to be called their God, for he has prepared for them a city" (Heb 11:16). Gratitude wells as we contemplate personalized dwellings in glory—each uniquely suited to our Savior's creative care. This imagery transforms funeral sermons: loss becomes a family member moving into a home built by the Master for eternal comfort. Churches can teach on this promise through baptistery murals or "housewarming" celebrations for new believers, symbolizing entry into the Father's estate. Every "farewell" in ministry transitions into a "welcome home," as we affirm that Christ's departure was to arrange eternal accommodations, not to abandon His own. Thus every hearth and hearthside prayer can praise Jesus for His meticulous preparation of our heavenly abode.

Unstained and Unfading Reward (Jude 1:24; Revelation 3:21)

Jude concludes with praise that God "is able to keep you from stumbling and to present you blameless before the presence of his glory with great joy" (Jude 1:24). Revelation echoes this promise to the overcomer: "To the one who conquers, I will grant to sit with me on my throne, as I also conquered and sat down with my Father on his throne" (Rev 3:21). These assurances depict not dangling carrots but divine pledges that every trial-tested believer will stand pure and share in Christ's majesty. Gratitude deepens when we recognize that our reward is not earned by flawless performance but secured by Christ's flawless obedience and satisfying sacrifice. Ministry leaders can frame stewardship renewals and milestone anniversaries around these texts, reminding servants that God's commendation never fades. Mentoring programs can include reflections on "throne-sharing," cultivating long-term faithfulness with the eye on heavenly celebration. Each act of perseverance thus becomes a down payment on an unstained, unfading reward—kindling praise for Jesus, who guarantees our place in His eternal fellowship.

14.5 Living Hope

Born Again to a Living Hope (1 Peter 1:3–5)

Peter describes believers as "born again… to a living hope through the resurrection of Jesus Christ from the dead" (1 Pet

1:3–5). This living hope is dynamic—active, life-giving, and sustaining—distinguished from fleeting human optimism. Gratitude arises as we realize that our hope springs not from wishful thinking but from the historical fact of Christ's resurrection. This hope anchors us amid storms, providing an inner spring that never runs dry even when life's wells go dry. Church liturgies can amplify this theme by incorporating sunrise services, symbolizing hope's dawning that darkness cannot quench. Personal devotions might include journaling "resurrection moments"—connections with new life in Christ—that reinforce thankfulness. When congregations share testimonies of deliverance and renewal, they substantiate this living hope for one another. Each confession of "Christ is risen!" becomes a trumpet call, reminding the Body that our hope is alive and unfading because of Jesus.

An Anchor for the Soul (Hebrews 6:19–20)

Hebrews pivots from warning to assurance: "We have this as a sure and steadfast anchor of the soul… that enters the inner place behind the curtain, where Jesus has gone as a forerunner on our behalf" (Heb 6:19–20). In ancient seafaring, an anchor secured the ship against turbulent waves; similarly, Christ's priestly presence in heaven secures our souls against life's tempests. Gratitude deepens when we recognize that no emotional squall—anxiety, grief, discouragement—can uproot us from the anchored hope we hold in Christ. Churches can help believers grasp this by teaching guided meditations on anchoring truths—Christ's intercession and heaven's firm foundation—and by creating visual anchors (e.g., anchor symbols on prayer walls). Small groups might practice "anchor prayers," proclaiming Hebrews 6 truths together when storms hit. As members remind one another, "Our anchor holds," thankfulness emerges organically, cementing communal confidence that Jesus, our Priest and Pioneer, never relinquishes His post.

Hope That Purifies and Perseveres (Romans 5:3–5; Titus 2:13)

Paul instructs: "we rejoice in our sufferings, knowing that suffering produces endurance, and endurance produces character, and character produces hope, and hope does not put us to shame" (Rom 5:3–5). Titus urges us to await the "blessed hope and appearing of the glory of our great God and Savior Jesus Christ" (Titus 2:13). Gratitude for this refining process embraces trials as means by which God purges selfishness and strengthens faith. Each hardship—personal loss, conflict, failure—becomes a verse in a purification hymn, leading to hope that shines even brighter in affliction. Discipleship programs can include "trial testimonies," where believers share how suffering produced godly character. Retreats focused on refining fire encourage participants to submit to the Spirit's sanctifying work, thanking Jesus that purity, not comfort, is the ultimate goal. As endurance evolves into hope that outlasts uncertainty, the church witnesses a faith sealed by testing—proof that our hope in Christ is both precious and unfading.

14.6 Hall of Faith

Cloud of Witnesses Encouraging Us On (Hebrews 12:1)

Hebrews 12 begins by calling us to "lay aside every weight, and sin which clings so closely," and then to "run with endurance the race that is set before us, looking to Jesus, the founder and perfecter of our faith" (Heb 12:1–2). Before that exhortation, the author evokes a great "cloud of witnesses" who have gone before—Old Testament heroes whose lives testify to God's faithfulness (Heb 11). Picture a stadium packed with saints, cheering us on as we press toward the finish line. Gratitude arises when we remember that our struggles are not unseen or solitary; we run under the gaze of those who endured by trusting God's promises. Their stories—Abraham's journey to a promise land, Moses' choice of reproach over privilege, Rahab's faith amid fear—reverberate through history, reminding us that faithfulness always triumphs. In moments of weariness, we can mentally file a list of these "witnesses," drawing courage from their examples. Churches can honor this cloud by sharing brief biographies of faith heroes in worship or maintaining a "Hall of Faith" display, prompting congregants to give thanks for those who have blazed the trail. Each name recalled becomes a note in our chorus of gratitude to Jesus, who sustains our race by the communion of saints.

Heroes Who Endured by Faith (Hebrews 11)

Hebrews 11 catalogs a gallery of patriarchs and prophets who "obtained a good testimony through faith" (Heb 11:2). From Abel's offering that still speaks (Heb 11:4) to Sarah conceiving in old age (Heb 11:11), each narrative reveals trust in unseen realities over present limitations. Noah built an ark on dry land in obedience to a promise he had never physically seen (Heb 11:7), while Abraham left his homeland, "looking forward to the city that has foundations" (Heb 11:10). Gratitude for these giants of faith moves our hearts to emulate their courage: when we face uncertainties, we declare, "By faith, we step forward trusting God's word." Small groups might adopt one hero each month, diving into their stories and rehearsing prayers of thanksgiving for their perseverance. Children's ministries can dramatize these accounts, helping the next generation stand on ancestry of faith. Every time a believer chooses God's promise over personal convenience, they echo the ancestors' faith and join the symphony of praise: "Thank You, Jesus, that You reward those who diligently seek You."

Christ, Author and Perfecter of Our Faith (Hebrews 12:2)

Amid the Hall of Faith, the book of Hebrews directs our gaze upward: "looking to Jesus, the founder and perfecter of our faith" (Heb 12:2). The Greek terms *archēgós* (originator) and *teleiōtēs* (completer) portray Christ as both the pioneer who blazed the trail and the finisher who brings faith to maturity. Gratitude deepens when we realize that our faith does not rest on human effort alone but on Jesus' own obedience through suffering to glory. His life models perfect trust in the Father, His death secures our redemption, and His resurrection guarantees our vindication. In moments of doubt or failure, we look not inward but to Christ's flawless record, trusting that He continues to perfect our faith by the power of His Spirit. Worship gatherings that emphasize Jesus' priestly intercession (Heb 7:25) reinforce our confidence that He prays our faith into wholeness. When we face trials, we remember that Christ endured hostility from sinners yet "for the joy set before him endured the cross" (Heb 12:2), prompting us to thank Jesus for authoring our spiritual journey and completing the work He began in us.

14.7 Glory through Suffering

Light Afflictions Preparing Eternal Weight (2 Corinthians 4:16–18)

Paul contrasts "light momentary affliction" with "an eternal weight of glory beyond all comparison" (2 Cor 4:17). Though present sufferings feel crushing, they are brief in the span of eternity and serve to prepare us for a glory that vastly outshines our pain. Gratitude for this perspective transforms our response to hardship: rather than curse the trial, we thank Jesus for using every difficulty to shape us into vessels fit for His glory. This does not minimize real suffering but locates it within the overarching narrative of redemption and renewal. Personal testimonies of endurance—health battles, relational losses, ministry setbacks—become markers of God's refining fire, chipping away dross to reveal the brilliance of His workmanship. In pastoral care settings, counselors point care-receivers to this promise, framing struggles as spiritual training grounds. Corporate worship that includes "testimony nights" allows the Body to celebrate how the Lord's grace has turned affliction into an avenue of glory preparation. Each tear shed, each groan offered to God, becomes a sacrificial seed that yields a harvest of eternal praise.

Filling Up What Is Lacking in Christ's Afflictions (Colossians 1:24)

Paul writes that he "rejoices in my sufferings for your sake, and in my flesh I am filling up what is lacking in Christ's afflictions" (Col 1:24). This enigmatic phrase has been understood not as adding to Christ's redemptive work but as participating in its ongoing outpouring of grace to the nations. Gratitude surfaces when we recognize our trials connect us to the sufferings of Christ and to the global church's mission. Our personal hardships extend the reach of Christ's compassion, drawing others to the hope that transcends pain. Missionaries who face persecution, pastors who endure criticism, and everyday believers bearing injustice participate in this filling-up of Christ's afflictions. Discussion groups can explore how local service among the marginalized echoes Paul's experience—viewing hardships as dividends on the cross that unlock fresh streams of gospel impact. When we embrace suffering as a means of grace rather than a mere burden, we echo Paul's joy: "I rejoice… for your sake," and we thank Jesus for knitting our pains into the grand tapestry of His redemptive labor.

Sharing in His Sufferings, Then in His Glory (1 Peter 5:10; Romans 8:18)

Peter assures believers that "after you have suffered a little while, the God of all grace… will himself restore, confirm, strengthen, and establish you" (1 Pet 5:10). Paul likewise anticipates that "the sufferings of this present time are not worth comparing with the glory that is to be revealed to us" (Rom 8:18). Suffering and glory thus form a continuum: our shared fellowship in Christ's trials preludes our communal participation in His triumph. Gratitude emerges when we realize that our fellowshipping in suffering is a divine apprenticeship for reigning with Jesus. In small-group settings, sharing stories of hardship and restoration fosters solidarity and hope. Worship through lament—psalms of sorrow—gives way to hymns of praise, modeling the trajectory from suffering to glory. Each testimony of deliverance becomes a living emblem of the promise: "Suffer now, reign later." As we embrace this divine rhythm, our hearts join the apostolic chorus: "Thank You, Jesus, that Your glory is coming, and that You let me glimpse it most clearly in the valley of suffering."

14.8 Worship in Eternal Glory

Heaven's Throne Room and Living Creatures (Revelation 4:1–11)

John's apocalyptic vision transports us "immediately in the Spirit" before the throne of God, where the One seated radiates emerald and jasper brilliance, surrounded by a rainbow of covenant promise (Rev 4:2–3). Before Him stand four living creatures—lion, ox, man, eagle—each with six wings, calling day and night, "Holy, holy, holy, is the Lord God Almighty" (Rev 4:8). Their ceaseless doxology anchors heaven's liturgy, reminding us that worship is the universe's primary function. Gratitude wells within the redeemed as we imagine joining the cherubim's chorus, our voices merging with angelic and cosmic praise. The throne's center, a molten sea of glass, symbolizes purity and undisturbed peace—reflecting God's holiness back to Himself. Every detail—the creatures' eyes, the elders' crowns—points to a worship reality beyond mortal imagination, yet promised to those who love Jesus. As earthly liturgies echo these themes—incense, lights, acclamations—we taste heaven's atmosphere of reverent joy. In gratitude, we lift our eyes beyond temporal concerns and covenant ourselves to join the eternal symphony of adoration around the Lamb's throne.

The Lamb Enthroned and the New Song (Revelation 5:8–14)

In the next vision, the heavenly court shifts focus from the Father to the Lamb "looking as though it had been slain," now standing in victory, holding the scroll of redemption (Rev 5:6). Each creature and elder falls before Him, wielding harps and golden bowls of incense—the prayers of the saints—singing a new song: "Worthy are you to take the scroll and to open its seals, for you were slain, and by your blood you ransomed people for God" (Rev 5:9). This anthem weaves together justice and mercy: the Lamb's slaughter enacts divine justice, His shedding of blood extends mercy to every tribe. Gratitude for this dual triumph compels the Church to craft fresh expressions of worship—hymns, liturgies, visual art—as a perpetual new song. Every communion celebration becomes a microcosm of this scene: the broken bread and poured cup retelling the Lamb's worth. When we hear organ pedals roll and voices rise in unison to proclaim the Lamb's worthiness, our hearts echo the cosmic choir, each "Amen" a personal note of thanks to the Savior-King.

Unending Hallelujahs of the Redeemed (Revelation 19:1–6)

Revelation culminates in heaven's grand hallelujah: "Salvation and glory and power belong to our God, for his judgments are true and righteous" (Rev 19:1–2). A myriad voices answer, "Hallelujah!... The smoke from her goes up forever and ever" (Rev 19:3), celebrating the downfall of Babylon—symbol of all that opposes God's reign. Then the twenty-four elders and four creatures join, saying, "Amen! Hallelujah!" (Rev 19:4), unleashing an unstoppable wave of praise that precedes Christ's return to judge and reign. Gratitude for this vision ignites our corporate worship with anticipation: every hymnbook and every liturgical response can carry an undertone of "foretaste and prophesy." Worship gatherings that conclude with "Hallelujah!" remind congregants that no earthly circumstance can silence heaven's song. When the congregation stands—voices intertwined in a final flourish of praise—it becomes a foretaste of that unending hallelujah fest, where creatures great and small exalt the Lamb without pause, and every tongue joins the eternal chorus of thanksgiving.

14.9 Communion with the Redeemed

The Marriage Supper of the Lamb (Revelation 19:6–9)

John hears a voice like a great multitude, "Hallelujah! For the Lord our God the Almighty reigns" (Rev 19:6), and is invited to the marriage supper of the Lamb—a feast symbolizing the intimate union between Christ and His Bride. This supper is not a mere banquet but the consummation of covenant promises, where the redeemed dine at victory's table, clothed in fine linen representing righteous deeds (Rev 19:8). Gratitude for this everlasting fellowship pervades every celebration of Eucharist, as we "proclaim the Lord's death until he comes" (1 Cor 11:26). Each shared meal—whether in cathedral settings or humble potlucks—becomes an emblem of that great feast, uniting diverse believers in one banquet hall. As we taste bread and wine, we anticipate the fullness of communion when sorrow, pain, and separation yield to unbroken union. Worship teams and liturgists can weave in wedding imagery, hymns of betrothal, and art that captures the feast's joy—reminding congregations that communion is both present grace and future promise. In gratitude, we lift our glasses, mindful that the Lamb's table waits for us beyond time's horizon.

Feast of Rich Fare and Aged Wine (Isaiah 25:6–9)

Isaiah paints a lush portrait of the Messiah's banquet: "On this mountain the LORD of hosts will make for all peoples a feast of rich food… and aged wine" (Isa 25:6). This prophetic feast declares that death's veil will be lifted—a banquet not of scarcity but of abundance, prepared by the God of provision. Gratitude for such imagery deepens our understanding of divine hospitality: God does not merely serve sustenance but celebrates our joy with the finest fare. Churches can host "Isaiah Feasts," inviting communities to share meals in remembrance of this promise. Culinary ministries—community dinners and food justice programs—embody this banquet's spirit, demonstrating that the gospel feeds both body and soul. When believers break bread together, laugh, and share stories, they enact Isaiah's vision, and their collective thanksgiving echoes the prophet's assurance that God will "swallow up death forever" (Isa 25:8).

A Multitude from All Nations at the Table (Revelation 7:9–10)

John beholds "a great multitude that no one could number, from every nation, tribe, people, and language," standing before the throne and the Lamb, clothed in white robes, crying out, "Salvation belongs to our God who sits on the throne, and to the Lamb!" (Rev 7:9–10). This scene affirms that the marriage supper and the magnificent feast include all who believe, transcending every barrier. Gratitude for this multiethnic fellowship compels congregations to craft inclusive communion liturgies: bilingual prayers, cross-cultural elements, and shared traditions. When churches invite immigrants, refugees, and indigenous peoples to break bread at the Lord's table, they honor the tapestry of redemption. Each hand clasped across a cultural divide, each shared hymn in multiple tongues, becomes an act of worship to the King whose banquet table is open to all. In these moments, thanksgiving becomes as diverse as the redeemed multitude itself.

14.10 Renewal of Creation

A New Heaven and a New Earth (Revelation 21:1–5)

John's climactic vision reveals "a new heaven and a new earth, for the first heaven and the first earth had passed away" (Rev 21:1). The sea—symbol of chaos—is gone; the city of God, adorned like a bride, descends prepared (Rev 21:2). The Creator's former works of beauty are superseded by a fresh canvas where righteousness dwells (2 Pet 3:13). Gratitude for this promise spurs ecological stewardship as a foretaste of cosmic renewal: tree plantings, habitat restoration, and sustainable living become acts of worship celebrating the King's restorative power. Churches can partner in community greening initiatives, integrating liturgies of creation care into worship services. Each step toward environmental reconciliation echoes the eschatological promise that every broken corner of creation will be made new, and our gratitude for this assurance becomes part of our mission to honor the Lord's handiwork.

River of Life and Tree of Life (Revelation 22:1–2)

Descending from God's throne is "the river of the water of life, bright as crystal," flanked by the tree of life bearing twelve kinds of fruit, its leaves healing nations (Rev 22:1–2). These images reprise Eden's lost paradise, now offered without hindrance—no more curse or barrier. Gratitude for access to this life-giving water transforms baptismal liturgies: each immersion can be envisioned as a personal step into the river. Gardens around worship spaces, planted with edible trees and medicinal herbs, become microcosms of the riverbank, offering tangible reminders of the healing to come. When congregants sip water from blessed fountains or partake of community garden produce, they foretaste the eternal banquet and testify, "Thank You, Jesus, for restoring Eden's gifts in limitless abundance."

Cursed Things Removed Forever (Revelation 22:3–5; Romans 8:21)

The final bookends of Scripture declare that "no longer will there be anything accursed" (Rev 22:3), that night will never fall, and that God's servants "will reign forever and ever" (Rev 22:5). Likewise, Paul affirms that creation itself will be set free from its bondage to decay (Rom 8:21). Gratitude for the removal of sin's chain motivates present labors to alleviate suffering—advocacy for the oppressed, care for the sick, and campaigns against injustice—knowing these efforts anticipate a curse-less world. Churches can host "Heaven-and-Earth Sabbath" services—days of simultaneous worship and creation-care projects—symbolizing that the removal of curse is both spiritual and material. When communities celebrate the end of pandemics, the collapse of war zones, or the revitalization of polluted rivers, they enact the coming reality of a world unmarked by curse, prompting communal thanksgiving for Christ's final victory over every form of decay.

14.11 Eternal Service and Sustenance

Priests Serving Before God's Throne (Revelation 22:3)

In the new creation, John sees that "his servants will worship him. They will see his face, and his name will be on their foreheads" (Rev 22:3–4). Believers, now priests, serve continually before the throne, offering worship and seeing God's presence unveiled. Gratitude for our priestly calling reshapes our understanding of service: it is not merely duty but perpetual privilege. Ecclesial liturgies that emphasize communal intercession and personal dedication mirror this heavenly reality. Churches can create prayer altars and dedicate "worship rooms" where members practice priestly intercession. Each moment of prayer, each sung hymn, and each lifted intercession becomes a downpayment on that eternal service, prompting thankful praise for Jesus who makes us priests in His kingdom.

No More Need of Sun or Moon (Revelation 21:23–25)

Revelation depicts the New Jerusalem needing no sun or moon, for "the glory of God gives it light, and its lamp is the Lamb" (Rev 21:23). This perpetual radiance signifies that our eternal needs are met in divine presence, eliminating every fear of darkness or uncertainty. Gratitude for this unceasing light prompts churches to incorporate candlelit vigils, sunset services, and "light of the world" thematic worship. Personal devotional practices—morning prayers before sunrise— become symbolic anticipations of living in the King's radiance. When congregations gather under electric lights singing "You are the light of the world," they both acknowledge present illumination and worship the Lamb who forever dispels darkness.

Sustained by the Lamb's Provision (Revelation 7:16–17)

John hears that the redeemed "shall hunger no more, neither thirst anymore... for the Lamb in the midst of the throne will be their shepherd, and he will guide them to springs of living water" (Rev 7:16–17). The Lamb's provision transforms us from wayfarers into cared-for sheep, forever sustained. Gratitude for this care motivates ministries that nourish body and soul—food pantries, community cafés, counseling services—underscoring that in Christ's kingdom, no one is neglected. Churches can host "Shepherd Sundays," focusing offerings on holistic care ministries and inviting local agencies to share resources. Each mission meal served and each counseling session offered becomes an expression of eternal provision, inspiring praise that the Lamb Shepherds His own into unending life and sustenance.

14.12 Crown of Unfading Hope

Crown of Righteousness for Faithful Finishers (2 Timothy 4:8)

Paul anticipates the "crown of righteousness" that awaits those who long for Christ's appearing (2 Tim 4:8). This imperishable reward honors those who finish their race with integrity and eager expectancy. Gratitude for this crown fuels perseverance; each milestone in personal holiness and ministry accomplishment becomes a step closer to that heavenly accolade. Churches can incorporate "finish-line services"—celebrations for long-serving staff or volunteers—where the congregation prays thanksgiving and envisions the crown laid at Jesus' feet. Every recommitment vow or life-review testimony thus becomes an opportunity to recall Paul's words and to say, "Thank You, Jesus, for promising a reward for those who run well."

Crown of Glory for Shepherd-Servants (1 Peter 5:4)

Peter assures faithful elders that "when the chief Shepherd appears, you will receive the unfading crown of glory" (1 Pet 5:4). This crown recognizes those who lead with selfless care, not for personal gain but for the flock's well-being. Gratitude for these shepherd-servants spills over into communal affirmation—laying on of hands in commissioning services, gifts of honor, and public declarations of thanks. Mentorship celebrations, ordination anniversaries, and pastoral recognition events become liturgical moments, inviting all to praise Jesus for raising true shepherds. Each accolade bestowed reflects the kingdom's values, and every "thank you" echoes end-time applauses for faithful under-shepherds.

Crown of Life for Enduring Persecution (James 1:12; Revelation 2:10)

James writes, "Blessed is the man who remains steadfast under trial, for when he has stood the test he will receive the crown of life" (Jas 1:12). Revelation warns believers to be faithful unto death, and they will receive this crown (Rev 2:10). Gratitude for this promise reframes martyrdom and martyrdom-like sufferings—not as defeats but as assured conquests. Memorial services for persecuted saints and tearful retreats for those facing hostility become hallows of hope rather than monuments of despair. Churches can dedicate "Persecution Remembrance Sundays," sharing stories from the global church, praying for the faithful under fire, and singing hymns that affirm life's victory through death. Each commemoration becomes a solemn, grateful affirmation that no trial can extinguish the crown of life won by the Lamb's own blood.

Conclusion

Eternal glory stands at the heart of Christian hope—an inheritance impervious to decay, a home built by the Master, and a destiny crowned with unfading honors. From the Shekinah's radiance above the Tabernacle to the New Jerusalem's crystal river, Scripture unfurls visions that beckon weary pilgrims toward a reality far surpassing earthly splendor. In Christ's resurrection we grasp the firstfruits of our own rising; in our finite bodies we anticipate transformation into imperishable glory. Our present trials become portals to eternal weight, our worship embodies foretaste of heaven's chorus, and our service echoes the Lamb's priestly care. As citizens of a kingdom that is "righteousness and peace and joy in the Holy Spirit" (Rom 14:17), we now live by values that timelessly affirm justice, mercy, and grace. To say "Thank You, Jesus, for eternal glory—hope unfading" is to acknowledge that every tear will be wiped away, every curse removed, and every sorrow healed in the light of His radiant presence. May this unwavering hope propel us forward, with hearts full of gratitude, eyes fixed on the eternal city, and voices lifted in endless praise to the One who makes all things new.

www.ingramcontent.com/pod-product-compliance
Lightning Source LLC
Chambersburg PA
CBHW070848050426
42453CB00012B/2089